Praise for

Rules for International Monetary Stability: Past, Present, and Future

"How can monetary policy harm or support the functioning of the international monetary system? And is monetary policy cooperation desirable? These are the perennial questions revisited in this thoughtful volume by some of the leading economists in the field, with special reference to the role that rule-based policies can play. An excellent read for anyone interested in this important topic and in the challenges the global economy is facing."

—Claudio Borio, *head of the Monetary and Economic Department, Bank for International Settlements*

"A thought-provoking mix of interesting historical, theoretical, and empirical papers on the theme of how heterodox post-financial-crisis monetary policies might have led to greater instability in the global financial system. Overall, the book makes the case that significant adverse international spillovers are far less of a concern in a rule-based world (e.g., a Taylor rule) than when monetary policy deviates sharply from a rule-based system, as it arguably has done in recent years, especially as central banks have struggled to contend with the zero bound on interest rates."

—Kenneth Rogoff, *Thomas D. Cabot Professor, Harvard University*

"There is new interest in rules for the conduct of monetary policy, first and foremost in the United States but also more broadly. Is this just a reaction against the exceptional steps taken by central banks in the wake of the global financial crisis, or does it reflect historical lessons learned and advances in the theory and analysis of optimal monetary policy? This book provides an ideal introduction to the debate."

—Barry Eichengreen, *University of California, Berkeley*

"This excellent volume offers a panoramic view of international monetary spillover and coordination issues, current and historical. It will be an essential reference for anyone wanting to understand the interdependence of national central banks, the pitfalls of monetary union, and the unique role of the Fed."

—Maurice Obstfeld, *economic counsellor, International Monetary Fund*

Rules for **International Monetary Stability**

The Hoover Institution gratefully acknowledges the following individuals and foundations for their significant support of the ***Working Group on Economic Policy*** *and this publication:*

Lynde and Harry Bradley Foundation

Preston and Carolyn Butcher

Stephen and Sarah Page Herrick

Michael and Rosalind Keiser

Koret Foundation

William E. Simon Foundation

John A. Gunn and Cynthia Fry Gunn

Rules for **International Monetary Stability**

Past, Present, and Future

EDITED BY

Michael D. Bordo
John B. Taylor

CONTRIBUTING AUTHORS

David Beckworth
James Bullard
Richard Clarida
Christopher Crowe
Sebastian Edwards
Pierre-Olivier Gourinchas
Patrick J. Kehoe
Allan H. Meltzer
Catherine Schenk
John B. Taylor
John C. Williams
Michael D. Bordo
Varadarajan V. Chari
John H. Cochrane
Alessandro Dovis
Christopher Erceg
Robert Kaplan
Dennis Lockhart
David H. Papell
George P. Shultz
Harald Uhlig

WITH ADDITIONAL DISCUSSANTS

HOOVER INSTITUTION PRESS
STANFORD UNIVERSITY STANFORD, CALIFORNIA

With its eminent scholars and world-renowned library and archives, the Hoover Institution seeks to improve the human condition by advancing ideas that promote economic opportunity and prosperity, while securing and safeguarding peace for America and all mankind. The views expressed in its publications are entirely those of the authors and do not necessarily reflect the views of the staff, officers, or Board of Overseers of the Hoover Institution.

www.hoover.org

Hoover Institution Press Publication No. 679
Hoover Institution at Leland Stanford Junior University,
Stanford, California 94305-6003

First printing 2017
25 24 23 22 21 20 19 18 17 9 8 7 6 5 4 3 2 1

Manufactured in the United States of America

The paper used in this publication meets the minimum requirements of the American National Standard for Information Sciences—Permanence of Paper for Printed Library Materials, ANSI/NISO Z39.48-1992. ♾

Cataloging-in-Publication Data is available from the Library of Congress.
ISBN-13: 978-0-8179-2054-8 (cloth)
ISBN-13: 978-0-8179-2056-2 (EPUB)
ISBN-13: 978-0-8179-2057-9 (Mobipocket)
ISBN-13: 978-0-8179-2058-6 (PDF)

Contents

Preface

The Hoover Institution held a conference entitled International Monetary Stability: Past, Present, and Future on May 5, 2016. This conference was the third in a series of conferences on key issues of monetary policy put on by the Economic Policy Working Group at the Hoover Institution under the direction of John B. Taylor. These conferences were organized by Hoover Senior Fellows John Taylor, Michael Bordo, John Cochrane, and Lee Ohanian.

This year's forum drew an impressive list of participants, including four Federal Reserve bank presidents and numerous representatives from the Federal Reserve, academia, the financial sector, and business media. Five presentations of monetary research projects and two panel discussions focused on the deepening links of international monetary policy regimes, exchange rate volatility, and international capital flows as well as next steps for central banks as they assess the results of unconventional monetary interventions.

For invaluable help in organizing this conference, we thank Daniel Robertson and Marie-Christine Slakey, and, for a great deal of additional help in putting the conference volume together, we also thank Kyle Palermo and Barbara Arellano.

MICHAEL D. BORDO

JOHN B. TAYLOR

Introduction

Since the end of the Great Recession in 2009 the central banks of the advanced countries have taken unprecedented actions to reflate and stimulate their economies. There have been significant differences in the timing and pace of these actions. These independent monetary policy actions have had significant spillover effects on the economies and monetary policy strategies of other advanced countries. In addition, the monetary policy actions and interventions of the advanced countries have had a significant impact on the emerging market economies, leading to the charge of "currency wars."

The perceived negative consequences of spillovers from the actions of national central banks has led to calls for international monetary policy coordination, including one by the general manager of the Bank for International Settlements, Jamie Caruana, another from the former chair of the Federal Reserve, Paul Volcker, and a number in papers at the European Central Bank's policy conference in Sintra, Portugal, in June 2016. The arguments for coordination based on game theory are the same today as they were back in the 1980s, when they led to the Plaza and Louvre accords of 1987 and 1988, respectively. Both accords, which required that participant countries follow policies to improve global welfare at the expense of domestic fundamentals, led to disastrous consequences, especially the Japanese boom and bust of 1991 (Taylor 2016).

An alternative approach to the international spillovers of national monetary policy actions is to view them as deviations from rules-based monetary policy. In this view, a return to rules-based monetary policy and a rolling back of the "global great deviation" by each country's central bank would lead to a beneficial policy outcome without the need for explicit policy coordination.

In this book, we report the results from a recent conference which brought together academics, market participants, and policymakers to focus on these issues. The consensus of much of the conference was on the need for a classic rules-based reform of the international monetary system.

The book contains five chapters that cover international monetary policy interactions from different perspectives: theoretical, empirical, and historical. It is followed by two chapters that contain the discussions of policy panels by practitioners and policymakers. All of the chapters contain an edited transcript of the general discussion by all participants in the conference.

In chapter 1, Sebastian Edwards demonstrates that Federal Reserve monetary policies had significant spillovers on the emerging market countries of Latin America and East Asia despite floating exchange rates. This raises questions about the ability of the central banks of these countries to exercise independent monetary policies. David Papell in his comment considers whether this was due to recent departures from optimal policy rules in the United States, concentrating on the concluding lines of Edwards's paper, which assert that "to the extent that the advanced country central bank (that is, the Fed) pursues a destabilizing policy, this will be imported by the smaller nations, creating a more volatile macroeconomic environment at home."

In chapter 2, David Beckworth and Christopher Crowe demonstrate some of the destabilizing impacts of such policy spillovers, especially when the United States is "banker to the world," with a large portfolio of longer-term assets financed by short-term liabilities. They consider ways in which more rules-based policy could alleviate these international instabilities. In his comment, Christopher Erceg raises some empirical issues and notes that the results imply a positive effect of US policy deviations (shocks to policy rules) on real gross domestic product abroad.

In chapter 3, V. V. Chari and Patrick Kehoe examine rules-based policy in the context of a currency union such as the European Monetary Union. They show that currency unions bring about more rules-based and less discretionary monetary policy, but note that such unions have disadvantages in dealing with incentives to bail out the debt of member countries. In his comment, Harald Uhlig explains in detail the nature of the assumptions and notes that some of the price-stability effects of monetary unions observed in the countries of Europe are also observed in the United States.

In chapter 4, Pierre-Olivier Gourinchas, Ricardo Caballero and Emmanuel Farhi discuss the results of their model, which shows the existence of the zero lower bound on the central bank interest rate combined with a shortage of safe assets in the global economy. This gives rise to the current account imbalances that we have observed in recent years. John Cochrane in his comment questions the relevance of the zero lower bound, and he argues that real factors such as the marginal product of capital provide a better explanation of what is going on in the world today. While praising the paper for laying out a model that could be discussed substantively, he also questions the existence of an aggregate deficiency so many years after the crisis.

In chapter 5, Michael Bordo and Catherine Schenk provide an historical overview of central bank cooperation and coordination, with focus on the importance of rules. They cover a range of different international monetary regimes, from the classical gold standard and interwar gold exchange standard, to Bretton Woods, to the 1980s and 1990s, looking at particular episodes of formal policy coordination. Their overriding finding is that systems that are more rules based and do not require active coordination of policy actions work better than more discretionary systems. Their discussant, Allan Meltzer, delved into some of the reasons underlying their findings based on his studies of the history of the Federal Reserve.

Chapter 6 contains the discussion from a panel of three economists with experience with international economic policy coordination at the US Treasury—Richard Clarida, George Shultz, and John Taylor. They discussed "Rules-Based International Monetary Reform." Clarida explained how his own research led to the conclusion that a nearly optimal rules-based international system could be generated by optimal rules in each country. He also emphasized, however, that certain inherently global developments—such as a change in the equilibrium real interest rate—required an analysis of trends in other countries. George Shultz described how international reforms that first brought about flexible exchange rates were implemented in practice during his own experience as Treasury secretary. John Taylor reviewed his proposal for a rules-based international monetary system in which each country announces and commits to its own policy rule.

Chapter 7 contains the discussion of the final panel on international monetary policy and reform in practice by four current members of the Federal Open Market Committee: James Bullard of St. Louis, Robert Kaplan of Dallas, Dennis Lockhart of Atlanta, and John Williams of San Francisco. Despite some mild disagreement, there seemed to be a lot of consensus that the equilibrium real interest rate (r^*) had declined. This did not have much bearing on their current interest rate decisions, but it meant that gradual normalization would be to a lower rate than expected. In addition, Jim Bullard presented an analysis in which deviations from optimal rules-based policy could cause instabilities in other countries, a possibility raised by Sebastian Edwards in chapter 2. Considerable discussion with the other conference participants led to a general consensus, summarized by George Shultz, in favor of a rules-based monetary policy and international monetary system, although there was some disagreement on what the rule would be.

References

Caruana, J. 2012. Policymaking in an interconnected world. Paper presented at Federal Reserve Bank of Kansas City policy symposium, The Changing Policy Landscape, Jackson Hole, August 31.

Taylor, J. B. 2016. A rules-based cooperatively managed international monetary system for the future. In *International monetary cooperation: Lessons from the Plaza Accord after thirty years,* ed. C. Fred Bergsten and Russell A. Green, 217–36. Washington, DC: Peterson Institute for International Economics.

Volcker, P. A. 2014. Remarks. Bretton Woods Committee Annual Meeting, Washington, June 17.

CHAPTER ONE

Monetary Policy Independence under Flexible Exchange Rates

The Federal Reserve and Monetary Policy in Latin America—Is There Policy "Spillover"?

Sebastian Edwards

ABSTRACT

I use historical weekly data from 2000 to 2008 to analyze the way in which Federal Reserve policy actions have affected monetary policy in a group of Latin American countries: Chile, Colombia, and Mexico. I find some evidence of policy spillover during this period, in Chile and Colombia, but not in Mexico. In addition, I analyze whether changes in the slope of the yield curve in the United States have affected policy rates in these emerging markets (EMs). I also investigate the role of global financial markets' volatility and capital mobility on the extent of monetary policy "spillovers." I provide some comparisons between these Latin American countries and a group of East Asian nations during the same period. The results reported here call into question the notion that under flexible exchange rates countries exercise a fully independent monetary policy.

1. Introduction

For central bankers from around the world, the years 2013 to 2015 were years of great apprehension as they waited for the Federal Reserve to make up its mind and to begin raising policy rates. As time passed without the Fed taking action, central bank governors became increasingly anxious. The first sign of apprehension came

This paper was prepared for presentation at the Hoover Institution Monetary Policy Conference held on May 5–6, 2016. I thank John Taylor for encouragement and Ed Leamer for very helpful discussions. I am grateful to David Papell for his comments.

in June 2013 during the so-called “taper tantrum.”[1] Soon afterward, a number of influential central bankers from the periphery called for the Fed to normalize monetary policy once and for all. They wanted the “waiting game” to be over and for the Fed to begin hiking interest rates. On August 30, 2015, the governor of the Reserve Bank of India, Ragu Rajan, told the *Wall Street Journal*, “[F]rom the perspective of emerging markets . . . it’s preferable to have a move early on and an advertised, slow move up rather than, you know, the Fed being forced to tighten more significantly down the line.”

The wait was finally over on December 17, 2015, when the Fed raised the federal funds policy target range by 25 basis points, from 0 to 0.25 to 0.25 to 0.50 percent. During the next few weeks many Latin American countries—Chile, Colombia, Mexico, and Peru, for example—followed suit, and their respective central banks raised interest rates.[2] In contrast, during that same short period most of the East Asian central banks remained “on hold.” An important question in this regard is, Why do some central banks “follow” the Fed, while others act with what seems to be a greater degree of independence?

During the first few weeks of 2016, and as the world economy became more volatile and questions about China mounted, anxiety returned. In particular, many EMs’ central bankers became concerned about the rapid depreciation of their currencies, a phenomenon that they associated with the expectation that the Fed would continue to hike rates during 2016. For example, in an interview published in the *Financial Times*, Agustín Casterns, the governor of the Bank of Mexico, publicly argued that the peso had weakened too much—it had “overshot”—and predicted that, eventually, it would

1. On the effects of the tapering on the EMs see, for example, Aizenman, Binici, and Hutchison (2014) and Eichengreen and Gupta (2014).

2. In most of the Latin American countries, the Fed action was seen as contributing to the depreciation of their currencies.

go through a period of significant strengthening.[3] During February 2016, the degree of apprehension among periphery central bankers increased when the Bank of Japan moved its policy rate to negative terrain. In part as a result of this action, long rates declined, and the yield curve became flatter. On February 10, 2016, the *Wall Street Journal* said, "A little more than a month after the Federal Reserve lifted its benchmark rate from near zero, rates across the market are *falling*. The yield on the 10-year US Treasury note, a benchmark for everything from corporate rates to corporate lending this week fell below 1.7%, its lowest level in a year. (Emphasis added.)"

At a policy level, an important issue is how emerging markets are likely to react when advanced countries' central banks (and, in particular, the Federal Reserve) change their monetary policy stance.[4] According to received models of international macroeconomics (i.e., the Mundell-Fleming model, in any of its versions), the answer to this question depends on the exchange rate regime. Countries with pegged exchange rates cannot pursue independent monetary policy, and any change in the advanced countries' central bank policy rates will be transmitted into domestic rates (with the proper risk adjustment). However, under flexible exchange rates countries are able to undertake independent monetary policies and don't face the "trilemma." In principle, their central bank actions would not have to follow (or even take into account) the policy position of the advanced nations, such as the United States.[5] More recently, however, some authors, including, in particular, Taylor (2007, 2013, 2015) and Edwards (2012, 2015), have argued that even under flexible exchange rates there is significant policy interconnectedness across countries. In a highly globalized setting, even when there

3. See *Financial Times*, January 17, 2016. http://www.ft.com/intl/cms/s/0/968bd686-ba02-11e5-bf7e-8a339b6f2164.html#axzz3zyDnMPnT.

4. In the recent World Economic Outlook (2015), the International Monetary Fund devotes a long discussion to this issue.

5. On the "trilemma," see, for example, Obstfeld, Shambaugh, and Taylor (2005) and Rey (2013).

are no obvious domestic reasons for raising interest rates, some central banks will follow the Fed. This phenomenon may be called policy "spillover," and could be the result of a number of factors, including the desire to protect domestic currencies from "excessive" depreciation.[6] The late Ron McKinnon captured this idea when, in May 2014, he stated at a conference held at the Hoover Institution that "there's only one country that's truly independent and can set its monetary policy. That's the United States."[7] Of course, not every comovement of policy rates should be labeled as "spillover." It is possible that two countries (the United States and a particular EM, say, Colombia) are reacting to a common shock—a large change in the international price of oil, for example. "Spillover" would happen if, after controlling by those variables that usually enter into a central bank policy reaction function—the Taylor rule variables, say—there is still evidence that the EM in question has followed the Fed.

The purpose of this paper is to use data from three Latin American countries—Chile, Colombia, and Mexico—to analyze the issue of policy "spillover" from a historical perspective. More specifically, I am interested in answering the following questions: (*a*) Have changes in the Fed policy rate historically affected the policy stance of these countries' central banks, even after controlling for other variables? (*b*) If the answer is yes, how strong has the policy pass-through been? (*c*) What is the role played by the yield curve in the policy "spillover" process? Does it make a difference if the policy rate hike is accompanied by a flattening or steepening of the global yield curve? (*d*) What has been the role of global instability in the transmission mechanism of policy interest rates? and (*e*) Has this process been affected by the degree of capital mobility in the spe-

6. This is related to "fear of floating." See, for example, Calvo and Reinhart (2000). On the effect of advanced central banks' actions on EMs, see also Ince, Molodstova, Nikolsko-Rzhevskyy, and Papell (2015), Molodstova and Papell (2009), and Nikolsko-Rzhevskyy, Molodstova, and Papell (2008).

7. I thank John B. Taylor for making the transcript of Ron McKinnon's remarks available to me.

cific countries? In order to put my findings in perspective, in the final section of the paper, I compare the results obtained for the three countries in the sample to a group of East Asian nations. Although the analysis presented here is based on historical data (2000 to 2008), the answers are particularly pertinent for the current times, as an increasing number of central banks in the emerging nations are considering the issue of whether to react to Fed policy moves.

This paper differs from previous work on the subject in several respects: (*a*) I concentrate on individual countries. This allows me to detect differences across nations. Most analyses of related subjects have relied on either pooled (panel) data for a group of countries—often pooling countries as diverse as Argentina and India—or have based their simulations on a "representative EM." (*b*) I use short-term (weekly) time series data. As a consequence, I am able to follow the granularity of the transmission from interest rates in the United States to interest rates in the EMs of interest. (*c*) As noted, I focus on the important issue of the slope of the yield curve, and I analyze how changes in the policy rate and the long rate have interacted to affect the three central banks' policy stance. (*d*) I explicitly investigate how changing conditions in the global economy—including the volatility of global financial markets—affect (if they do at all) the transmission process. (*e*) I investigate whether the degree of capital mobility affects the transmission process.[8] And (*f*) I provide an explicit comparison between a group of Latin American countries and a group of Asian nations.

2. Preliminaries

Before moving forward, a note on the sample is in order. Chile, Colombia, and Mexico are the three Latin American countries with

8. I have previously addressed some of these issues in Edwards (2011, 2012, 2015).

available weekly data for the variables of interest. In addition, they have three important characteristics in common: (*a*) they followed inflation targeting during the period under study (2000 to 2008); (*b*) they had a relatively high degree of capital mobility (more on this below); and (*c*) the three had independent central banks. In this sense, they constitute a somewhat homogenous group.

In figure 1.1, I present weekly data for the federal funds target rate from 1994 through 2008, just before it was reduced to (almost) zero and quantitative easing was enacted. Between January 2000 and September 2008, there were 40 changes in the federal funds policy (target) rate. Twenty were increases, and in 19 of them the rate hike was 25 basis points; on one occasion the Fed Funds rate was increased by 50 basis points (in the week of May 19, 2000). The other 20 policy actions correspond to cuts in the federal funds rate. In seven cases it was cut by 25 basis points; in 11 cases it was cut

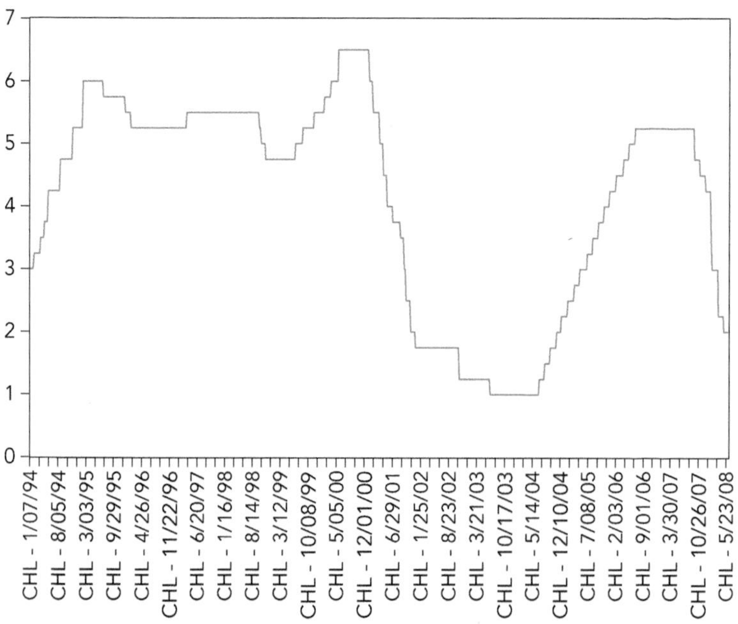

FIGURE 1.1. Federal funds target rate, 1994–2008

by 50 basis points; and on two occasions it was reduced by 75 basis points (both of them in early 2008: the week of January 25th and the week of March 21st).

In figure 1.2, I include weekly data on the policy rate for the three countries in this study: Chile, Colombia, and Mexico. As noted, the key question in this paper is the extent to which these EMs' central banks took into account the Fed's policy stance when determining their own monetary policy. In other words, with other givens, did (some of) these countries take into account Fed action when deciding on their own policies, or did they act with complete independence?

Standard tests indicate that it isn't possible to reject the null hypothesis that the policy interest rates have unit roots. For this reason in the analysis that follows, I rely on an error correction specification. This is standard in the literature on interest rate dynamics.[9] Not surprisingly, it is not possible to reject the hypothesis that the Federal Fund's rate "Granger causes" the EMs' policy rates; however, the null that these rates "cause" Fed policy actions is rejected, in every case, at conventional levels. The details of these tests are not reported here due to space considerations; they are available on request.

A brief discussion on the use of the term *spillover* is in order. As the reader may have noticed, I have used it in quotation marks. There are two reasons for this: First, central bankers usually reject—and sometimes quite strongly—the notion that their decisions are subject to direct influence from abroad. They argue that in making decisions they take into account all available informa-

9. See, for example, Frankel, Schmukler, and Serven (2004), and Edwards (2012) for analyses of the transmission of interest rate shocks. These studies are different from the current paper in a number of respects, including the fact that they concentrate on market rates and don't explore the issue of "policy spillover." Other differences are the periodicity of the data (this paper uses weekly data) and the fact that in the current work individual countries are analyzed. Rey (2013) deals with policy interdependence, as does Edwards for the case of one country only (Chile).

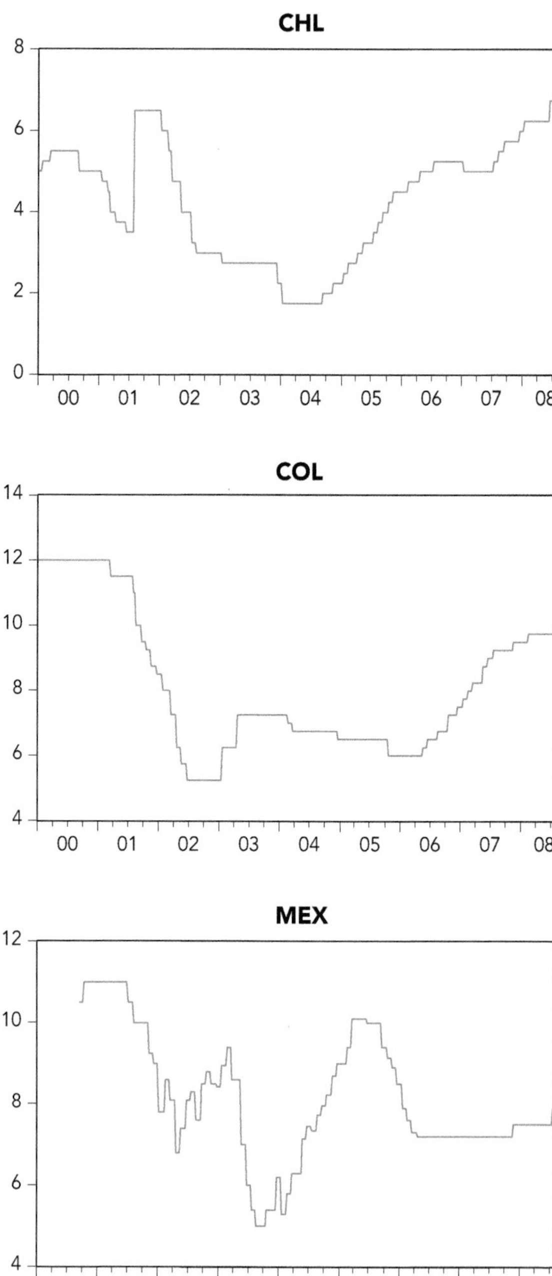

FIGURE 1.2. Monetary policy rates, selected Latin American countries, 2000–2008

tion, including global interest rates, but they point out that they don't follow, as a matter of policy, any other central bank, be it the Fed or the ECB. For example, this point has been made recently by Claro and Opazo (2014) with respect to Chile's central bank. Second, and as noted, it is possible that even if there are strong comovements in policy rates, these don't constitute "spillover" but are the reflection of both banks reacting to common shocks. In the analysis presented below, I do make an attempt to control by the type of variables that would constitute common shocks and, thus, to separate "spillover" from policy rates' comovements.[10]

3. On policy "spillover": A conceptual framework

Consider a small open economy with risk-neutral investors. Assume further, in order to simplify the exposition, that there are controls on capital outflows in the form of a tax of rate τ.[11] Then, the following condition will hold in equilibrium (one may assume without loss of generality that the tax is on capital inflows, or both on inflows and outflows; see the discussion in Edwards 2015a):

$$\frac{r_t - r_t^*}{(1 + r_t^*)} = E_t\{\Delta e_{t+1}\} - (1 + E_t\{\Delta e_{t+1}\})\tau \qquad (1)$$

Where r_t and r_t^* are domestic and foreign interest rates for securities of the same maturity and equivalent credit risk and $E_t\{\Delta e_{t+1}\}$ is the expected rate of depreciation of the domestic currency. (This assumes perfect substitutability of local and foreign securities. If these are not perfect substitutes, we could multiply r_t^* by some

10. In previous work—and in the version of this paper presented at the conference—I have used the terms "spillover" and "contagion" interchangeably. "Contagion" is usually interpreted as being suboptimal. From a theoretical point of view, however, there are some circumstances under which taking into account a foreign country's policy rate is optimal. See, for example Clarida (2014).

11. Parts of this section draw on Edwards (2015a, b).

parameter θ). In a country with a credible fixed exchange rate, the expected rate of depreciation is always equal to zero, $E_t\{\Delta e_{t+1}\} = 0$. If, in addition, there is full capital mobility $\tau = 0$ and, thus, $r_t \approx r_t^*$. That is, under these circumstances, local interest rates (in domestic currency) will not deviate from foreign interest rates. In this case, changes in world interest rates will be transmitted in a one-to-one fashion into the local economy. It is in this sense that with (credible) pegged exchange rates there cannot be an independent monetary policy; the local central bank cannot affect the domestic rate of interest. If $\tau \geq 0$, then there will be an equilibrium wedge between domestic and international interest rates, but still the domestic monetary authorities will be unable to influence local rates over the long run. Of course, how fast the domestic rates will converge to the international rate will vary from country to country. This is, indeed, the typical case of the "trilemma" or the "impossibility of the Holy Trinity."

Under flexible rates, however, $E_t\{\Delta e_{t+1}\} \neq 0$, and local and international rates may deviate from world interest rates. Assume that there is a tightening of monetary policy in the foreign country—i.e., the Fed raises the target federal funds rate—that results in a higher r_t^*. Under pegged exchange rates this would be translated into a one-to-one increase in r_t; the pass-through coefficient is equal to one, even if $\tau \geq 0$. However, if there are flexible rates, it is possible that r_t remains at its initial level and that all of the adjustment takes place through an expected appreciation of the domestic currency, $E_t\{\Delta e_{t+1}\} < 0$. As Dornbusch (1976) showed in his celebrated "overshooting" paper, for this to happen it is necessary for the local currency to depreciate on impact by more than in the long run. Under flexible rates, then, the exchange rate will be the "shock absorber" and will tend to exhibit some degree of volatility.[12]

12. The shock absorber role of the exchange rate goes beyond monetary disturbances. Edwards and Levy-Yeyati (2005) show that countries with more flexible rates are able to accommodate better terms of trade shocks.

If central banks want to avoid "excessive" exchange rate variability, they may take into account other central banks' actions when determining their own policy rates. That is, their policy rule could include a term with other central banks' policy rates.[13] In a world with two countries, this situation is captured by the following two policy equations, where r_p is the policy rate in the domestic country, r_p^* is the policy rate in the foreign country, and the x and x^* are vectors with the traditional determinants of policy rates (the elements in standard Taylor rules, for example), such as deviations of inflation from their targets and the deviation of the rate of unemployment from the "natural" rate:

$$r_p = \alpha + \beta r_p^* + \gamma x \tag{2}$$

$$r_p^* = \alpha^* + \beta^* r_p + \gamma^* x^*. \tag{3}$$

In equilibrium, the monetary policy rate in each country will depend on the other country's rate.[14] For the domestic country the equilibrium policy rate is (there is an equivalent expression for the foreign country):

$$r_p = \frac{\alpha + \beta\alpha^*}{1 - \beta\beta^*} + \left(\frac{\gamma}{1 - \beta\beta^*}\right) x + \left(\frac{\beta\gamma^*}{1 - \beta\beta^*}\right) x^*. \tag{4}$$

Changes in the drivers of the foreign country's policy interest rate, such as α^*, β^*, γ^*, or x^*, will have an effect on the domestic policy rate. This interdependence is illustrated in figure 1.3, which includes both reaction functions (2) and (3); PP is the policy function for the domestic country and P*P* is for the foreign nation.

13. In Edwards 2006, I argue that many countries include the exchange rate as part of their policy (or Taylor) rule. Taylor (2007, 2013) has argued that many central banks include other central banks' policy rates in their rules. The analysis that follows in the rest of this section owes much to Taylor's work.

14. The stability condition is $\beta\beta^* < 1$. This means that in figure 1.3 the P*P* schedule has to be steeper than the PP schedule.

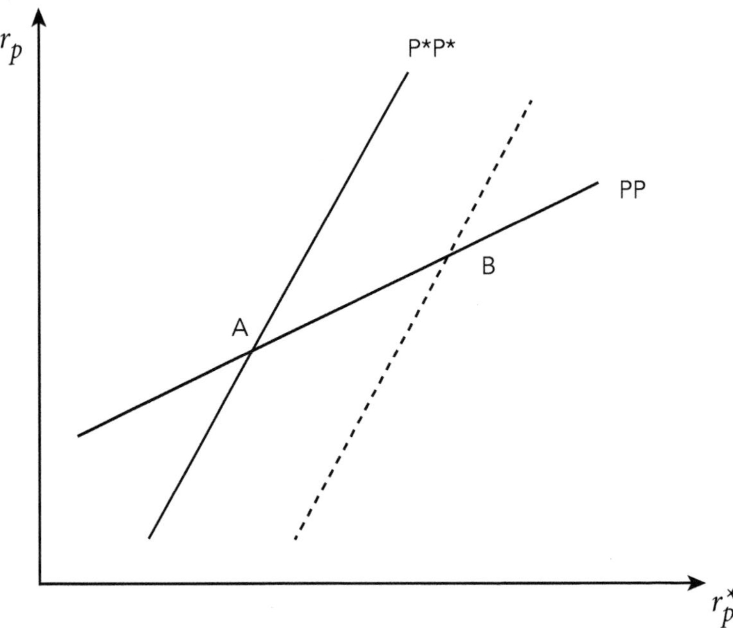

FIGURE 1.3. Policy rates equilibrium under policy "spillover" and large countries

The initial equilibrium is at point A. As may be seen, a higher x^* (say the gap between the actual and target inflation rate in the foreign country) will result in a shift to the right of P*P* and in higher equilibrium policy rates in both countries; the new equilibrium is given by B.[15] Notice that in this case the final increase in the foreign policy rate gets amplified; it is larger than what was originally planned by the foreign central bank. The extent of the effect of the foreign country's policy move on the domestic country policy rate will depend on the slopes of the two curves; these, in turn, depend on the parameters of equations (1) and (2).

Figure 1.3 is for the case when both countries take into consideration the other nation's actions. But this need not be the case.

15. The new equilibrium will be achieved through successive approximations, as in any model with reaction functions of this type, where the stability condition is met.

Indeed, if one country is large (say, the United States) and the other one is small (say, Colombia), we would expect policy "spillover" to be a one-way phenomenon. In this case, and if the foreign country is the large one, β* in equation (2) will be zero, and the P*P* schedule will be vertical. A hike in the foreign country's policy rate will impact the domestic country rate, but there will be no feedback to the large nation and, thus, no amplifying effect.[16] As noted, the magnitude of the policy "spillover" will depend on the slope of the PP curve. The steeper this curve, the larger is policy "spillover"; if, on the contrary, the PP curve is very flat, policy "spillover" will be minimal. In the limit, when there is complete policy independence in both countries, the PP schedule is horizontal and the P*P* is vertical.

In traditional analyses $\beta = \beta^* = 0$. That is, once central banks have taken into account the direct determinants of inflation (and unemployment, if that is part of their mandate), there is no role for the foreign policy rate when determining the domestic policy stance. It is in this regard that in this paper I call a situation where β or β* are different from zero policy "spillover." At the end of the road, the extent to which specific countries are affected by a foreign country's policy stance is an empirical matter.

Given the discussion in the introduction to this paper, and the concerns that have emerged in central banks from around the world in 2015–2016, it is possible to think that in some countries the actual policy rate would include other global variables, including the "long" rate in the world economy (r^{*L}) and the extent of uncertainty in global financial markets (μ). In this case, equation (2) would become

$$r_p = \alpha + \beta r_p^* + \gamma x + \delta r^{*L} + \theta\mu. \tag{5}$$

16. Of course, if neither country considers the foreign central bank actions, PP will be horizontal and P*P* will be vertical.

In the sections that follow I use data from three Latin American countries to investigate whether the key coefficients in equation (5) have been different from zero, as the "spillover" analysis suggests, or whether once other variables are incorporated they are no longer relevant, as suggested by traditional analyses. To put it simply, then, the goal of this paper is to determine, using historical data, whether, once the appropriate controls are introduced into the empirical analysis, $\beta \neq 0$.[17]

4. An empirical model

In this section I report the results from the estimation of a number of equations for monetary policy rates for the three countries in the sample—Chile, Colombia, and Mexico. I assume that each central bank has a policy function of the form of equation (5) and that central banks don't necessarily adjust their policy rates instantaneously to new information, including changes in policy rates in the advanced nations. More specifically, I estimate the following error correction model that allows central banks to make adjustments at a gradual pace:

$$\Delta r_t^p = \alpha_0 + \alpha_1 FF_t + \alpha_2 \Delta r_{t-1}^p + \alpha_3 r_{t-1}^p + \sum \rho_j x_{jt} + \varepsilon_t. \quad (6)$$

In this expression, r_t^p is the policy rate in each of the three countries in period t; FF_t is the federal funds (target) interest rate; and the x_{jt} are other variables that affect the central bank policy actions, including, in particular, the long rate in the foreign country (the United States), inflationary pressures, global perceptions of coun-

17. In previous work—and in the version of this paper presented at the conference—I used the terms "spillover" and "contagion" interchangeably. "Contagion" is usually interpreted as being suboptimal. From a theoretical point of view, however, there are some circumstances under which taking into account a foreign country's policy rate or the exchange rate may be optimal. See, for example, Clarida (2014) for a discussion on optimal monetary policy in open economies.

try risk, and expectations of global inflation; that is, these variables capture what we would normally expect to be included in an expanded Taylor rule type of equation. If there is policy "spillover," the estimated α_1 would be significantly positive. The extent of long-term policy "spillover" is given by $-(\alpha_1/\alpha_3)$. If, for example, $-(\alpha_1/\alpha_3) = 1$, then there will be full importation of Fed policies into domestic policy rates. Parameter γ allows for the adjustment to a new equilibrium policy rate to be cyclical; this, however, is unlikely. In equation (6), the timing of the variables is contemporaneous. However, in the estimation and as explained below, alternative lag structures were considered.

4.1. Reduced form results

In table 1.1, I report results for a basic *bivariate* dynamic specification of equation (6) for all three countries, using least squares. The federal funds variable is entered contemporaneously. If it is included with a one-week lag, the results don't change in any significant way.[18] These preliminary estimates should be interpreted as a *reduced form* for a significantly more complex system. Indeed, these results are consistent with a number of models and hypotheses. For example, they are consistent with the case where vector x in equation (1) includes variables that indirectly depend on the foreign country's policy rate r_p^*. An example of this is when x includes domestic inflation, or its deviations from target, which, through a pass-through equation, may depend on the rate of depreciation of the domestic currency, a variable that, in turn, depends on the interest rate differential between the home and the

18. The issue of timing here is important. The three central banks under study have monthly meetings; in contrast, the Federal Open Market Committee (FOMC) meets only eight times per year. Our data refer to each week's Friday. The FOMC never holds scheduled meetings on a Friday. This means that using contemporaneous data for the federal funds rate is fine in the sense that changes to the policy precede by at least a few days the policy rate that we are considering for our EMs.

TABLE 1.1. Monetary policy rates in Latin America, 2000–2008 (least squares)

Eq Name: Method:	Chile (1.1)	Colombia (1.2)	Mexico (1.3)
FF_POLICY	0.016	0.016	0.004
	[2.384]**	[3.373]***	[0.590]
C	0.044	0.055	0.090
	[1.505]	[2.055]**	[1.589]
POL_RATE(–1)	–0.024	–0.015	–0.013
	[–2.610]***	[–3.588]***	[–1.854]*
D(POL_RATE(–1))	0.005	–0.027	0.004
	[0.100]	[–0.525]	[0.073]
Observations	390	387	403
R-squared	0.019	0.038	0.009

Note: *, **, and *** refer to significance at 10%, 5%, and 1%, respectively.

foreign countries. Another model that is consistent with the reduced forms presented in table 1.1 is one where the monetary authorities in the EMs believe that the Fed has superior knowledge and/or information about world economic conditions, including global monetary pressures and/or the evolution of commodity prices. In this case, it is possible that the EMs' central banks follow the Fed in a way similar to the way in which firms follow a "barometric price leader" in the industrial organization literature.[19] In what follows, I try to disentangle the different effects at play, and I investigate whether the federal funds rate has an independent effect even when other variables are held constant (domestic inflationary pressures, US expected inflation, and so on).

As may be seen from table 1.1, in two of the three countries the estimated coefficients for the federal funds rate are positive and significant; the exception is Mexico. This provides some preliminary evidence suggesting that during the period under study (2000–2008) there may have been some policy "spillover" from the

19. Clarida (2014) develops a model of monetary policy in an open economy where the optimal policy rule includes the exchange rate. Interestingly, the optimal rule implies moving the exchange rate in a direction that is opposite from PPP.

United States to some of these EMs. The main insights from this table may be summarized as follows: (*a*) The impact effect—first week—of a Fed action on these countries' policy rates is small. This is not surprising, as the timing of central bank meetings doesn't necessarily coincide across countries. (*b*) The coefficient for Δr_{t-1}^{p} is never significant. And (*c*) the estimated long-run effect of a change in the "spillover" effect $-(\alpha_1/\alpha_3)$ ranges from 0.66 to 1.0 in the countries where there is "spillover." The individual point estimates for these (unconditional) long-term coefficients are 0.66 for Chile, 1.00 for Colombia, and non-significantly different from zero for Mexico. In some regards the result that US policy didn't affect Mexico's central bank stance during this period is surprising, given the proximity of the two countries and the traditional dependence of Mexico's economy on US economic developments.[20]

4.2 Multivariate analysis

In this subsection I report results from multilateral estimates using both least squares and instrumental variables for the three Latin American nations. I included the following covariates x_{jt} (in addition to the dynamic terms and the federal funds target rate):[21] (*a*) Year over year inflation rate, lagged between four and six weeks. Its coefficient is expected to be positive as central banks tighten policy when domestic inflation increases. (*b*) Annualized growth, lagged between four and six weeks. This is the second term of traditional Taylor rules, and its coefficient is also expected to be positive. (*c*) A measure of expected global inflationary pressures, defined as

20. It is important to emphasize that the period under consideration is 2000–2008. Indeed, at the time of this writing (April 2016), most analysts believe that the Bank of Mexico is particularly aware of the Fed's policy when determining its own policy stance.

21. Notice that for two of the regressors weekly data are not available. This is the case for inflation and growth. In these cases, I use monthly data for the four weeks in question. I constructed monthly growth data by combining quarterly data on gross domestic product growth and monthly data on manufacturing activity.

the breakeven spread between the five-year US Treasury Securities (Treasuries) and five-year Treasury Inflation-Protected Securities (TIPS). This is entered with one period lag, and its coefficient is expected to be positive.[22] (*d*) The yield on the ten-year US Treasury note. (*e*) An indicator of country risk premium, defined as the lagged Emerging Markets Bond Index spread for Latin America. Its expected sign is not determined a priori and will depend on how central banks react to changes on perceived regional risk.

The least squares estimates are reported in table 1.2 and confirm the results from table 1.1 in the sense that during this period there is evidence of policy "spillover" in Chile and Colombia. These results are quite satisfactory. This is especially the case considering that interest rate equations are usually very difficult to estimate. As may be seen, most coefficients are significant at conventional levels and have the expected signs. The R-squared is quite low, as is usually the case for interest rate regressions in first differences. In addition to the individual countries' regression, I report pooled results. In these estimates, fixed effects were included. The most salient findings in table 1.2 may be summarized as follows:

- In every regression the coefficients of the traditional Taylor rule have the expected positive sign, and in the great majority of cases they are significant at conventional levels. In Chile the long-run coefficient of inflation in the monetary policy equation is not significantly different from one; in Colombia and Mexico it is greater than one, as suggested by the original Taylor model for the United States. Also, in Colombia and Mexico, the (long-term) coefficient of the growth term is smaller than that of the inflation term, as in most empirical Taylor rules.

22. However, it is possible to argue that once the federal funds rate is included, the coefficient of the spread between Treasuries and TIPS should be zero since the federal funds rate already incorporates market expectations of inflation of the United States.

TABLE 1.2. Monetary policy rates in Chile, Colombia, and Mexico, 2000–2008 (least squares)

Eq Name	Chile (2.1)	Colombia (2.2)	Mexico (2.3)	Pooled (2.4)	Chile (2.5)	Colombia (2.6)	Mexico (2.7)	Pooled (2.8)
FF_POLICY	0.0196	0.0456	0.0079	0.0093	0.0206	0.0469	0.0034	0.0122
	[2.0085]**	[4.2431]***	[0.6498]	[1.8590]*	[1.7156]*	[4.2860]***	[0.2133]	[1.8874]*
C	–0.5328	–0.5984	–0.4487	–0.2747	–0.5232	–0.5386	–0.4857	–0.2425
	[–3.2323]***	[–2.9346]***	[–1.9778]**	[–2.7266]***	[–2.9127]***	[–2.4059]**	[–2.0091]**	[–2.1953]**
POL_RATE(–1)	–0.0147	–0.0644	–0.0306	–0.0104	–0.0142	–0.0609	–0.0292	–0.0104
	[–1.2218]	[–5.5324]***	[–2.6834]***	[–2.2504]**	[–1.1130]	[–4.7588]***	[–2.4805]**	[–2.2497]**
D(POL_RATE(–1))	–0.0433	–0.0669	–0.0204	–0.0185	–0.0440	–0.0719	–0.0215	–0.0194
	[–0.8376]	[–1.2512]	[–0.3793]	[–0.6026]	[–0.8463]	[–1.3306]	[–0.4003]	[–0.6317]
GROWTH(–6)	0.0246	0.0153	0.0173	0.0090	0.0247	0.0137	0.0186	0.0086
	[2.7747]***	[2.3254]**	[2.1148]**	[2.2095]**	[2.7628]***	[1.9655]**	[2.1405]**	[2.0997]**
INF_YOY(–6)	0.0141	0.1043	0.0363	0.0116	0.0134	0.0996	0.0344	0.0113
	[1.2449]	[5.1164]***	[2.2374]**	[2.1245]**	[1.0645]	[4.6140]***	[2.0489]**	[2.0582]**
EMBI_LATAM(–1)	0.0196	–0.0047	0.0171	0.0075	0.0199	–0.0037	0.0162	0.0082
	[3.0001]***	[–0.8207]	[1.8373]*	[1.8684]*	[2.8769]***	[–0.6318]	[1.6918]*	[1.9904]**
TIPS_INF_USA(–1)	0.1208	0.1128	0.1597	0.0809	0.1208	0.1211	0.1500	0.0831
	[2.5283**	[1.9791]**	[2.1605]*	[2.4940]**	[2.5237]**	[2.0716]**	[1.9450]*	[2.5494]*
UST_10YR(–1)	—	—	—	—	–0.0033	–0.0172	0.0160	–0.0104
					[–0.1368]	[–0.6505]	[0.4472]	[–0.7107]
Observations	390	331	351	1072	390	331	351	1072
R-squared	0.0590	0.1257	0.0440	0.0272	0.0590	0.1268	0.0446	0.0277
F-statistic	3.4205	6.6332	2.2548	4.2484	2.9876	5.8465	1.9933	3.7788

Note: *, **, and *** refer to significance at 10%, 5%, and 1%, respectively.

- In six of the eight regressions, the coefficient of the federal funds rate (FF-Policy) is significantly positive, indicating that during the period under study there was a pass-through Fed policy rates into policy interest rates in Chile and Colombia. These coefficients are positive and significant, even when other determinants of the monetary policy stance—including the traditional Taylor rule components—are included in the regressions. Once other covariates are included, the coefficient for the federal funds for Mexico continues to be nonsignificant (see, however, the instrumental variables results reported below). This suggests that in Chile and Colombia there was some form of "spillover" during the period under study.[23]
- The impact coefficient for the Fed's federal funds rate is significantly larger in Chile (0.0196 and 0.0206) than in Colombia (0.0456 and 0.0469). That is, during this period Chile's central bank had a tendency to react more slowly to changes in the Fed's policy stance than Colombia's did.
- The extent of long-term policy "spillover," measured by $-(\alpha_1/\alpha_3)$, is rather large in both Chile and Colombia. The point estimates for the long-run effect is greater than one for Chile—this is the case both in equations (1) and (5). For Colombia, this long-term coefficient is smaller than one: point estimates are 0.707 and 0.770 in equations (2) and (6). This means that as a consequence of a Fed policy rate hike, Chile will react more slowly but in the end will tend to implement a higher increase in its own policy rates.
- Consider a 100 basis point increase in the federal funds rate. According to the point estimates in the two first columns in table 2, after 26 weeks, the pass-through into Chile is 41 basis points (bps), on average, and 58 bps in Colombia. After 52 weeks, the transmission is 71 bps in Chile and only 69 in Colombia. After 104 weeks

23. In a recent paper Claro and Opazo (2014) argue that the Central Bank of Chile has been fully independent, and has not directly responded to Fed policy moves.

the pass-through is 103 bps in Chile; in Colombia the process is finished with a rate increase, on average 71 bps.[24]

- The coefficients of the other covariates are significant at conventional levels in almost every case. These results indicate that perceptions of higher regional risk, measured by the spread of the EMBI index for Latin America, tend to result in defensive monetary policy—that is, in higher domestic interest rates—in Chile and Mexico but not in Colombia. A higher expected inflation in the United States, measured by the implied inflationary expectations in the spread between the five-year note and five-year TIPS, also generates a tightening in the domestic monetary policy. This is an interesting result as it suggests that central bankers in Chile and Colombia react to a Fed action even when we control for the market's expectations of inflation. This suggests that, during this period, central bankers in Chile and Colombia believed that the Fed had superior information and/or knowledge than the market.
- In the last four columns in table 1.2, I present estimates of policy reaction functions that include the yield on the ten-year Treasury note as an additional regressor. The issue, as noted, is the extent to which the slope of the yield curve matters in the transmission of policy rates. More specifically, I try to answer the following question: Does it make a difference if the federal funds rate is raised and the ten-year Treasury yield is constant or if it is allowed to adjust. As may be seen, the results provide some preliminary evidence that there is no role for the long rate in the policy transmission process (see, however, the discussion below for an analysis of the possible effects of Treasuries of other tenors).

24. Most (but not all) central banks conduct policy by adjusting their policy rates by multiples of 25 bps. The estimates discussed here refer to *averages*. Thus, they need not be multiples of 25 bps.

4.3 Instrumental variables and commodity prices

In this subsection I discuss issues related to possible endogeneity, and I present a set of regressions estimated with instrumental variables. I also report the results obtained from some extensions of the analysis.

For countries such as Chile, Colombia, and Mexico, the federal funds rate, the yield on TIPS, and the yield on Treasuries are clearly exogenous to their monetary policy decisions. It is possible to argue, however, that some of the domestic variables, in particular growth, may be subject to some degree of endogeneity.[25] In order to explore this angle, I estimated instrumental variables versions of some of the equations in table 1.2. The results are presented in table 1.3 and confirm the results reported previously in the sense that during the period under study Chile and Colombia were subject to considerable policy "spillover."[26] This is not the case for Mexico. Most of the coefficients of the other covariates continue to have expected signs and are estimated with the standard level of precision. Table 1.3 also has a dynamic panel estimate; country fixed effects were included.

Notice, however, that there are some differences between the results in tables 1.2 (least squares [LS]) and 1.3 (instrumental variables [IV]) in terms of the point estimates of the coefficients of interest. In the IV estimates the impact coefficient for Chile is larger than under LS. More important, perhaps, the long-term pass-through is now significantly smaller than one; it has a point

25. It is possible for lagged growth to be endogenous. This may especially be the case in a dynamic panel, like the ones in columns (2.4) and (2.8) of table 1.2 and in the sections that follow.

26. The following instruments were used: log of lagged commodity prices (copper, coffee, metals, energy, West Texas Intermediate oil), lagged US dollar to euro rate, six periods lagged effective devaluation, lagged expected depreciation, and lagged rates for the United States at a variety of maturities.

TABLE 1.3. Monetary policy rates in Chile, Colombia, and Mexico, 2000–2008 (instrumental variables)

Eq Name	Chile (3.1)	Colombia (3.2)	Mexico (3.3)	Pooled (3.4)
FF_POLICY	0.0251	0.0342	0.0061	0.0016
	[2.3351]**	[3.3445]***	[0.5007]	[0.2608]
C	–0.2963	–0.4893	–0.5750	–0.3663
	[–1.5060]	[–2.4593]**	[–2.5843]**	[–3.4398]***
POL_RATE(–1)	–0.0343	–0.0514	–0.0317	0.0032
	[–2.1021]**	[–4.5398]***	[–2.8138]***	[0.4043]
TIPS_ INF_USA(–1)	0.1151	0.0694	0.1799	0.0585
	[2.3749]**	[1.2124]	[2.4719]**	[1.6974]*
EMBI_LATAM	0.0111	–0.0039	0.0258	0.0141
	[1.4476]	[–0.6573]	[2.6270]***	[2.8582]***
D(POL_RATE(–1))	0.0027	–0.0692	–0.0375	–0.0417
	[0.0474]	[–1.2705]	[–0.6905]	[–1.2614]
INF_YOY(–6)	0.0196	0.0870	0.0391	0.0022
	[1.7463]*	[4.4663]***	[2.3166]**	[0.2993]
GROWTH(–6)	–0.0045	0.0219	0.0321	0.0309
	[–0.2612]	[2.3886]**	[2.4868]**	[2.8406]**
Observations	378	331	351	1060
R-squared	0.0309	0.0986	0.0485	0.0017
F-statistic	2.1018	6.1147	3.1841	4.9113

Note: *, **, and *** refer to significance at 10%, 5%, and 1%, respectively.

estimate of 0.732. The long-term pass-through for Colombia is now 0.661. To summarize: the results in table 1.3 indicate that during the period under analysis the central banks in Chile and Colombia tended to follow the Federal Reserve; the pass-through coefficient was, in both countries, lower than one.

An interesting question is whether monetary policy in these countries has been historically affected by the behavior of commodity prices. In order to analyze this issue, I included in each regression the log of the detrended commodity prices of greater relevance for each of the three countries: copper for Chile, energy and coffee for Colombia, and energy for Chile. The detrending of

TABLE 1.4. Monetary policy rates and commodity prices in Chile, Colombia, and Mexico, 2000–2008 (instrumental variables)

Eq Name	Chile (4.1)	Colombia (4.2)	Mexico (4.3)
FF_POLICY	0.0250	0.0322	0.0057
	[2.3188]**	[3.1479]***	[0.4680]
C	–0.3158	–0.4560	–0.5721
	[–1.5972]*	[–2.2955]**	[–2.5676]**
POL_RATE(–1)	–0.0332	–0.0500	–0.0315
	[–2.0353]**	[–4.4307]**	[–2.7994]**
TIPS_ INF_USA(–1)	0.1171	0.0598	0.1795
	[2.4069]**	[1.0489]	[2.4628]**
EMBI_LATAM	0.0118	–0.0042	0.0255
	[1.5316]*	[–0.7035]	[2.5911]**
D(POL_RATE(–1))	0.0006	–0.0575	–0.0361
	[0.0103]	[–1.0554]	[–0.6649]
INF_YOY(–4)	0.0196	0.0841	0.0391
	[1.6357]*	[4.3230]***	[2.3180]**
GROWTH(–4)	–0.0030	0.0221	0.0319
	[–0.1753]	[2.4394]**	[2.4741]**
LOG_COPPER_W(–4)	0.1209	—	—
	[0.3886]		
LOG_ENERGY_W(–4)	0.1095	–0.4262	–0.1425
	[0.4069]	[–1.9246]*	[–0.4375]
LOG_COFFEE_W(–4)	—	0.2938	—
		[1.4902]	
Observations	378	331	351
R-squared	0.0344	0.1137	0.0493
F-statistic	1.6665	5.5445	2.7953

Note: *, **, and *** refer to significance at 10%, 5%, and 1%, respectively.

these indexes was obtained using the Hodrick-Prescott filter. The results are in table 1.4. Broadly speaking, we can say that the results obtained confirm our earlier findings regarding "spillover." There is no strong evidence that commodity prices affected monetary policy during this period. Only one of the commodity coefficients is significant at conventional levels: energy in Colombia, with a negative coefficient.

5. Extensions, refinements, and robustness

In this section I present a number of extensions to the analysis. First, I investigate whether the yield on Treasuries of shorter maturities than 10 years have had an effect in the policy "spillover" process. In particular I consider the yield on two- and five-year Treasuries. It is possible that central banks' authorities in these countries take into account rates in the middle rather than at the long end of the yield curve. Second, I investigate if the volatility conditions in global financial markets have historically had an effect on the transmission of policy rates from the Fed to the countries in the sample. Third, I investigate the extent to which the degree of capital mobility has historically affected the extent of policy "spillover." Fourth, I present a number of robustness tests.

In the analyses presented in this section, I focus on a dynamic panel for Chile and Colombia, the two nations that in the results in the previous section appeared to have been subject to some policy "spillover" during the period under study. There are a number of advantages of using a panel, including the fact that in a panel some of the covariates exhibit greater variability (this is particularly the case for the index of capital mobility).

5.1 Moving along the yield curve

The results in the preceding section for individual countries suggested that the yield on the long Treasury note (10 years) hadn't affected, historically, monetary policy in the three countries in the sample. In this subsection I investigate this issue further by incorporating the yields of other Treasury securities along the yield curve. In particular, I estimate dynamic panel regressions (with instrumental variables and fixed effects) for Chile and Peru, with the yield on the two-, five-, and ten-year Treasuries as additional

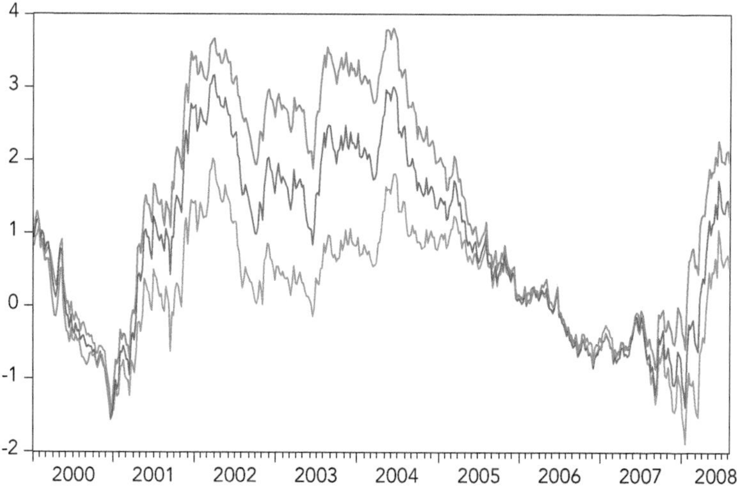

FIGURE 1.4. Spread between two-, five-, and ten-year Treasuries and federal funds rates, weekly, 2000–2008

regressors. Before proceeding further, let us look at how the spreads between the federal funds rate and these longer-term Treasury securities behaved during the period under investigation (see figure 1.4). As may be seen, the spreads (slopes of the yield curve at different points) are fairly high between mid-2001 and mid-2005; they were quite low during late 2000 and late 2007.

The results from the instrumental variables dynamic panel analysis are in table 1.5 and may be summarized as follows:

- The coefficient of the federal funds rate is always significant, confirming the existence of policy "spillovers" in the two countries that make up the panel. It is interesting to notice that the point estimate of the coefficient of the federal funds is higher in the regressions where the yield on longer-term Treasuries is incorporated. This indicates that the "spillover" effect is larger when we control for longer-term yields, and a hike in the federal funds makes the yield curve flatter.

TABLE 1.5. Monetary policy rates in Latin America and the yield curve, dynamic panel (Chile and Colombia), 2000–2008 (instrumental variables)

Eq Name	(5.1)	(5.2)	(5.3)	(5.4)
FF_POLICY	0.0141	0.0846	0.0421	0.0253
	[2.1931]**	[3.3751]***	[2.8125]***	[2.4035]**
C	–0.2987	–0.0639	–0.0976	–0.1300
	[–2.2316]**	[–0.4022]	[–0.5878]	[–0.7080]
POL_RATE(–1)	–0.0206	–0.0246	–0.0205	–0.0201
	[–2.4229]**	[–2.7927]***	[–2.3970]**	[–2.3629]**
TIPS_ INF_USA(–1)	0.0688	0.1009	0.0903	0.0811
	[1.9609]*	[2.6842]***	[2.4531]**	[2.2328]**
EMBI_LATAM	0.0083	0.0022	0.0077	0.0092
	[1.6130]*	[0.3919]	[1.4865]	[1.7716]
D(POL_RATE(–1))	–0.0338	–0.0306	–0.0306	–0.0325
	[–0.8611]	[–0.7602]	[–0.7737]	[–0.8263]
INF_YOY(–4)	0.0204	0.0101	0.0136	0.0169
	[2.6494]***	[1.6910]*	[1.6212]*	[2.0742]**
GROWTH(–6)	0.0171	–0.0044	0.0020	0.0086
	[1.6648]*	[–0.3255]	[0.1528]	[0.6823]
UST_2YR	—	–0.0935	—	—
		[–2.9143]***		
UST_5YR(–1)	—	—	–0.0573	—
			[–2.0730]**	
UST_10YR(–1)	—	—	—	–0.0402
				[–1.3436]
Observations	709	709	709	709
R-squared	0.0529	0.0082	0.0424	0.0520
F-statistic	4.1658	4.7380	4.2026	3.9069

Note: *, **, and *** refer to significance at 10%, 5%, and 1%, respectively.

- The coefficient of longer-term yields is always negative, and significantly so for the two- and five-year tenor. Moreover, the null hypothesis that the federal funds and longer Treasury yield sum up to zero cannot be rejected at conventional levels. This indicates that during the period under analysis a raise in the federal funds rate that was not accompanied by an increase in longer-term yields had a greater effect on these countries' monetary policy than a hike in the policy rate that results in a parallel shift of the midsection of the US yield curve.

5.2 Global financial conditions and monetary policy "spillover"

Has policy "spillover" worked in a similar way when the global economy is in turmoil as compared to when it is going through a tranquil period? In order to investigate this issue, I used the "TED spread," defined as the spread between the three-month London Interbank Offered Rate (LIBOR) and the effective (as opposed to policy) federal funds rate, as an indicator of market volatility. During periods of financial turbulence the TED spread increases; it declines during periods of tranquility. In figure 1.5 I present the weekly evolution of the TED spread for 2000 to 2008. During this period the mean was 0.21 (21 bps), the median was 0.18, and the standard deviation was 0.228. In the analysis I proceeded as follows: I estimated dynamic panel IV equations for two subsamples: "low volatility" (low TED spread) and "high volatility" (high TED spread). The definition of "high" and "low" was determined by the median value of the TED spread.

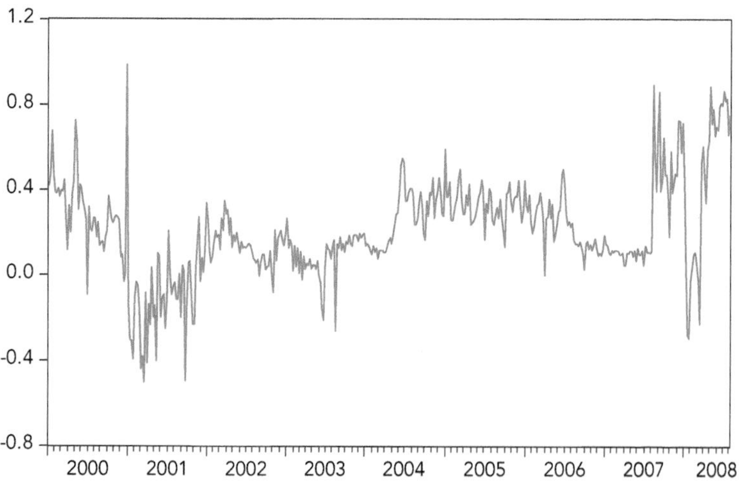

FIGURE 1.5. TED spread, weekly, 2000–2008

TABLE 1.6. Monetary policy rates in Latin America and global volatility, dynamic panel (Chile and Colombia), 2000–2008 (instrumental variables)

Eq Name	(6.1) High Ted	(6.2) High Ted	(6.3) Low Ted	(6.4) Low Ted
FF_POLICY	0.0986	0.0510	0.0165	0.0090
	[2.9686]***	[2.4409]**	[0.3983]	[0.3732]
C	–0.3545	–0.3029	–0.3113	–0.3538
	[–2.4117]**	[–1.9718]**	[–0.9305]	[–1.0117]
POL_RATE(–1)	0.0065	0.0026	–0.0170	–0.0163
	[0.4792]	[0.1810]	[–0.9142]	[–0.8863]
TIPS_INF_USA(–1)	0.0974	0.0996	0.0710	0.0675
	[2.3381]**	[2.3090]**	[1.1402]	[1.0910]
EMBI_LATAM	0.0141	0.0186	0.0101	0.0109
	[2.1733]**	[2.3505]**	[0.8774]	[0.9896]
D(POL_RATE(–1))	–0.1971	–0.1734	–0.0293	–0.0306
	[–2.9552]***	[–2.6999]***	[-0.4997]	[–0.5223]
INF_YOY(–4)	0.0059	0.0066	0.0150	0.0167
	[0.5185]	[0.5225]	[0.9771]	[1.1639]
GROWTH(–6)	0.0337	0.0268	0.0221	0.0259
	[4.1462]***	[3.0269]***	[0.6433]	[0.7682]
UST_2YR	–0.1235	—	–0.0068	—
	[–2.6501]***		[–0.1342]	
UST_5YR	—	–0.0819	—	0.0044
		[–1.9496]*		[0.1058]
Observations	301	301	382	382
R-squared	0.1151	0.1475	0.0365	0.0343
F-statistic	7.9707	7.4637	1.5386	1.5378

Note: *, **, and *** refer to significance at 10%, 5% and 1%, respectively.

The results from these regressions are in table 1.6. They indicate that "spillover" is a phenomenon that occurs during periods of higher global financial volatility. Indeed, these estimates suggest that there is no policy "spillover" during periods when global financial markets are calm. A possible explanation for this is that EMs' central bankers become particularly defensive during periods of global financial turmoil. It is during these times that they become particularly sensitive to global shocks and decide to follow the advanced countries' central banks. This notion is supported by the estimated coefficients of the EMBI variable: in the high-volatility regressions they are significantly higher than in the regressions for the complete sample, and their p-values are significantly lower; indeed, these coefficients are not significant during the low-volatility periods.

A preliminary analysis of the case of Mexico—remember that in the previous section I found no evidence of "spillover" for that country—indicates that there was indeed some response by its central bank to federal funds changes during high-volatility periods. However, in order to determine the robustness of this result, further research is required.

5.3 Policy "spillovers" and capital controls

In equation (1) I assumed that there was a tax of rate τ on capital leaving the country. Alternatively, it is possible to think that there is a tax on capital inflows of the type popularized by Chile during the 1990s.[27] If this is the case, equation (1) becomes[28]

$$r_t - r_t^*(1 - t) + t = E_t\{\Delta e_{t+1}\}, \tag{1'}$$

where t is the rate of the tax on capital inflows.

As pointed out above, the three countries in this study had varying degrees of capital mobility during the period under investigation, with Chile being the most open, and Colombia being the least open, to capital movement. In addition, during the (almost) 500 weeks covered by this analysis there were some adjustments to the extent of mobility in all nations. This was especially the case with Chile, a country that in early 2001, and during the negotiation of the

27. On the Chilean tax on capital inflows, see De Gregorio, Edwards, Valdes (2000) and Edwards and Rigobón (2009).

28. See, for example, Edwards (2012).

Free Trade Agreement with the United States, opened its capital account further. In figure 1.6 I present the evolution of a comprehensive index of capital mobility. In constructing this index I took as a basis the indicator constructed by the Fraser Institute; I then used country-specific data to refine it. A higher number denotes a higher degree of capital mobility in that country in that particular year.

An interesting question, then, is whether the degree of capital mobility affects the extent of pass-through from federal funds rates into policy interest rates in emerging countries. In order to address this issue, I estimated a number of IV dynamic panel regressions similar to those reported above, with two additional regressors: an index of capital mobility and a variable in which this index interacts with the federal funds rate. The results reported in table 1.7 should be considered preliminary and subject to further research for a number of reasons, including the fact that the index of capital mobility is an aggregate summary that includes different modalities of capital controls. To understand better the role of mobility on interest rate pass-through, it is necessary to construct more detailed and granular indexes. Furthermore, in order to investigate this issue fully, a broader sample that includes countries with greater restrictions would be required.

The results in table 1.7 are interesting. Overall they tend to confirm the findings reported above: there continues to be evidence of a pass-through from federal funds rates into domestic policy rates, even after controlling for other variables. As may be seen, the capital mobility index is significant and positive when entered on its own; in this case the federal funds coefficient continues to be significant and positive. The interactive variable is negative and significant at the 10% level in all regressions. This suggests that the higher the degree of mobility, the lower the effect of a change in the policy rate. A possible reason for this is that a higher degree of capital mobility is acting as a proxy for the sophistication of domestic capital markets. It is possible that with deeper domestic

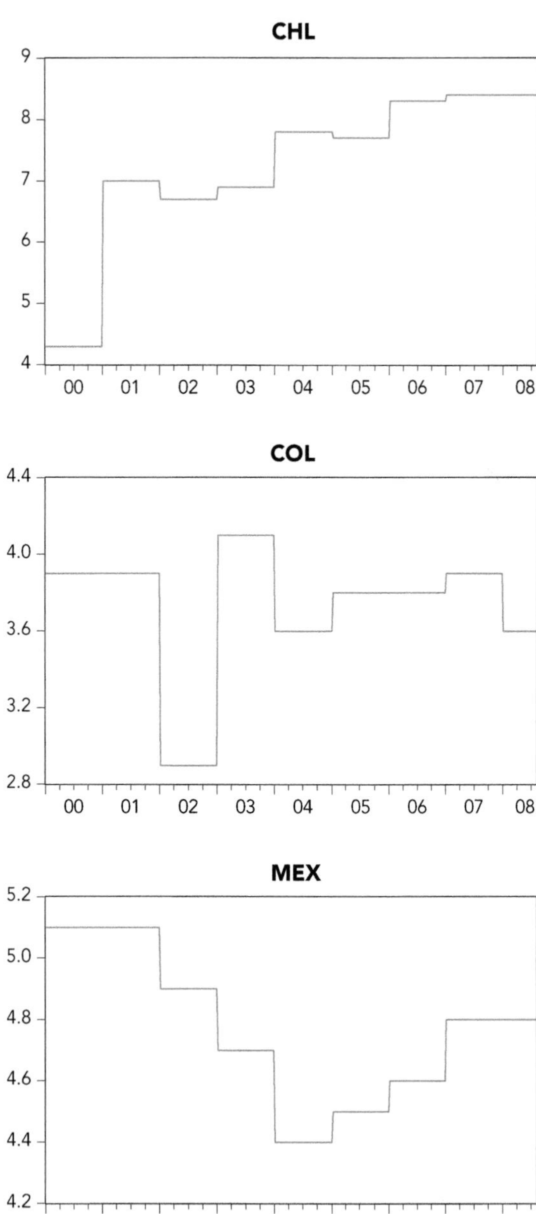

FIGURE 1.6. Capital mobility index for selected Latin American countries, 2000–2008

TABLE 1.7. Monetary policy rates in Latin America and capital mobility, dynamic panel (Chile and Colombia), 2000–2008 (instrumental variables)

Eq Name	**(7.1)**	**(7.2)**	**(7.3)**
FF_POLICY	0.0667	0.0759	0.0768
	[2.0288]**	[2.2010]**	[2.2153]**
FF_POLICY* CAP_CONT_NEW	–0.0105	–0.0120	–0.0113
	[–1.6174]*	[–1.8036]*	[–1.7841*]
C	–0.7534	–0.8726	–0.8849
	[–2.6063]***	[–2.7140]***	[–2.6975]***
POL_RATE(–1)	–0.0284	–0.0307	–0.0303
	[–3.1544]***	[–3.2514]***	[–3.2627]***
TIPS_ INF_USA(–1)	0.0194	0.0104	0.0123
	[0.4195]	[0.2216]	[0.2648]
EMBI_LATAM	0.0123	0.0124	0.0117
	[2.2361]**	[2.3016]**	[2.2101]**
D(POL_RATE(–1))	–0.0444	–0.0457	–0.0455
	[–1.1274]	[–1.1554]	[–1.1507]
INF_YOY(–4)	0.0375	0.0410	0.0393
	[2.5593]**	[2.7218]***	[2.7474]***
GROWTH(–6)	0.0228	0.0261	0.0258
	[2.1012]**	[2.2547]**	[2.2569]**
CAP_CONT_NEW	0.0805	0.0925	0.0890
	[2.1365]**	[2.3415]**	[2.3811]*
UST_2YR	0.0166	—	—
	[0.7575]		
UST_5YR	—	0.0265	—
		[1.1307]	
UST_10YR	—	—	0.0289
			[1.1355]
Observations	709	709	709
R-squared	0.0477	0.0403	0.0429
F-statistic	3.6382	3.7074	3.7081

Note: *, **, and *** refer to significance at 10%, 5%, and 1%, respectively.

financial markets a central bank could maintain a higher degree of independence. As noted, however, this is an issue that merits further analysis.

5.4 Other extensions

In order to determine the robustness of the results, I considered a number of alternative specifications, and I introduced additional regressors. Here I summarize some of the results.

Federal funds rate. I considered different lags in the federal funds rate (from contemporaneous to two-week lags). This had no discernable effect on the results. Also, the results were basically unaffected if the estimation period was altered somewhat and if the *effective* federal funds rate was used instead of the *target* rate.

Additional global financial variables. An interesting question is whether other variables related to global economic conditions enter these three countries' policy rules. I address this issue by considering two additional covariates: a stock market index for the United States (first differences of the log) and the first difference in the (log of the) euro-US dollar (USD) exchange rate. In two of the individual countries' regressions (Colombia and Mexico), the coefficient of the (one period lagged) euro-USD exchange rate is significantly positive. The inclusion of this variable, however, doesn't affect the main findings regarding policy "spillover" discussed above. The stock market covariate is not significant.

Short-term deposit rates. I also investigated the extent to which Fed policies were translated into (short-run) market interest rates. The results obtained—available on request—show that there is a significant and fairly rapid pass-through from Federal Reserve policies into three-month certificate of deposit rates in the three countries in the Latin American sample. This is the case even after controlling for expected depreciation, country risk, and global financial conditions such as the USD-euro exchange rate and commodity prices—for a preliminary analysis on this issue see, for example, Edwards (2012) and the literature cited there.

6. A comparison with East Asian nations

How characteristic are the Latin American countries in this study? How does their central banks' behavior compare to that of central banks in other EMs? In order to address this issue, I estimated a number of IV dynamic panel equations for a panel of three East Asian nations: Korea, Malaysia, and the Philippines. These three nations constitute a slightly more varied group than our group of Latin American countries is: Korea and the Philippines had (some degree of) currency flexibility during the period 2000–2008 while during most of the period under study Malaysia had fixed exchange rates (relative to the USD); the three East Asian nations' central banks were de facto (but not necessarily de jure) quite independent from political pressure; and Korea and the Philippines followed inflation targeting.[29]

The results for the East Asia panel are presented in table 1.8. The most important findings may be summarized as follows: (*a*) In contrast to the Latin American nations discussed above, for the East Asian nations the coefficients of the traditional Taylor rule components (inflationary pressures and domestic growth) are not significant, suggesting that during this period these countries implemented monetary policy following a criterion that differed from traditional Taylor rules. (*b*) There is, however, evidence that changes in the policy stance in the United States were transmitted, to some extent, to these East Asian nations. (*c*) But the most interesting result is that the magnitude of the monetary policy "spillover" is much smaller in East Asia than in Latin America. This becomes particularly clear when we compare the results in tables 1.5 and 1.8.

29. For indexes of central bank transparency and independence see Dincer and Eichengreen (2013).

TABLE 1.8. Monetary policy rates in East Asia, dynamic panel, 2000–2008 (instrumental variables)

Eq Name	(8.1)	(8.2)	(8.3)	(8.4)
FF_POLICY	0.0116	0.0149	0.0115	0.0114
	[4.0109]***	[2.0996]**	[3.0940]***	[3.8950]***
C	0.2523	0.2483	0.2524	0.2494
	[3.2841]***	[3.2271]***	[3.2776]***	[3.2262]***
POL_RATE(–1)	–0.0399	–0.0407	–0.0400	–0.0417
	[–4.6058]***	[–4.6363]***	[–4.5188]***	[–4.4447]***
TIPS_INF_USA(–1)	–0.0199	–0.0175	–0.0200	–0.0212
	[–1.2329]	[–1.0432]	[–1.2150]	[–1.2906]
EMBI_ASIA	0.0003	0.0006	0.0003	–0.0002
	[0.0371]	[0.0747]	[0.0340]	[–0.0220]
D(POL_RATE(–1))	–0.0020	–0.0031	–0.0019	0.0006
	[–0.0521]	[–0.0802]	[–0.0484]	[0.0163]
INF_YOY(–4)	0.0004	0.0008	0.0004	0.0004
	[0.1587]	[0.2890]	[0.1548]	[0.1549]
GROWTH(–6)	–0.0064	–0.0045	–0.0065	–0.0079
	[–1.6088]*	[–0.8470]	[–1.3051]	[–1.5894]
UST_2YR	—	–0.0053	—	—
		[–0.5097]		
UST_5YR	—	—	0.0003	—
			[0.0305]	
UST_10YR	—	—	—	0.0054
				[0.5058]
Observations	676	676	676	676
R-squared	0.0244	0.0321	0.0240	0.0180
F-statistic	3.8769	3.4716	3.4411	3.4715

Note: *, **, and *** refer to significance at 10%, 5%, and 1%, respectively.

The coefficients for the impact effect are smaller in the East Asian case. But, more important, the long-term pass-through coefficient is significantly smaller in East Asia than in Latin America. Compare, for instance, columns (5.1) and (8.1), which have the same specification. According to (5.1) the long-run pass-through in the Latin American nations is a relatively high 0.68, while it is only 0.29 in the East Asian nations. Interestingly, this historical difference in response is consistent with the behavior of EMs' central banks during late 2015 and early 2016 that was discussed above: the Latin American countries tended to follow the Fed and raise their policy rates while the East Asian nations stayed "on hold."

7. Concluding remarks

In December 2015 the Federal Reserve raised interest rates for the first time since 2006. At the time an important question was—and continues to be—how the tightening process would affect the emerging markets. Underlying that question was a bigger issue: To what extent do emerging markets follow an independent monetary policy? In this paper I attempt to provide a (partial) answer to this question by investigating the extent to which Fed policy actions have, in the past, been passed into monetary policy interest rates in a group of Latin American nations–Chile, Colombia, and Mexico—during the period 2000–2008.

The results indicate that two of the three countries—Chile and Colombia—were subject to policy "spillovers" during this period. Even after controlling for other determinants of monetary policy stance—including the traditional Taylor rule variables—changes in the Fed policy rate were transmitted into these countries' own policy rates. Interestingly, there is no evidence for "spillovers" for Mexico.

The finding of a nonzero pass-through from the Fed to monetary policy in two of the three countries in the sample with exchange rate flexibility is important for the debate on optimal exchange rate regimes. Indeed, according to traditional models, one of the key advantages of flexibility is that the country in question can run its own monetary policy. The results in this paper question that principle by indicating that at least for two out of three countries there is a fairly high degree of policy "spillover"—there is also some evidence of "spillover" in the three East Asian countries discussed in section 6. A possible explanation for the results reported in this paper is "fear to float" that is not captured fully by the covariates included in the analysis.[30] According to models in the Mundell-Fleming tradition, if there is less than perfect capital mobility, a hike in the global interest rate—generated by, say, Federal Reserve action—will result in an incipient external deficit and in a depreciation of the domestic currency. Indeed, it is currency adjustment what reestablishes equilibrium. If, however, there is "fear to float," the local authorities will be tempted to tighten their own monetary stance (that is, hike policy rates) as a way of avoiding the weakening of the currency. Further investigation along these lines should shed additional light onto the question of the "true" degree of monetary independence in small countries with flexible exchange rates. A particularly important point that follows from this analysis is that, to the extent that the advanced country central bank (that is, the Fed) pursues a destabilizing policy, this will be imported by the smaller nations, creating a more volatile macroeconomic environment at home.[31]

Data Sources

Interest rates: Policy rates were obtained from various issues of each country's central bank. Data on US Treasuries and federal funds rate were also obtained from *Datastream*. All the figures correspond to the Friday of that particular week.

Exchange rates: For the Latin American countries, they correspond to units of domestic currency per US dollar. Expected devaluation is constructed as the 90-day forward discount also relative to the US dollar. The euro-USD rate is defined as euros per US dollar. The source is *Datastream*.

Commodity Price Indexes: Obtained from the JP Morgan data set.

Country risk: Defined as the EMBI premium above Treasuries, measured in percentage points. The data were obtained from *Datastream*.

Inflation and growth: Individual countries' central bank bulletins.

30. Calvo and Reinhart (2000) is the classical reference on this subject.

31. For a discussion along these lines, see, for example, Taylor (2013). See also Edwards (2012) and Rey (2013).

References

Aizenman, J., M. Binici, and M. M. Hutchison. 2014. *The transmission of Federal Reserve tapering news to emerging financial markets.* National Bureau of Economic Research.

Calvo, G. A., and C. M. Reinhart. 2000. *Fear of floating* (no. w7993). National Bureau of Economic Research.

Cetorelli, N., and L. S. Goldberg. 2011. Global banks and international shock transmission: Evidence from the crisis. *IMF Economic Review* 59 (1): 41–76.

Clarida, R. H. 2014. Monetary policy in open economies: Practical perspectives for pragmatic central bankers. *Journal of Economic Dynamics & Control* Dec.: 21–29.

Claessens, S., H. Tong, and S. J. Wei. 2012. From the financial crisis to the real economy: Using firm-level data to identify transmission channels. *Journal of International Economics* 88 (2): 375–87.

Claro, S. and L. Opazo. 2014. Monetary policy independence in Chile. *BIS* paper no. 78.

De Gregorio, J., S. Edwards, and R. O. Valdes. 2000. Controls on capital inflows: Do they work? *Journal of Development Economics* 63 (1): 59–83.

Devereux, M. B., P. R. Lane, and J. Xu. 2006. Exchange rates and monetary policy in emerging market economies. *Economic Journal* 116 (511): 478–506.

Dincer, N., and B. Eichengreen. 2013. Central bank transparency and independence: Updates and new measures. Working paper.

Dornbusch, R. 1976. Expectations and exchange rate dynamics. *Journal of Political Economy,* 1161–76.

Edwards, S. 2006. *The relationship between exchange rates and inflation targeting revisited* (no. w12163). National Bureau of Economic Research.

———. 2012. The Federal Reserve, the emerging markets, and capital controls: A high-frequency empirical investigation. *Journal of Money, Credit and Banking* 44 (s2): 151–84.

———. 2015. Monetary policy independence under flexible exchange rates: An illusion? National Bureau of Economic Research working paper 20893.

Edwards, S., and E. Levy-Yeyati. 2005. Flexible exchange rates as shock absorbers. *European Economic Review* 49 (8): 2079–2105.

Edwards, S., and R. Rigobón. 2009. Capital controls on inflows, exchange rate volatility and external vulnerability. *Journal of International Economics* 78 (2): 256–67.

Eichengreen, B., and P. Gupta. 2014. Tapering talk: The impact of expectations of reduced Federal Reserve security purchases on emerging markets. World Bank Policy Research working paper 6754.

Frankel, J., S. L. Schmukler, and L. Serven. 2004. Global transmission of interest rates: Monetary independence and currency regime. *Journal of International Money and Finance* 23 (5): 701–733.

Glick, R., R. Moreno, and M. M. Spiegel. 2001. Financial crises in emerging markets (no. 2001–2007). Cambridge University Press.

Goldberg, L. S. 2009. Understanding banking sector globalization. *International Monetary Fund Staff Papers,* 171–97.

Ince, O., T. Molodtsova, A. Nikolsko-Rzhevskyy, and D. H. Papell. 2015. Taylor rule deviations and out-of-sample exchange rate predictability. Working paper.

Justiniano, A., and B. Preston. 2010. Monetary policy and uncertainty in an empirical small open-economy model. *Journal of Applied Econometrics* 25 (1): 93–128.

Miniane, J., and J. H. Rogers. 2007. Capital controls and the international transmission of US money shocks. *Journal of Money, Credit and Banking* 39 (5): 1003–35.

Molodtsova, T., and D. H. Papell. 2009. Out-of-sample exchange rate predictability with Taylor rule fundamentals. *Journal of International Economics* 77 (2): 167–80.

Molodtsova, T., A. Nikolsko-Rzhevskyy, and D. H. Papell. 2008. Taylor rules with real-time data: A tale of two countries and one exchange rate. *Journal of Monetary Economics* 55: S63–S79.

Monacelli, T. 2005. Monetary policy in a low pass–through environment. *Journal of Money, Credit and Banking,* 1047–66.

Obstfeld, M., J. C. Shambaugh, and A. M. Taylor. 2005. The trilemma in history: Tradeoffs among exchange rates, monetary policies, and capital mobility. *Review of Economics and Statistics* 87 (3): 423–38.

Rey, H. 2013. Dilemma not trilemma: The global financial cycle and monetary policy independence. Jackson Hole Economic Symposium.

Rogoff, K., S. J. Wei, and M. A. Kose. 2003. Effects of financial globalization on developing countries: Some empirical evidence (vol. 17). Washington, DC: International Monetary Fund.

Spiegel, M. M. 1995. Sterilization of capital inflows through the banking sector: Evidence from Asia. *Economic Review-Federal Reserve Bank of San Francisco* 3:17.

Taylor, J. B. 2007. Globalization and monetary policy: Missions impossible. In *International dimensions of monetary policy*, ed. M. Gertler and J. Gali, 609–624. Chicago: University of Chicago Press.

Taylor, J. B. 2013. International monetary coordination and the great deviation. *Journal of Policy Modeling* 35 (3): 463–72.

Taylor, J. B. 2015. Rethinking the international monetary system. Remarks at the Cato Institute conference, Rethinking Monetary Policy.

Tesar, L. L. 1991. Savings, investment and international capital flows. *Journal of International Economics* 31 (1): 55–78.

DISCUSSION BY DAVID PAPELL

It is a pleasure to read and discuss this interesting and well-written paper by Sebastian Edwards. There is a lot of detail in the paper that I'm not going to comment on here, so I highly recommend that you read it. The organizing principle of the paper is the impossible trinity or, equivalently, the macroeconomic policy trilemma. As first discussed by Mundell (1963), the idea of the trinity/trilemma is that, while countries would prefer to have fixed exchange rates, high capital mobility, and independent monetary policy, they can only attain two of the three objectives.

The paper considers the part of the trilemma that applies to emerging market economies with high degrees of capital mobility. Countries that do not restrict capital flows have two choices. One is to fix the exchange rate. We learned from the series of exchange rate crises in the 1990s and early 2000s that fixed exchange rates that can be changed do not work. You need a hard fix such as dollarization or a single currency that, in turn, totally dictates monetary policy. For countries that want to have monetary policy independence, the only choice is to have flexible exchange rates. A modern version is discussed by Taylor (2001), who proposes his own trinity, the possible trinity. For emerging market economies that do not choose to permanently fix their exchange rates, the only sound monetary policy is one based on a flexible exchange rate, an inflation target, and a policy rule.

The results of the paper can be considered in the context of the following policy rule:

$$r_p = \alpha + \beta r_p^* + \gamma x \qquad (1)$$

where r_p is the policy rate for the emerging market country, r_p^* is the policy (federal funds) rate for the United States, and x are the variables, such as inflation and the output gap, that enter a standard

Taylor (1993) rule. The coefficient α is determined by the inflation target, the equilibrium real interest rate, and the coefficient on inflation. Monetary policy independence is defined by the coefficient β being equal to zero so that the US federal funds rate does not affect the emerging market country's policy rate.

Edwards first estimates Taylor rules for three Latin American countries. The US federal funds rate is significant for Chile and Colombia, but not significant for Mexico. The long-term coefficients are substantial, and the results are robust to many controls. He then estimates Taylor rules for a panel of East Asian countries. While the results are also significant, they are not as large. The conclusion is that flexible exchange rates do not provide monetary policy independence.

What does monetary policy independence mean? From the perspective of this paper, it means that if a country has a policy rule, it should only have domestic variables in its rule, which would be contradicted by having either the US federal funds rate or the real exchange rate in the Taylor rule. This perspective receives support from Taylor (1999), who argues that, based on simulations of macroeconomic models, there is only a weak case for having an exchange rate in a policy rule. It also receives support from Clarida (2014), who shows that optimal policy in a two-country model would have a Taylor-type rule, where each country pays attention only to its own variables.

But there is another perspective. Why does monetary policy independence mean that a country cannot be concerned about the value of its exchange rate? In Mundell (1963) the central bank can still intervene in the foreign exchange market under flexible exchange rates; it just can't announce an exchange rate that it is going to defend. In Taylor's 2001 paper on advice for emerging market economies, flexible exchange rate policy doesn't mean that the exchange rate plays no important role in interest rate decisions or in a policy rule. Clarida, Gali, and Gertler (1998) found significant coefficients on either the federal funds rate or the real dollar exchange rate in Taylor rules for Germany and Japan, and there are many subsequent examples.

Suppose that all countries include foreign interest rates in their Taylor rules. Why is this a matter for concern? The basis for the concern comes from Taylor (2009). Suppose you have two countries, each of which responds to the other country's interest rate. In addition to equation (1), there would also be a policy rule for the foreign country:

$$r_p^* = \alpha^* + \beta^* r_p + \gamma^* x^* \tag{2}$$

where x^* are the variables that enter the foreign country's Taylor rule. Substituting equation (1) into equation (2), and vice versa, produces the following reaction functions:

$$r_p = \frac{\alpha + \beta\alpha^*}{1 - \beta\beta^*} + \left(\frac{\gamma}{1 - \beta\beta^*}\right) x + \left(\frac{\beta\gamma^*}{1 - \beta\beta^*}\right) x^* \tag{3}$$

$$r_p^* = \frac{\alpha^* + \beta^*\alpha}{1 - \beta\beta^*} + \left(\frac{\gamma^*}{1 - \beta\beta^*}\right) x^* + \left(\frac{\beta^*\gamma}{1 - \beta\beta^*}\right) x. \tag{4}$$

Assume that β and β^* are both between zero and one, so that each country raises its policy rate when the other country's policy rate increases, but less than point-for-point. Then $0 < \beta\beta^* < 1$ so that $1 - \beta\beta^* < 1$. The important characteristic of the reaction function is that the term that multiplies domestic variables is magnified for both countries. For the domestic country with a policy rule defined by equation (1), the coefficient γ is the desired response to the domestic variables x in the Taylor rule. Since $1 - \beta\beta^* < 1$, the actual response in equation (3) is larger than the desired response in equation (1). The same argument applies to the foreign country in equations (2) and (4). Because each country responds to the other country's interest rate, the policy responses are magnified.

The problem with this analysis, however, is that equations (1) and (2) can't possibly be the correct model for thinking about Latin American or Asian countries. When I think about the future path of the US federal funds rate, one thing that doesn't come to mind is what the interest rates in Chile, Colombia, or Mexico are going to be. Consider an alternative model, which is also discussed in Taylor (2009). What happens if the emerging market country responds to the US federal funds rate, but the United States doesn't respond to the emerging market country's policy rate? The policy rule for the emerging market country is still described by equation (1), but the policy rule for the United States is the standard Taylor rule:

$$r_p^* = \alpha^* + \gamma^* x^*. \tag{5}$$

Substitute equation (5) into equation (1):

$$r_p = \alpha + \beta(\alpha^* + \gamma^* x^*) + \gamma x. \tag{6}$$

The emerging market country responds to the US interest rate, which means that it responds to US macro variables, but there is no magnification effect. While concern about the exchange rate will affect monetary policy independence in the sense that it causes emerging market economies to respond to US variables, it does not affect monetary policy independence in the sense that it does not cause them to increase the policy response to their own inflation rates and output gaps.

In the context of flexible exchange rates and high capital mobility, I am not convinced that a policy response to the US federal funds rate based on concern about the exchange rate or capital flows is as important a problem as is represented by the paper because, since there is no magnification, emerging market economies do not have to increase the response to their own variables.

This assumes that the Fed follows its own policy rule. But what happens if the Fed deviates from its rule? While Sebastian talks about this at the end of the paper, saying it will create a more volatile macroeconomic environment, the paper is about "spillover" or contagion between policies. What I think is potentially more important is "spillover" or contagion between policy rule deviations. If the Fed deviates from its policy rule, does this create pressure on other countries to deviate from their policy rules? This is not an easy question to answer for developed economies, and I am doubtful that it can be answered with the span of data available for emerging market economies. But the question is worth asking. If flexible exchange rates do not insulate countries from US policy rule deviations, then monetary policy independence would truly be a mirage.

References

Clarida, R. 2014. Monetary policy in open economies: Practical perspectives for pragmatic central bankers. *Journal of Economic Dynamics and Control* 49: 21–30.

Clarida, R., J. Gali, and M. Gertler. 1998. Monetary policy rules in practice: Some international evidence. *European Economic Review* 42: 1033–67.

Mundell, R. 1963. Capital mobility and stabilization policy under fixed and flexible exchange rates." *Canadian Journal of Economics* 29: 475–85.

Taylor, J. B. 1993. Discretion versus policy rules in practice. *Carnegie-Rochester Conference Series on Public Policy* 39: 195–214.

Taylor, J. B. 1999. The robustness and efficiency of monetary policy rules as guidelines for interest rate setting by the European Central Bank. *Journal of Monetary Economics* 43: 655–79.

Taylor, J. B. 2001. Using monetary policy rules in emerging market economies. In *Stabilization and monetary policy: The international experience.* Proceedings of a conference at the Central Bank of Mexico.

Taylor, J. B. 2009. Globalization and monetary policy: Missions impossible. In *The international dimensions of monetary policy,* ed. M. Gertler and J. Gali, 609–624. Chicago: University of Chicago Press.

GENERAL DISCUSSION

SEBASTIAN EDWARDS: Let me tackle two issues that David Papell raises. The first one—something that John Taylor and I have discussed over the years and that comes up every time I go to an emerging market and talk to central bankers either as an advisor or just in a conversation—is about what to do with the exchange rate in respect to monetary policy. So the exchange rate, even in the most simple Taylor rule, is already indirectly in the monetary policy, because, of course, what happens to the exchange rate affects inflation through some pass-through mechanism. It doesn't have to be one-to-one. And the pass-through, as John Taylor has documented, has been declining around the world in the last 30 years. But, of course, every time Argentina devalues its currency, and the exchange rate just went from nine pesos to 14 or 15 pesos to the dollar, domestic inflation in Argentina goes up, because they are wired for a number of historical reasons to react to changes in the exchange rate. So the question is, Should the exchange rates play a role over and above this indirect role in monetary policy, or should we allow the exchange rates to do whatever it has to do and react as a shock absorber to different shocks in the world economy? That's a big, big question, and I don't think we have time to solve it during my two minutes here. But the point that I want to make is that even in any of these models, exchange rates already are there once you have local inflation.

The second point I want to raise—and I will just leave it open—is, Why should we worry about this monetary policy "spillover"? Is this a concern? There are two different approaches to this at least. One is the welfare approach. The United States does not take into account what Colombia does. Many of you guys are or have been in the FOMC. I'm sure that you've never spent even one millisecond talking about Colombia. And you haven't spent any time talking about what Chile does, a well-behaved country that is not about to go belly up, and even if it did, it is so small that no one would worry. And so in this case, as I point out in the paper, there is a one-way amplification effect, that only concerns the developing countries.

So why worry? One question is whether there are negative welfare implications by the way these central banks are behaving. And a related one is whether we should worry that, even if they are doing the right thing, because the exchange rate does truly belong in the augmented Taylor rule in order to minimize the volatility of nominal GDP, that is not what they are saying. And I think that it is important, and we should worry, because they are saying that they do something that they don't appear to be doing. And I think that for the markets to operate properly, the understanding of what central banks are doing is important, and we should match to some extent—and this has to do with, of course, transparency and communications—what central banks say with what they do. And what I think I'm doing here is unveiling the fact that indeed they say one thing while they do another thing. Now why would they say, "We don't pay attention to what the Fed does"? It's beyond me. There's no loss in dignity or honorability by saying, "Yeah, we look at what the Fed does." It's a big country, and it's very important.

HAROLD UHLIG: I have two questions. One is a conceptual one, the other is an econometric one. The conceptual one is this notion of independence here. So let me start with an analogy. When I was a child, my parents didn't really allow me to get drunk on weekends. And now that I'm an adult and independent from my parents, I still try not to get drunk on weekends. But it's not because I'm dependent on somebody else. It's because it's a good idea not to do that. And so you wonder if the central banks in these countries do what they do because it's a good idea or because they are dependent in some ways. The very essence of the Taylor rule in some ways is that central banks don't set interest rates arbitrarily. They set them according to economic circumstances, and maybe that's all that they're doing, and we just have to wrap our mind around why they're doing what they're doing. So I think the welfare question, to answer whether there's a lack of independence, is really at the heart of the whole discussion, and bringing that out more in the paper maybe would be nice, some theory.

The other one is the econometric question. It looks like you put the contemporaneous federal funds rate and the contemporaneous US policy stance on the right-hand side in the regression. But you have the lag policy rates in this regression. So for short horizons, it may not be all that surprising that news about monetary policy will result in news about domestic monetary policy. That's a little different from saying the stands of US monetary policy drive the stands of the monetary policy in the country. So the question is, What happens if you put in the stands of US monetary policy, say, with four lags? I notice there are a bunch of lag variables in there. But if it still shows up significantly there, you would have a much stronger case.

RICHARD CLARIDA: David Papell mentioned my 1998 paper with Gali and Gertler, and it actually addresses a couple of the issues here. So in that paper, we actually had a forward-looking Taylor rule. We were precisely interested in the issue of whether the real exchange rate enters into the Bundesbank's or the Bank of Japan's equations because it's useful in forecasting inflation, or whether it enters with an independent effect. And our generalized method of moments approach actually allowed us to test that hypothesis. And what we found is entering over and above its ability to forecast. So at least in our original work, we were directly focused on this issue of a reduced form of correlation from a forecasting role. But we found the independent role.

But the second point, I think, to Harold's observation: it's actually not hard to write down a model—as in my paper in this volume—where you can get a relationship between, say, Colombia's or Chile's interest rate and the US interest rate, because essentially there's a global dimension to the neutral policy rates. In the original Taylor formulation, the neutral rate's a constant, but you can write down models where not only is it time varying, but there's actually a global dimension to it, and then it's very easy for the foreign interest rate to enter, because it's essentially a proxy for that unobservable global factor. But nice paper.

SEBASTIAN EDWARDS: Harold Uhlig, Rich Clarida, and also David Papell raise the question of what really is independence here? And the answer is that I'm defining it in a particular way, which is very clear in the paper, which you may not agree with, but that's the way I define it. It's not fuzzy. It has to do with after estimating an augmented Taylor rule that includes some foreign or external or global variables, and I will get back in a second, once you estimate that Taylor Rule, whether the federal funds rate still plays a role. And here let me just add that I must apologize for not citing the Clarida, Gali paper, which, of course, is a very important paper on this topic. So this is the way I define independence, and that's why "contagion" or "spillover" is in quotation marks. It is a very particular way of doing it, and one can indeed write models where the foreign interest rate enters. But the question I think is what Vasco said, which is: Is it entering because it's an additional target, or is it entering because it affects the objective function of the central bank, which is to minimize the variability of nominal GDP over time?

ALLAN MELTZER: I've read Sebastian's paper. It's really very interesting. And it intrigued me that Mexico was so different. And I came up with this possible explanation, which I want to try on you. Mexico went through some really tough times up through 1994. And now it's 20 years past that, and it's followed a policy of noninflation during that period under sometimes difficult circumstances. So it has embedded in the holders of the peso the idea that Mexico will not inflate, just as holders of the dollar currently think the United States may never inflate again. Anyway, they have that strong belief, and they have more independence as a result. Whereas in Chile and certainly in Colombia, US pressure is very strong. And I end that by saying in my experience with the Bank of Japan over a very long time, I remember when Larry Summers came as the US undersecretary of the Treasury, came to Tokyo and told them, look, you're not allowed to change your exchange rate. And so it went back up. And he said you have to use fiscal policy.

SEBASTIAN EDWARDS: I think that I agree basically with what Allan said. Mexico is one of the few—not the only but one of the few—Latin American countries that had long, long, long periods of price and exchange rate stability: about 20 years of the peso when the old peso to the dollar was fixed at 12 pesos and fifty cents. That created a whole literature—most of you are too young to even remember it—the "peso problem" literature. The peso was at a discount every year for 20 years, and it never actually devalued, until it did. And when it did, it was gigantic. So I think that after the 1994–95 crisis in Mexico, that possibility became very clear. It was internalized by the market. I was a chief economist for Latin America at the World Bank, and I remember a good friend, Guillermo Ortiz, who was at the time secretary of the Treasury, sweating. This was a totally traumatic experience for Mexico. And they decided it would never happen again.

MICHAEL HUTCHISON: I'm wondering about the commodity prices in Chile. Isn't it the case that these kinds of exogenous shocks can be responded to immediately, while the lag of GDP takes some time? And officials also don't observe contemporaneous GDP and do observe commodity prices. Is it possible that you've underestimated the effect because you've left out commodity prices—Chile is an important example. Could you include other variables which are contemporaneously observable for policy rules?

SEBASTIAN EDWARDS: Mike Hutchinson makes some important points about commodity prices, and Chris asked the question: Why do the Latin American countries behave differently from the Asian countries? I think that part of it has to do with commodity prices. So the main difference between these countries—the Latin American and the East Asian countries—is that the Latin American currencies are commodity currencies and the East Asian currencies are not commodity currencies. And the commodity markets are denominated in dollars. So the price of copper in dollars, which has a role in the Chilean economy and the Peruvian economy, or the price of oil in Mexico and Columbia is affected in the world markets when the dollar changes in the world market and the dollar changes and responds in general to interest rate differentials. So interest rates in the United States have an important effect. And it also has an effect in expectations. So maybe that's an avenue that one has to continue to look into: the role of commodities.

CHRISTOPHER CROWE: I thought the finding that US policy was more important to Latin American countries than Asian countries was interesting and very plausible. I was wondering if we could have your thoughts on the reason why that is. I also wanted to give what might be a reason, which is the suggestive evidence that I saw when I was looking at a related issue: that if you look at overall capital flows to EMs and then look at capital flows from the United States to each of those EMs, in general, they're not very highly correlated. The exception is Latin American countries, where flows from the United States really drive flows in and out of those countries, and particularly in bank flows and debt securities, which presumably are the most interest rate sensitive parts of those flows. To my mind, that sounds like a plausible rationale why this is the case. So I'd be interested in your thoughts.

VASCO CURDIA: Sebastian's paper seems to be implying that you don't input the exchange rate because it's implicitly there, because you have local inflation. Through the indirect effects, you could argue the same thing about the federal funds rate to the extent that it affects financial conditions. That is already transmitted through the economy. So the question is whether they are there because they are a separate target or because they are some sort of summary statistic for other financial conditions or global conditions, So it would be interesting if you could dig a bit further, by including both exchange rates and the federal funds rate, because one of the arguments you mention for including the federal funds rate is maybe just to defend the currency. But if that's the case, just include the currency itself in there, right, with lags and so on.

Another thing which is partially there already is to include expectations for inflation in the United States, which maybe could be used as a proxy for inflation in the world. Why don't you use, let's say, International Monetary Fund forecasts for global demand and global inflation, or try to use some sort of trade-weighted measure of all those conditions. That's what should be in all those countries in a way, right, other than for financial conditions. So that will be an interesting thing.

WILLIAM ENGLISH: I wanted to follow up on Harald Uhlig's question. It seems to me that US policy or the exchange rate may matter because they affect the outlook for inflation or the outlook for the output gap, say. And because central banks should be forward-looking, it's not a surprise that these things enter into the policy rule in these countries. I guess the question is whether there's an overreaction relative to what you should expect based on the anticipated economic effects of the change in the US rate.

SEBASTIAN EDWARDS: Bill English raises the question of introducing forward-moving expectations and the global versus local economic effects. I do have in all of the estimates, as I said, the breakeven between either the five-year or the ten-year note and the five- or ten-year corresponding TIPS. And that is the market expectations of US inflation, which for these countries is an important forward-looking measure of the global inflation. So that is already in the paper.

As to Harald's point about different lags: I have tried, of course, different lags. Reporting is a complication. Sometimes you report, sometimes you don't. I should, as Harald says, report results with additional lags.

EVAN KOENIG: I have a colleague—Scott Davis—at the Federal Reserve Bank of Dallas who's made the argument that in trying to understand which countries are going to follow the Fed's lead and which aren't, it's really important to allow for the amount of dollar-denominated debt the country has and also the size of their foreign exchange reserves. So the underlying concern is the real burden of their debt.

SEBASTIAN EDWARDS: Evan Koenig makes a good point. And in terms of the empirical strategy, we have to look at what happens to reserves in these countries, and we have to look at the degree of dollarization of their debt, and so the balance sheet effect and the fear to float. The dilemma or the tradeoff in this research is whether to bring in the cross-section variability and improve the data and have a panel or whether to accept them as the unhappy families in Tolstoy's *Anna Karenina* sense: each country is different, and you have to focus on each country separately. And there is very little variability during any period of time that is not long, long, long, long, long in terms of dollarization. So let's take into account, for example, Colombia. Liabilities of dollarization may have gone in this period from 0.239 to 0.235. So it's really very hard to do it. So that's a tradeoff. And I realize that that's an important question.

CHAPTER TWO

The International Impact of the Fed When the United States Is a Banker to the World

David Beckworth and Christopher Crowe

ABSTRACT

The past few decades of globalization have seen a sharp rise in cross-border capital flows as the world has become more financially integrated. These changes have brought to light two important roles the US financial system has come to play in the globalized economy. First, the US financial system has become the main producer of safe assets for the global economy. Second, the US financial system's central bank, the Federal Reserve, has become a monetary superpower that to a large extent sets global monetary conditions. In this paper we document these two important roles of the US financial system and show how they have evolved over the past few decades. We then consider how the banker to the world and monetary superpower roles interact, specifically in light of the safe asset shortage problem that has emerged within the past decade.

1. Introduction

The past few decades of globalization have seen a sharp rise in cross-border capital flows as the world has become more financially integrated. Countries' gross external positions have ballooned, while net positions—referred to as global imbalances—have widened. These changes have brought to light two important roles the US financial system has increasingly come to play in the globalized economy.

The views expressed in this paper are those of the authors and do not necessarily reflect those of any Capula entity.

First, the US financial system has become the main producer of safe assets for the global economy. It does this by acting as banker to the world: it borrows short from foreigners and invests long abroad. In so doing, the US financial system creates the safe assets the rest of world craves but cannot create in sufficient volumes on its own. This global safe asset shortage has tended to push down yields and prompt investors' substitution into riskier assets. Attempts by the US private sector to create new types of safe assets (such as through mortgage securitization) or to issue existing safe assets in greater volumes (such as corporate bonds) have generally backfired: the securitization market collapsed, and only two US corporations now issue AAA-rated paper.[1] Safe asset supply is therefore increasingly concentrated in the safest public and publicly guaranteed assets, but the public sector has struggled to meet global safe asset demand amid political constraints on debt issuance. Meanwhile, the decline in yields globally has created new challenges for monetary policy.

Second, the US financial system's central bank, the Federal Reserve, has become a monetary superpower that to a large extent sets global monetary conditions. It, more than any other central bank, shapes the path of global nominal spending growth. Even though the Federal Reserve's mandate is domestic, its influence is increasingly global. In this paper we illustrate this global role through a number of channels: the increasing share of the global economy that uses or fixes its currency to the dollar; the dollar's increasing role in global credit flows; and episodes such as the "Taper Tantrum" and China's reserves sell-off that demonstrate how expectations of Fed policy changes quickly translate into a change in global financial conditions.

These two related roles mean that the world economy is very dependent on the US financial system to get it right. The world depends on the US financial system to provide an adequate amount

1. Those corporations are Microsoft and Johnson and Johnson (Karian 2016).

of safe assets and needs the Federal Reserve to maintain stable global monetary conditions. Some, although by no means all, of the strains in the global economy in recent decades can be attributed to failures on this score.

In this paper we document these two important roles of the US financial system and show how they have evolved over the past few decades. Critically, we also spend some time considering how the banker to the world and monetary superpower roles interact. Looking at historical cases, vector autoregressions, and a counterfactual exercise, we show that these two roles do interact sometimes in a destabilizing manner. We specifically examine them in light of a global safe asset shortage problem that has become more pronounced within the past decade.

We then conclude the paper by considering a proposal that we believe could mitigate some of the problems that arise when the banker to the world and monetary superpower roles interact. We also assess whether the United States could face competition for its dual role in the global economy in the near future and conclude that this is unlikely—making it all the more critical that the United States is able to perform these roles more effectively.

2. Banker to the world

One of the defining features of the US financial system is the role it plays in providing financial intermediation to the global economy. The United States tends to borrow short-term at low interest rates from the rest of the world while investing long-term on riskier assets abroad that earn a higher yield. By doing this, the US financial system provides safe, liquid assets to the rest of the world while funding economic development abroad. This tendency was first observed by Kindleberger (1965) and Despres at al (1966), who saw these activities as nothing more than the maturity transformation service of a bank. They therefore called the United States the "banker to the world."

These early observations of the United States acting as banker to the world occurred under the Bretton Woods System where the dollar was the key asset in the global financial system. The banker to the world role, however, continued after the Bretton Woods System broke down and, as noted by Poole (2004) and Gourinchas and Rey (2007), even intensified as globalization led to a sharp rise in cross-border capital flows.[2] This increased financial integration, though, was not matched by a similar deepening of financial markets in many parts of the world. Developing countries such as China and India saw their economies rapidly grow but were unable to grow their capacity to produce safe stores of value at a similar pace. Even advanced economies had uneven growth in their financial deepness (Mendoza et al. 2009).

As a result, there was increased demand for global financial intermediation services, and the US financial system stepped up to fill much of this void. Its deep financial markets and relatively robust institutions gave the United States a comparative advantage in issuing safe assets. It was well suited to serve as a banker to the world.

Gourinchas and Rey (2007) argue that not only is the US financial system acting as banker to the world, it is increasingly acting as a venture capitalist to the world. They note that over the past few decades an increasing share of US foreign investments, funded by its short-term liabilities to foreigners, became directed toward riskier assets. They see this as the natural evolution of the United States' banker to the world role as the global financial system becomes increasingly integrated.

Figures 2.1–2.4 document this banker to the world role by looking at the consolidated external balance sheet of the United

2. See Lane and Milesi-Ferretti (2001) and (2007) for a thorough documentation of this development. Goldberg (2011) provides further analysis of the US dollar's continuing dominant international role.

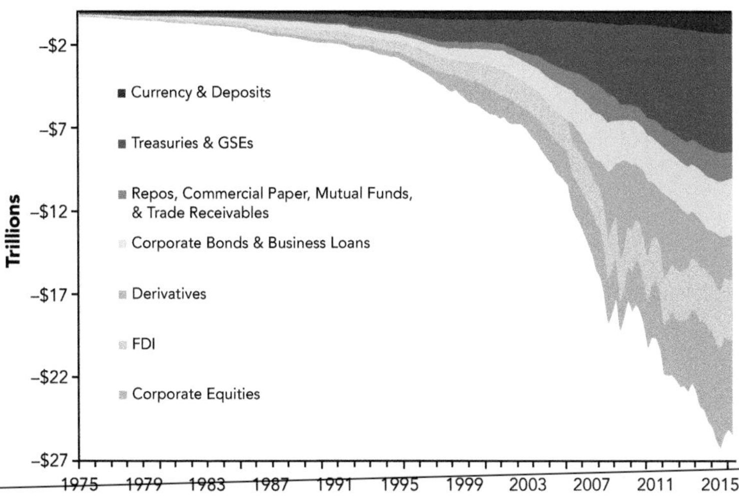

FIGURE 2.1. US Liabilities to the Rest of the World

Source: US Financial Accounts

States.[3] Figure 2.1, using data from the US financial accounts, shows in absolute dollar amount the liabilities the United States owes the rest of the world. The blue categories include everything from cash to treasuries to repurchase agreements and are generally considered safe assets. Derivatives issued by the United States to foreigners are arguably expected to be relatively safe assets, too—for example, recall AAA-rated Collateralized Debt Obligations pre-2008. The sum of these categories was $16.1 trillion at the end of 2015:Q4. This compares to $9.3 trillion of foreign direct investment (FDI) and equity foreigners owned in the United States at this time. US liabilities are disproportionately weighted toward the safe asset type.

Figure 2.2 shows the other side of the balance sheet: US assets owned abroad. Given the speculative nature of most US assets owned abroad, we assume here that the derivatives category

3. That is, the combined assets and liabilities of both the public and private sectors.

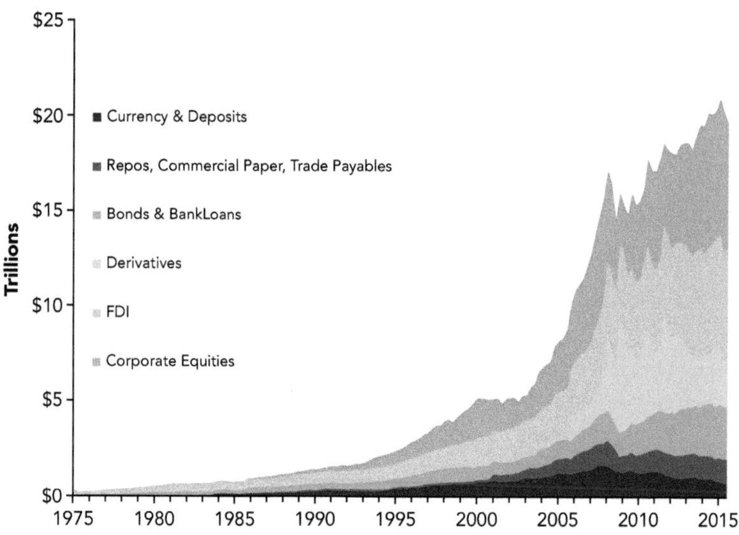

FIGURE 2.2. US Claims on the Rest of the World
Source: US Financial Accounts

represents higher-yielding riskier assets. If we add this to the FDI and equity categories, they make up $15.2 trillion out of a total US assets of $19.8 trillion. US assets are disproportionately weighted toward the riskier asset type.

Figure 2.3 summarizes these first two charts by showing the respective shares of risky assets and safe liabilities in terms of total assets and liabilities on the US balance sheet. The share of risky assets has trended upwards since the 1980s as financial globalization took root and now stands at 78% of total assets, while safe assets issued by the Unites States account for 63% of total external liabilities.[4] Just as a bank earns income on its net asset position from the spread between safe liabilities and riskier assets, so the United States earns positive income on its net international investment position (NIIP), as illustrated in figure 2.4. That the United States

4. Gourinchas and Rey (2007) find a similar pattern, hence their characterization of the United States as a venture capitalist.

FIGURE 2.3. Composition of US Balance Sheet

Source: US Financial Accounts, Authors' Calculations

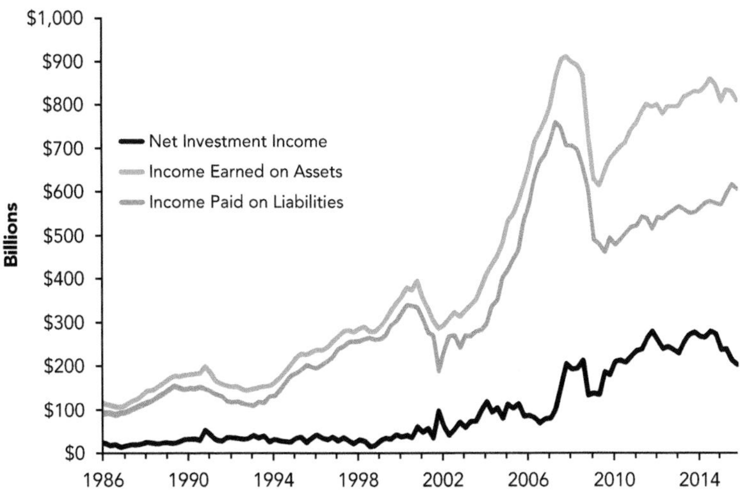

FIGURE 2.4. US Investment Income

Source: BEA

is able to earn positive income is all the more surprising when one considers that its external liabilities outweigh its assets by around 40% of gross domestic product (GDP).

To provide greater insight into how the United States is able to earn positive net returns on a negative net foreign asset portfolio, figure 2.5 decomposes the twelve-month net return (including valuation effects from changes in asset values) into contributions from the overall size of the NIIP (the level effect), the broad composition of assets versus liabilities (FDI, portfolio, and "other" investment —mostly bank flows), valuation effects from changes in exchange rates, and the residual, which reflects return differentials within broad asset classes not due to currency moves.[5] Overall net returns have been positive on average since 2007. The level effect is generally negative, reflecting the fact that the United States' liabilities outweigh its assets. The exception is the period of the global financial crisis, when average returns were negative and so a negative NIIP translated into a positive return.

Broad composition effects are highly procyclical, thanks to the greater skew towards riskier portfolio assets on the liability side relative to the asset side, and are slightly negative on average. The skew towards riskier assets is more pronounced within broad asset classes. For instance, within portfolio investment, US assets are skewed towards riskier equity while liabilities are skewed towards debt assets. Moreover, since US liabilities are overwhelmingly in

5. The levels effect applies the average return on all US liabilities to the net asset position and so captures the portion of net returns that is attributable to the overall size and sign of the NIIP. The broad composition effect shows the share of the return differential that is attributable to differences in the relative composition of assets and liabilities across the three broad asset classes (FDI, portfolio, and "other" investment) and is calculated using the return on US liabilities for each asset class. The remaining differential is attributable to the difference in returns between assets and liabilities within each asset class. This differential is broken down into differences in returns that are attributable to changes in exchange rates and the residual. Foreign exchange effects are estimated using the currency breakdown of US assets and liabilities provided by Benetrix et al. (2015) and show valuation effects attributable to changes in the US dollar effective exchange rate for assets and liabilities, where the latter is weighted by the currency composition of assets and liabilities respectively.

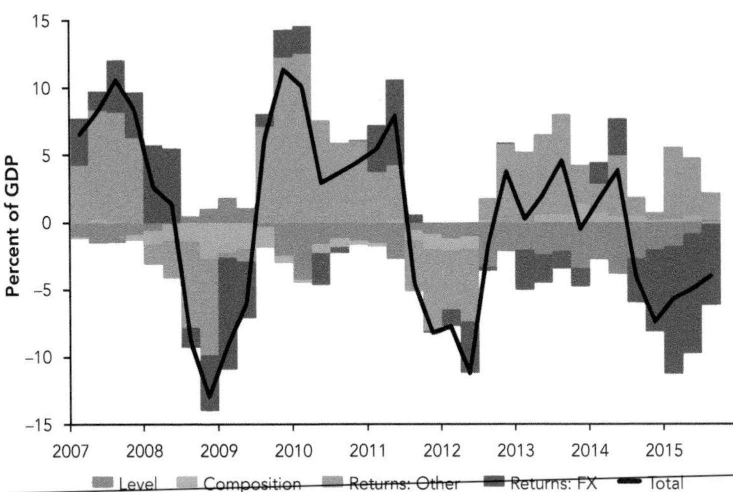

FIGURE 2.5. Decomposition of US Net Return on NFA

Notes: Annual (12m) returns on NIIP as % GDP Returns: FX: return thanks to differential returns on assets and liabilities thanks to FX moves. Assumes external assets denominated in foreign currencies with weights equal to WSJ USD index, while external liabilities denominated in USD Returns: Other: returns from coupon and valuation changes for assets vs liabilities, excluding impact of FX moves above Composition: returns thanks to differential composition of assets and liabilities Level: returns thanks to overall NIIP Total: total returns on NIIP

Source: Haver Analytics, Authors' Calculations

dollars (more than 80%) while assets are more likely to be denominated in foreign exchange (around 67%), the United States is exposed to foreign exchange risk. Both forms of risk exposure imply substantial returns volatility but also contribute to average returns, offsetting the negative contribution from running a negative overall NIIP.

The rapid swing of the United States' net returns from positive to negative in 2008–09 illustrates another facet of the US role, notably the provision of countercyclical "insurance" to global investors. Equivalent to 10% to 15% of US GDP on an annualized basis, the net wealth transfer from the United States provided a useful stabilizing role during the global crisis. Initially, the insurance was paid in the form of lower local currency returns on US holdings of foreign assets, notably thanks to big drops in equity prices. Later much of the payment came in the form of US dollar appreciation, as "flight to safety" concerns boosted the US currency and lowered the value of US asset holdings abroad. This insurance role has been dubbed "exorbitant duty" by Gourinchas et al. (2010).[6]

The observation that the United States fulfills this banker to the world role has a number of implications. First, it suggests that the United States has a greater debt capacity than would otherwise be the case. The United States' persistent current account deficit and resulting accumulation of liabilities is a result of global demand for "safe" US dollar assets, including demand for official reserves on the part of emerging market (EM) central banks as well as the savings needs of an ageing global population. As a number of authors have noted, the "exorbitant privilege" of issuing the global reserve currency allows the United States to fund a perennial current account deficit, just as a bank's role in the financial intermediation process allows it to perennially fund its assets and earn a spread through issuing cheap, less risky, debt (Gourinchas and Rey 2007).

One popular explanation for the United States' ability to adopt this role in the global financial system is that its deep and liquid financial markets endow it with a comparative advantage in issuing "safe" assets and in providing insurance against shocks for non-US residents faced with less-developed financial markets at home. For instance, Mendosa et al. (2009) develop a multicountry general equilibrium model with incomplete asset markets, where countries differ in their level of financial development (defined as the degree of enforceability of financial contracts). In their model, as globalization leads to greater financial integration of the countries with

6. Tille (2003) also notes the important role of currency movements on the US NIIP, thanks to the large gross positions that have built up and the differing currency composition of assets and liabilities.

more- and less-developed financial sectors, the country with the greater degree of financial development sees its net asset position deteriorate as the less-developed country builds up riskless claims against it—matching the experience of the United States described above.

Caballero et al. (2008) come to similar conclusions, although in their model the collapse in domestic asset values associated with the 1990s EM crises, as well as ongoing processes of financial integration, help to account for the flows into less risky US assets. Forbes (2010) provides some further empirical support for this argument, noting that investors in countries with relatively poorly developed domestic asset markets are more likely to hold US assets. These effects are significant and robust, whereas more traditional diversification arguments for cross-country asset holdings receive little empirical support.

A second implication is that a rapid reversal of this position is unlikely. The funding for the US current account deficit is not grudging or volatile but reflects a fundamental desire by non-US residents to build up stocks of safe assets, turning to the United States as banker to the world given its demonstrated comparative advantage in this area. The fact that this funding is freely given is most obviously reflected in the relatively poor returns that foreigners earn on their US assets. But the stickiness of this funding is also obvious when you consider whether there is any other country that could fulfil this role. As figure 2.6 shows, only the United Kingdom comes close in its share of global safe assets, but if the United States is run as a venture capital firm then the United Kingdom is arguably closer to a highly leveraged hedge fund, with 72% of its liabilities in the form of liquid assets, a much smaller economy, lower debt capacity, and no ability to print the global reserve currency.

A corollary of this is that a run on the US dollar prompted by concerns about the US current account deficit is unlikely. A

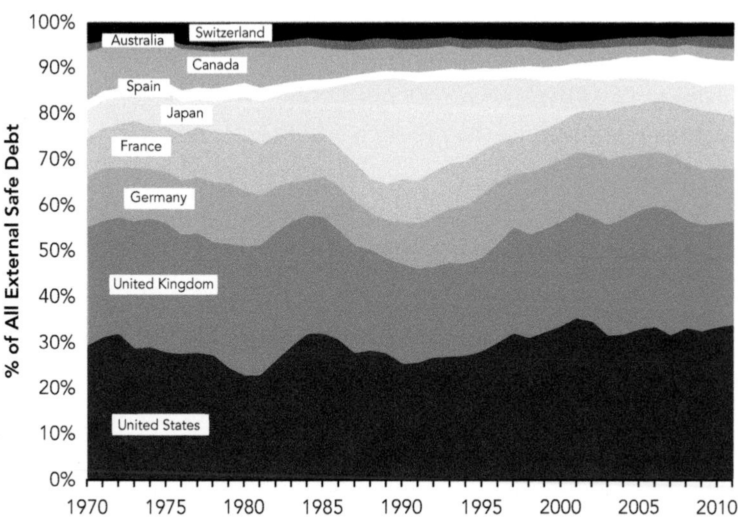

FIGURE 2.6. Share of World's Safe Assets
Source: Lane and Milesi-Ferretti (2007), Authors' Calculations

number of authors noted concerns about the sustainability of the US current account deficit in the run-up to the global financial crisis. Summers (2004) argued that "there is surely something odd about the world's greatest power being the world's greatest debtor," focusing on domestic savings-investment imbalances in the United States as the driver of the current account deficit rather than on the willing inflow of foreign capital that was its counterpart. Roubini and Setser (2005), Gros et al. (2006), and Krugman (2007) made similar arguments. These observers missed or failed to fully appreciate the banker to the world role played by the US financial system.[7] And while it is possible to have a run on a bank, it is unlikely to have a run on the main banker to the world when there are few good alternatives.

7. However, as we have argued elsewhere (Beckworth and Crowe 2012), some of the demand for US safe assets was recycled US monetary policy, and that proved to be distortionary. See the next section for more on this point.

3. Monetary superpower

Another defining feature of the US financial system is that its central bank, the Federal Reserve, has inordinate influence over global monetary conditions. Because of this influence, it shapes the growth path of global aggregate demand more than any other central bank does.

This global reach of the Federal Reserve arises for three reasons. First, many emerging and some advanced economies either explicitly or implicitly peg their currency to the US dollar given its reserve currency status. Doing so, as first noted by Mundell (1963), implies these countries have delegated their monetary policy to the Federal Reserve as they have moved towards open capital markets over the past few decades.[8] These "dollar bloc" countries, in other words, have effectively set their monetary policies on autopilot, exposed to the machinations of US monetary policy.[9] Consequently, when the Federal Reserve adjusts its target interest rate or engages in quantitative easing, the periphery economies pegging to the dollar mostly follow suit with similar adjustments to their own monetary conditions.

The extended reach of US monetary policy can be seen in figure 2.7. It shows the share of world GDP at purchasing power parity that is under the three largest currency blocs.[10] As of 2015, the dollar bloc made up 41% of world GDP compared to 16% that comes from the US economy alone. This is approximately a 2.5-fold increase in the reach of Federal Reserve policy. If it were not for these dollar bloc countries, the scope of US monetary policy

8. Chinn and Ito (2006) document this trend using an index on capital market openness for 182 countries. They show advance economies began opening up their capital accounts in 1980s while emerging and developing economies began doing so more in the 1990s.

9. Arbitrage in the foreign exchange markets leaves them no other choice but to follow US monetary policy if they want to maintain the peg. This is the "impossible trinity" or "macroeconomic trilemma" where countries can only accomplish two of three goals: peg to another currency, allow free capital flows, or conduct independent monetary policy.

10. Figure 2.7 is based on the de facto currency pegs in Ghosh et al. (2014). We are grateful to the authors for sharing their data.

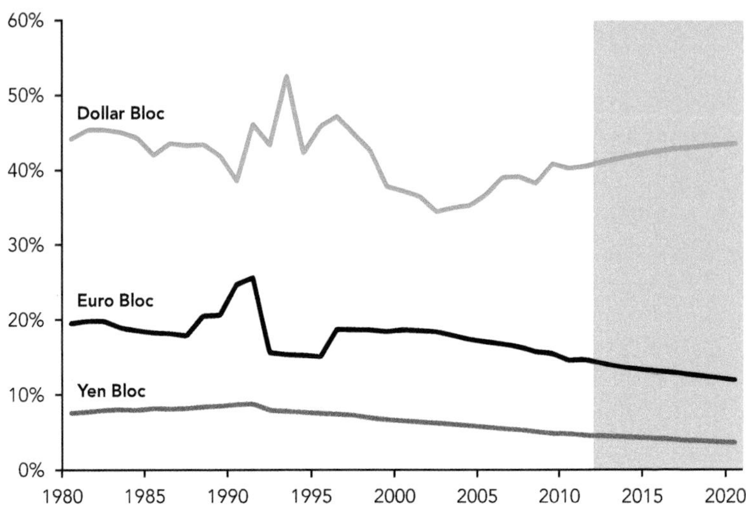

FIGURE 2.7. Share of World GDP at PPP for Currency Blocs

Note: De facto currency pegs based on Ghosh et al. (2014)
Source: PPP GDP data taken from IMF WEO database

would be similar in size to the euro bloc, which accounted for 15% of world GDP in 2015. In a distant third, the yen bloc comes in at 5% of world GDP. According to IMF estimates, this dollar bloc is expected to slightly grow as emerging economies become a larger share of the global economy.[11]

The second reason for the global reach of US monetary policy is that a large and growing share of global credit is denominated in dollars. That means the Federal Reserve's influence over the dollar's value gives it influence over the external debt burdens of many countries. For example, the Federal Open Market Committee's talking up of interest rate hikes from mid-2014 through the end of 2015 that caused the dollar to appreciate over 20% also sharply added to the debt burden for many economies.

11. This projection should be viewed with some caution as it assumes all dollar bloc countries will continue to maintain their dollar peg. Presumably, some of the emerging economies will eventually float their currencies.

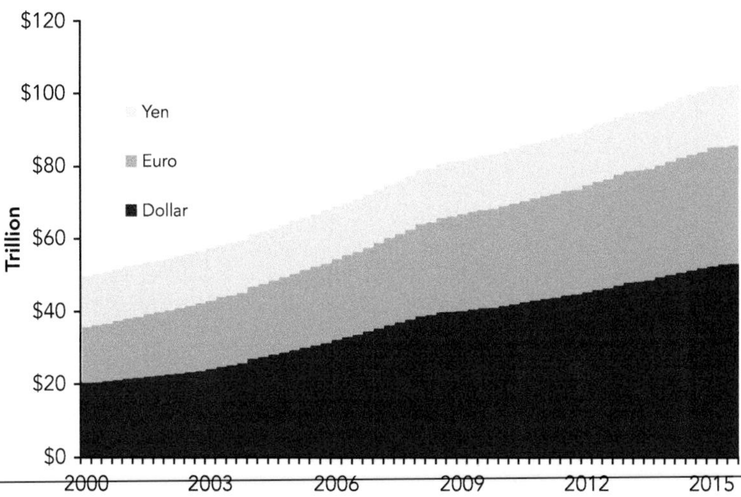

FIGURE 2.8. Currency-Denominated Lending (Bank Lending and Debt Securities)

Source: BIS data on global credit aggregates; Haver Analytics

The extent of this influence can be seen in figures 2.8 and 2.9. The first figure shows the Bank for International Settlements (BIS) measure of global aggregate credit comprised of bank lending and debt securities that is denominated in the yen, euro, and US dollar. The overall stock grew from $50 trillion in 2000:Q1 to $103 trillion in 2015:Q3. The dollar share of this measure grew from 41% to 52% over the same period, as the growth of euro- and yen-denominated credit failed to keep pace.

Figure 2.9 looks at credit extended to nonresidents (i.e., US dollar loans and debt securities issued to non-US residents) and reveals the increasingly dominant role of the US dollar. While credit to nonresidents more than tripled overall, from $3.7 trillion in 2000:Q1 to $13.0 trillion in 2015:Q3, the dollar share increased from 62% to 75%. This dominant share is why the Federal Reserve not only influences monetary but financial conditions for much of the world.

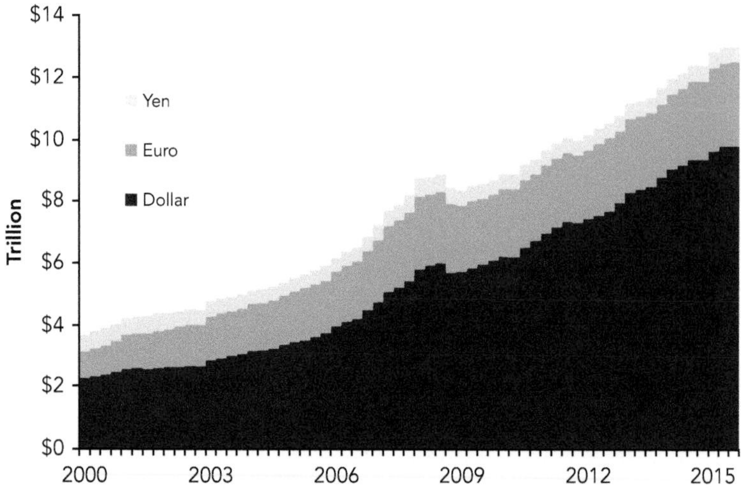

FIGURE 2.9. Currency-Denominated Lending Outside of Currency's Home Jurisdiction

Note: Lending includes bank lending and debt securities.
Source: BIS data on global credit aggregates; Haver Analytics

The third reason for the extended reach of US monetary policy is that other advanced-economy central banks are likely to be mindful of, and respond to, Federal Reserve policy given the large size of the dollar bloc. To see this, consider what could happen if the Federal Reserve decided to cut its interest rate target and engage in another round of quantitative easing. This easing of US monetary policy would be transmitted to the dollar bloc economies and cause their currencies, along with the US dollar, to depreciate relative to the yen and the euro. If the dollar bloc depreciation were big enough, it would force the Bank of Japan and the European Central Bank to begin easing monetary policy lest their currencies appreciate too much against the dollar bloc. Other advanced-economy central banks would follow suit. Other channels, such as the international risk-taking channel of Bruno and Shin (2014), may intensify this response.[12] This understanding

12. Bruno and Shin (2014) show how global banks are able to facilitate additional bank-funded leverage in other countries in response to easing by the Federal Reserve.

suggests that US monetary policy may be amplified beyond the dollar bloc's 41% of world GDP. Moreover, it implies that central banks in other advanced economies may be limited in their ability to conduct independent monetary policy.

A spate of recent studies provides evidence that supports this view. Belke and Gros (2005) and Beckworth and Crowe (2012) show that exogenous shocks to the federal funds rate Granger-cause innovations in the European Central Bank's marginal refinancing rate but not the other way around. Gray (2013) estimates the reaction function of twelve central banks—nine of which are in advanced economies—and finds that all of them systematically respond to changes in the federal funds rate.[13] McCauley et al. (2015) show that monetary conditions in both advanced economies and emerging economies were affected before and after the 2008 crash by US monetary policy.[14] Similarly, Chen et al. (2016) and Georgiadis (2016) show that the Federal Reserve's large-scale asset-purchase programs affected both advanced and emerging economies.[15]

Figure 2.10 provides evidence consistent with these findings. It shows the US Taylor rule gap—the Taylor rule federal funds rate minus the actual federal funds rate—plotted against the year-on-year growth of nominal spending for the countries of the Organisation of Economic Co-operation and Development (OECD) less the United States for the period of 1995:Q1 to 2015:Q4.[16] This figure plots, in other words, the stance of US monetary policy against

13. The twelve countries are Australia, Canada, South Korea, United Kingdom, Norway, New Zealand, Denmark, Israel, Brazil, Eurozone, China, and Indonesia. He shows the reaction function coefficient on the federal funds rate goes as high at 0.75%. Along these same lines, Taylor (2012) provides an interesting example of an advanced economy central bank, the Norges Bank, which explicitly states its actions are contingent on what the Federal Reserve does with its monetary policy.

14. They specifically look at US dollar credit growth outside the United States and find that prior to the crisis it was driven by foreign interest rate spreads over the federal funds rate. Since 2008 it has been more influenced by the foreign interest rate spread over the ten-year Treasury yield. They also show that advanced economies dollar credit growth was faster before 2008 but still makes up around 50% of outstanding dollar-denominated credit held by non-US residents.

15. Though in some cases the effect was greater for the emerging economies.

16. The construction of this Taylor rule is discussed in the next section.

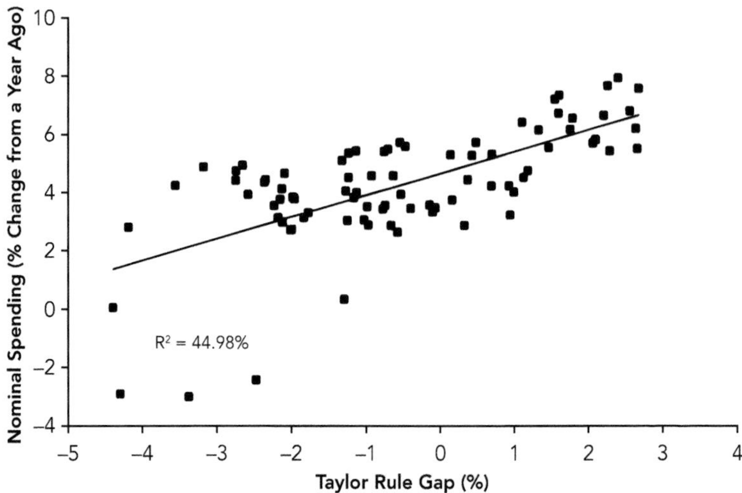

FIGURE 2.10. Fed Policy & OECD less USA Nominal Spending Growth (1995:Q1–2015:Q4)

Note: Nominal spending is measured by OECD's current price GDP (NGDP). The Taylor rule Gap equals the Taylor rule federal funds rate minus actual federal funds rate.
Source: Fred Database, IMF WEO, OECD Statistics, CBO, Authors' Calculations

aggregate demand growth in other mostly advanced economies.[17] Given the discussion above, the strong positive relationship shown in this figure indicates there is a strong linkage between Federal Reserve policy and monetary conditions in advanced economies.

These findings imply that even inflation-targeting central banks in advanced economies with developed financial markets are not immune from the influence of Federal Reserve policy. This has led Rey (2013, 2015) to argue that the standard macroeconomic trilemma view is incomplete. This trilemma says that in a financially integrated world with free capital flows a country can have an independent monetary policy and be insulated from external financial

17. The OECD countries less the United States are as follows: Australia, Austria, Belgium, Canada, Chile, Czech Republic, Denmark, Estonia, Finland, France, Germany, Greece, Hungary, Iceland, Ireland, Israel, Italy, Japan, Korea, Luxembourg, Mexico, Netherlands, New Zealand, Norway, Poland, Portugal, Slovak Republic, Slovenia, Spain, Sweden, Switzerland, Turkey, and United Kingdom.

shocks if it has a flexible exchange rate. Rey contends that if there are key "monetary policy centers" that shape "global financial cycles" then a flexible exchange rate will not be enough. She provides evidence that the key monetary center is the Federal Reserve.

Because of this inordinate influence the Federal Reserve has over global monetary conditions, Beckworth and Crowe (2013) and Gray (2013) have called it a "monetary superpower." They note that a key challenge the Federal Reserve faces as a monetary superpower is that it sets monetary policy for US economic conditions not global economic conditions. Consequently, it may inadvertently cause changes in the global monetary conditions that are too loose or too tight for the rest of the world.[18] Three examples since the early 2000s illustrate how the Federal Reserve can unintentionally be a destabilizing force in the global economy: the growth of global economic imbalances from 2002 to 2006, the emerging market boom of 2010–2011, and the emerging market slowdown of 2013–2015.

Global imbalances 2002–2006

Between 2002 and 2006 global current account imbalances rapidly grew with many emerging economies, commodity exporters, and some advanced economies running large current account surpluses while many advanced economies, especially the United States, ran large current account deficits. Prior to the crisis, many observers viewed this development with alarm as it portended a dollar crisis. After the crisis, many viewed it as a key factor behind the financial crisis of 2007–2009 since it implied a large inflow of capital to advanced economies, which, in turn, fueled the credit and housing boom.[19] As we discussed earlier, the precrisis critics were off since

18. Some observers, such as Taylor (2009) and Sumner (2011), argue the Fed sometimes fails to get even US monetary conditions right.

19. See Borio and Disyatat (2011) for a review of this argument and the literature behind it.

they missed the banker to the world role played by the US financial system. The postcrisis critics, however, also missed something. The world's demand for safe assets from the banker to the world during this time was partly an endogenous response to the actions of the monetary superpower.

To be clear, and as we alluded to earlier, there had been a growing demand for safe assets for some time. Caballero (2006) sees this "safe asset shortage" problem beginning with the collapse of Japanese asset values in the early 1990s and intensifying in the late 1990s as a result of the emerging market crises. These developments and the rapid growth of the emerging world had already increased the demand for safe assets. This structural shift in the demand for safe assets, however, was compounded by the actions of the Federal Reserve in the early to mid-2000s. This cyclical shift in the demand for safe assets happened, as argued by Borio and Disyatat (2011) and Beckworth and Crowe (2012), because of the Federal Reserve's monetary superpower status.

During this time the Federal Reserve engaged in a cycle of monetary easing that many considered excessive as it kept interest rates "too low for too long".[20] This easing put downward pressure on the dollar that the dollar bloc countries had to offset in order to maintain their dollar pegs. They did so by buying up dollars in the foreign exchange market and reinvesting most of them into US safe assets.[21] The demand, then, for the financial intermediation services of the banker to the world during this time was in part a response to the easing of Federal Reserve policy. Some of the global imbalance growth was simply recycled US monetary policy.

What made this monetary easing destabilizing was not just that it recycled monetary policy back into the US economy but

20. See, for example, Taylor (2009).

21. They also had to sterilize the increase in their own monetary base that resulted from buying up dollars in the foreign exchange market.

that it was overly expansionary given the state of the global economy. During this period the world got buffeted by a series of large positive supply shocks from the opening up of Asia and the technology innovations in the early 2000s.[22] The opening up of Asia significantly increased the world's labor supply while the technology gains increased productivity growth. This rapid growth of the global labor force and productivity both raised the expected return to capital. These developments, in turn, put upward pressure on the global natural interest rates while putting downward pressure on global inflation rates. Consequently, as noted by Beckworth (2008) and Selgin et al. (2015), a more stabilizing response from the Federal Reserve during this time would have been to avoid holding interest rates low for so long and allow the benign disinflationary forces to emerge. By failing to do so, the Federal Reserve inadvertently helped fuel a global credit and housing boom during this time.[23]

Emerging market boom of 2010–2011

Given the anemic US recovery following the Great Recession, the Federal Reserve engaged in series of large-scale asset-purchase programs known as quantitative easing (QE). While these expansionary programs may have been appropriate for the weak US economy, they were too expansionary for most of the dollar bloc countries, which had experienced faster recoveries. Then San Francisco Fed president Janet Yellen (2010) recognized this point in a 2009 speech she delivered during a trip to China:[24] "For all practical purposes,

22. The US productivity boom peaked between 2002 and 2004. See Selgin et al. (2015) for more on this development.

23. It arguably also encouraged easing in the Eurozone given the linkages described above.

24. Then Fed chair Ben Bernanke also acknowledged that US monetary policy was too expansionary for China in a lecture given to George Washington University students in 2012. See Peterson and Derby (2012).

Hong Kong delegated the determination of its monetary policy to the Federal Reserve through its unilateral decision in 1983 to peg the Hong Kong dollar to the US dollar. . . . Like Hong Kong, China pegs its currency to the US dollar, but the peg is far less rigid. . . . Because both the Chinese and Hong Kong economies are further along in their recovery phases than the US economy, current US monetary policy is likely to be excessively stimulatory for them. However, as both Hong Kong and the mainland are currently pegging to the dollar, they are both to some extent stuck with the policy the Federal Reserve has chosen to promote recovery."

This tension was not limited to dollar bloc countries. Other emerging countries, such as Brazil, felt the force of the Federal Reserve's QE programs as the resulting depreciation of the dollar created pressure among them to depreciate their currency, too. Because of this, Brazil's finance minister at the time, Guido Manega, famously quipped in 2010 that an "international currency war" had broken out (Wheatley and Garnham 2010). These concerns were reinforced by the advent of a second QE in the same year and drew strong rebukes from other emerging market officials, including ones in China (Evans-Pritchard 2010).

Ultimately, the global monetary stimulus from the Federal Reserve led to an overheating in emerging economies as shown by Chen et al. (2016). IMF data show GDP growth in emerging and developing economies increasing from a low of 3.0% growth in 2009 to an average of 6.9% growth in 2010 and 2011. Inflation rose from a low 5.0% to a high of 7.1% in 2011.[25] Accompanying this growth was the rapid expansion of dollar-denominated credit to the emerging world, which McCauley et al. (2015) show was driven by US monetary policy. Unsurprisingly, the conversation in emerging economies shifted from currency wars to concerns about inflation (Theunissen and McCormick 2011).

---

25. Data are taken from the IMF's World Economic Outlook database of April 2016.

Emerging market slowdown of 2013–2015

In May and June of 2013, Fed chair Ben Bernanke raised the possibility of the Federal Reserve tapering its asset purchases under a third QE program. Markets took this as a sign of an imminent rise in interest rates by the Federal Reserve. As a consequence, Treasury yields sharply rose over the rest of 2013—ten-year Treasury yields increased from around 1.7% in May to about 3.0% in December—as the market priced in the anticipated rate hikes. This was an effective tightening of monetary policy, and emerging markets were hit hard with sudden outflows of capital, especially the "fragile five": Turkey, Brazil, India, South Africa, and Indonesia. The monetary superpower had struck again.

Once again, emerging market officials spoke out against what they saw as the Federal Reserve's indiscriminate use of its monetary superpower. Raghuram Rajan, the governor of the Reserve Bank of India, said in 2014, "I have been saying that the US should worry about the effects of its policies on the rest of the world. We would like to live in a world where countries take into account the effect of their policies on other countries and do what is right, rather than what is just right given the circumstances of their own country" (Dasgupta and Nam 2014).

Concerns over the fragile five were eventually trumped by economic developments in China. China's economy was already slowing down as it was transitioning from the high growth of a developing economy to the more modest growth of a middle-income country. In addition, China saw a rapid debt buildup in the years after 2008 as credit creation was ratcheted up to maintain robust economic growth after the crisis. Though China had weathered the Taper Tantrum relatively well, it met its match once the Fed began talking up interest rates hikes in earnest.

Figure 2.11 shows that the expected federal funds rate 12 months ahead increased from 0.29% in June 2014 to 0.89% in December

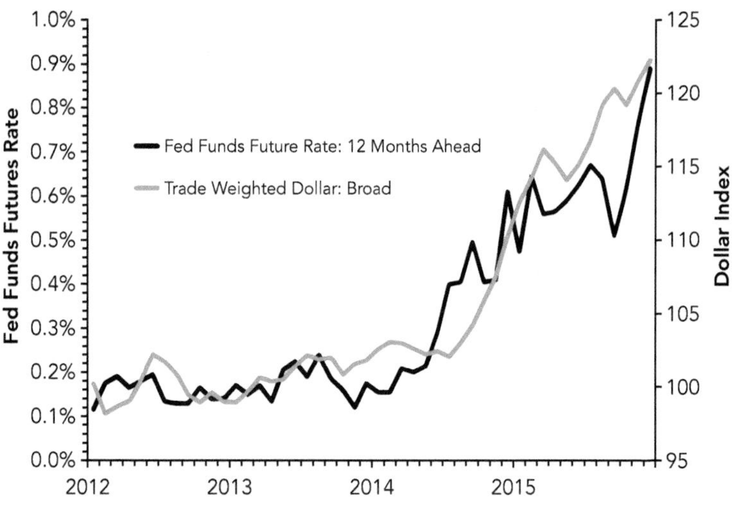

FIGURE 2.11. Expected Fed Policy and the Dollar
Source: Fred Data, Bloomberg

2015. This figure also shows that the sustained rise in the expected federal funds rate was accompanied by the dollar rising over 20%. Presumably, this expected tightening of US monetary policy caused the sharp rise in the dollar. The sharp appreciation of the dollar, in turn, caused the semipegged renminbi to appreciate just over 15% during this time.

The vulnerable and exposed Chinese economy could not handle this sudden appreciation of the renminbi. Officials from the People's Bank of China tried to offset this effective tightening of Chinese monetary conditions by cutting multiple times its benchmark lending rate and its required reserve ratio on banks. This attempt at domestic monetary easing plus the slowing growth created expectations that the renminbi was overvalued and would be devalued at some point. Consequently, investors began pulling capital at a rapid pace, with almost $1 trillion pulled out in 2015 (Bloomberg News 2016). Between June 2014 and December 2015, Chinese monetary authorities were forced to burn through almost $663 billion of foreign reserves to defend their peg. Figure 2.12 shows that the timing

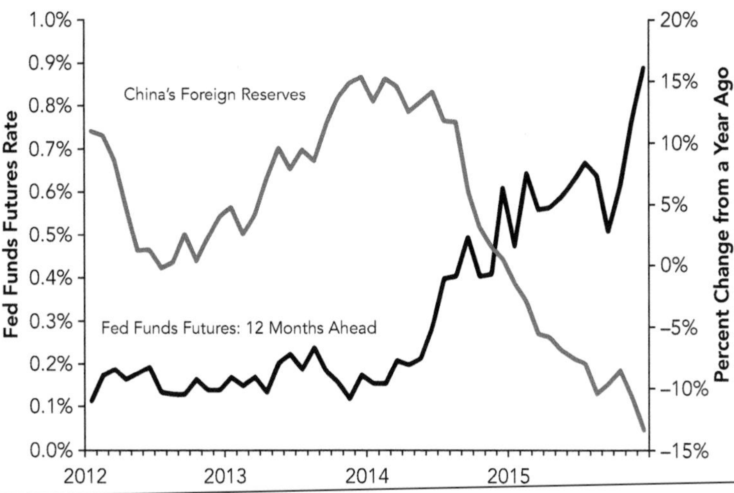

FIGURE 2.12. Expected Fed Policy and China's Foreign Reserves
Source: Fred Data, Bloomberg

of this capital exit and the increased fears of devaluation by China coincides closely with the talking up of interest rate hikes by the Federal Reserve.

The sharp rise in the dollar not only caused capital outflow problems for China, it arguably contributed to the financial turmoil in late August 2015 and early 2016. Moreover, some viewed it as weighing down global aggregate demand during this time, including the IMF (Mayeda 2015).

What these three episodes all illustrate is the inordinate influence of US monetary policy. The Federal Reserve is an unmatched monetary superpower. The March 2016 FOMC suggests the Fed is increasingly grappling with this reality. The FOMC believes that "global and financial developments continue to pose risks" and that policy would depend on, among other things, "financial and international developments."[26] While this is an interesting development, the Federal Reserve's domestic mandate and the complexities of

26. See www.federalreserve.gov/monetarypolicy/files/monetary20160316a1.pdf.

the global economy make it unlikely that US policymakers will ever be willing or able to explicitly respond to global economic conditions in a consistently stabilizing manner. What we can hope for is a more rules-based approach to US monetary policy that will make it easier for other central banks to plan for and respond to the monetary superpower in rules-based fashion themselves. As Taylor (2013) shows, this approach could mimic the stabilizing properties of an internationally coordinated monetary system for the global economy.

4. When monetary superpower status interacts with the banker to world role

In the previous two sections we documented that the US financial system acts as banker to the world and that the US central bank is a monetary superpower. A natural corollary to consider is how these two features of the US economy interact. Since the Federal Reserve can affect global monetary and financial conditions and therefore help shape global aggregate demand, it seems likely that US monetary policy could affect the demand for safe assets. Its actions could therefore affect the demand for the financial intermediation services provided by the banker to the world.

As we noted in section 2, this is the argument made by Borio and Disyatat (2011) and ourselves in earlier work (Beckworth and Crowe 2012). Both studies provide evidence that the easy stance of US monetary policy during the credit and housing boom period was recycled back into the US economy via purchases of safe assets by periphery countries. If this is the case, what effect did US monetary policy have on safe asset demand after the crash when many observers perceived US monetary policy to be effectively too tight for the US economy given the zero lower bound? Did it in any way contribute to worsening the safe asset shortage problem since 2008?

To answer these questions, we estimate a structural vector autoregression (VAR) in this section that looks at the effect the stance of US monetary policy has on the demand for US safe assets. Before doing that, though, it is useful to step back and take a closer look at the liquid assets on the liability side of the US balance sheet that was shown in figure 1. Figures 2.13 and 2.14 break these liquid assets out into publicly and privately provided categories for the period 1990:Q1 to 2015:Q4.

Figure 2.13 shows that during the housing boom period the main growth in publicly provided safe assets were in Treasury notes and bonds and government-sponsored-enterprise agency securities (GSEs). After the crisis in 2008, the growth in the world's demand for Treasury notes and bonds soars from holdings near $2.0 trillion in 2008 to roughly $4.5 trillion in 2015. Treasury bills have a sharp one-time demand spike and currency and deposits steadily grow after 2008.[27] Foreign holdings of GSEs sharply falls after 2008, going from about $1.6 trillion to almost $0.9 trillion.

Figure 2.14 shows the privately provided liquid assets.[28] The shortest-term category—the repurchase agreements, commercial paper, mutual funds, and trade receivables—rapidly grows during the housing boom period, as do the mortgage-backed securities (MBSs). As has been documented by Gorton (2010) and others, they began stumbling in 2007 and then entered free fall in 2008 as the run on the shadow banking system ensued. The shorter-term assets have since partially recovered while the MBSs continued to fall through 2013 and have remained flat since then. Corporate bonds also took a hit in 2008 but have fully recovered and returned to trend growth.

27. We include deposits in this category since they are insured by the government.

28. Here we ignore the financial derivatives because data is only available on it back to 2005:Q4. It is also an aggregated series that gives no sense of the underlying financial derivatives.

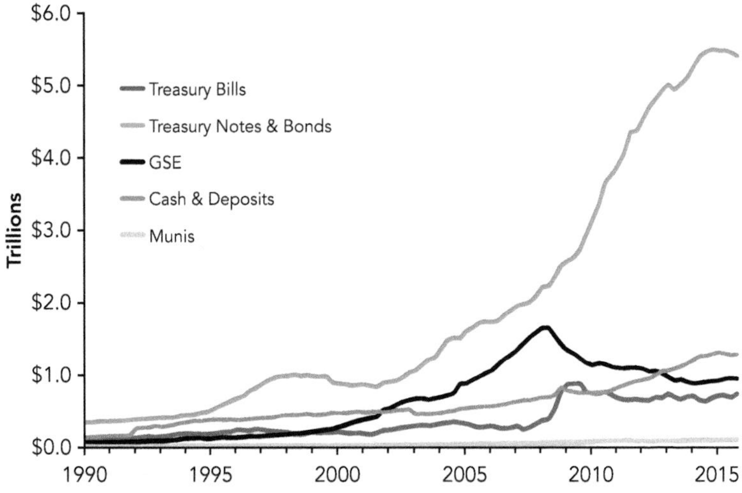

FIGURE 2.13. Public Liquid US Assets to Rest of the World
Source: US Financial Accounts, Authors' Calculations

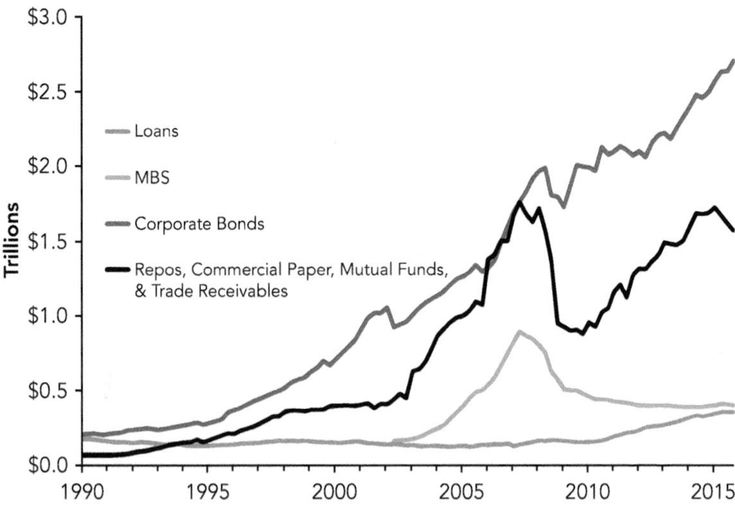

FIGURE 2.14. Private Liquid US Assets to Rest of the World
Source: US Financial Accounts, Authors' Calculations

Given these findings, we group the safest public assets—Treasuries, deposits, and currency—that continued to grow after the crisis into one category and place all other public and private liquid assets into another category. These categories are shown in figure 2.15. Interestingly, it shows the pattern among safe assets reported by Borio and Disyatat (2011): the growth of the safest, government-supplied assets declined in the early 2000s while the growth of the other liquid assets—mostly privately provided ones—rapidly grew during this time. The growing demand for safe assets, then, was focused mostly on the private-label assets (other than agencies) during the boom years. Thereafter, the roles are reversed. Going back to our original question, this suggests that the stance of US monetary policy may not only affect the overall demand for safe assets but also the composition of safe asset demand. We consider this possibility in our VAR estimation.

The stance of monetary policy

Before estimating our VAR, we need to come up with a consistent measure of monetary policy that works across both conventional and unconventional monetary policy periods. We opt for the Taylor rule gap: the difference between the federal funds rate prescribed by the Taylor rule and the actual federal funds rate. We believe our approach can handle both periods for the following reasons. First, we allow the neutral federal funds rate term in the Taylor rule—the intercept—to be time varying. We specifically use the New York Federal Reserve's five-year nominal risk-free yield estimate. This is equivalent to the expected average short term over the next five years after subtracting out the term premium.[29]

29. Put differently, this nominal risk-free yield plus the term premium make up the observable five-year Treasury yield. The data can be found at https://newyorkfed.org/research/data_indicators/term_premia.html.

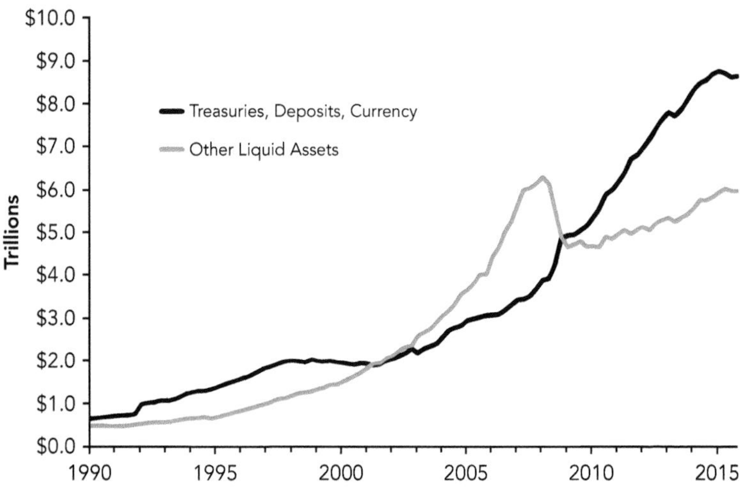

FIGURE 2.15. Liquid US Assets to Rest of the World
Source: US Financial Accounts, Authors' Calculations

The use of this time-varying neutral rate better allows the Taylor rule to reflect the changing state—including both boom and zero-lower-bound stages—of the economy. Second, to the extent the Federal Reserve's QE programs did meaningfully add monetary stimulus and change the economy, then it should affect both the time-varying neutral rate and the output gap and, consequently, be reflected in the Taylor rule gap. So whether it is during the boom period or the zero-lower-bound period, the Taylor rule gap should reflect the stance of monetary policy.

Figure 2.16 shows our Taylor rule alongside the actual federal funds rate. In addition to using a time-varying neutral rate, we also take the average of the output gap measures of the IMF, OECD, Congressional Budget Office (CBO), and Hodrick-Prescott (HP) filter to create a robust measure of the output gap. We use the GDP deflator for inflation and adopt the weights from the 1999 Taylor rule (Taylor 1999). As a robustness check on our Taylor rule, we estimated an aggregate demand (nominal GDP) gap measure—

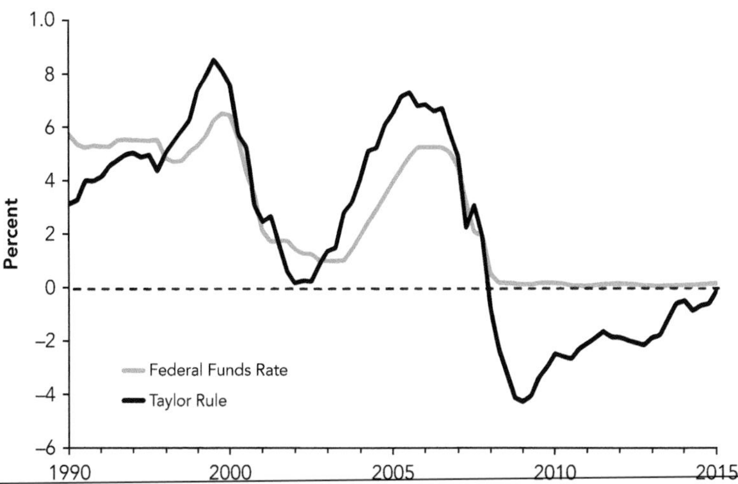

FIGURE 2.16. The Stance of Monetary Policy
Source: Fred Database, IMF WEO, OECD Statistics, CBO, Authors' Calculations

the difference between nominal spending needed to maintain full employment and actual nominal spending—for the same period and came up with a close fit (R^2 = 80%) as seen in figure A1 in the appendix. This suggests our Taylor rule gap measure is a reasonable measure of the stance of monetary policy.

The objective of this section is to examine whether Federal Reserve policy affects the rest of the world's demand for safe assets in the United States. As a first look at this question, we plot in figure 2.17 our Taylor rule gap against the US current account balance as a percent of GDP. Since the latter is just the flip side of the financial and capital account, it provides a summary measure of net capital flows into the US economy. Consistent with the arguments laid out in this paper, this figure shows a relatively strong and positive relationship between the stance of monetary policy and the current account balance. While suggestive, we need to better establish causality between Federal Reserve policy and capital flows. We do that next by estimating a VAR.

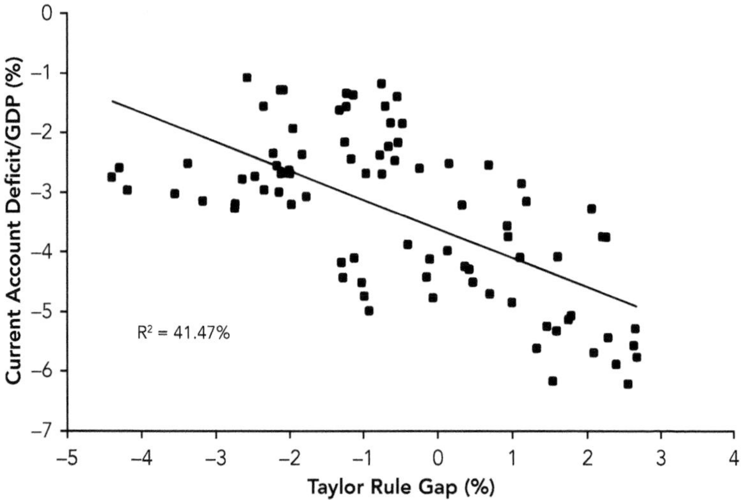

FIGURE 2.17. The Stance of Monetary Policy and Capital Flows (1995:Q1–2015:Q4)

Source: Fred Database, IMF WEO, OECD Statistics, CBO, Authors' Calculations

Empirical methods

Given the nature of our question and the relatively short sample period, one of the problems in estimating our VAR is ensuring there are adequate degrees of freedom. Consequently, we follow Lastrapes (2004, 2006), who shows how to estimate a VAR with a parsimonious set of core variables which can then be applied to a number of ancillary variables and thereby minimize the degrees-of-freedom problem. For us, this means estimating the following system of endogenous variables,

$$z_t = (TG_t, EM_t, USD_t, CA_t, A_t),$$

where TG_t is the Taylor Gap, EM_t is a real economic activity indicator for emerging markets, USD_t is the trade-weighted value of the dollar, CA_t is the current account deficit as a percent of GDP, and A_t

is the ancillary variable, all at time period t. The first four variables make up our core model and are fully endogenous. The motivation for this core group is to see the dynamic effects the Taylor rule gap has on the current account balance after controlling for the effects emerging market economies and the dollar have on it. Including these latter two variables should account for some of the structural pressures on the current account deficits discussed earlier. Also, note that by using the Taylor Gap measure, we are able to see how the stance of monetary policy, regardless of its cause, affects the current account balance.[30]

The ancillary variable is one that is affected by the core variables but cannot affect the core variables either contemporaneously or with a lag (because of restrictions we impose on the model). Therefore, no matter what variable we put into $A_{t,}$ the interactions among the core variables are unaffected and stay the same. This not only reduces the degrees of freedom needed, but it also allows us to estimate the model multiple times with different variables standing in the A_t slot.

For the EM_t variable we use the emerging market industrial production index produced by CPB Netherlands Bureau for Economic Policy Analysis. We use the Federal Reserve's broad dollar index for USD_t. The primary ancillary variables we examine in the A_t slot are the Treasuries, deposits, and currency series, the other liquid liability series, and the ten-year Treasury yield. We also plug in the US industrial production index as another robustness check on the Taylor Gap to see if it creates a response in US economic activity consistent with standard economic theory.

The model is estimated for the period 1999:Q1–2015:Q4. All variables are transformed into logs except for those already in percent form. Eight lags are used since the likelihood ratio test indi-

30. That is, the Taylor Gap reflects both passive changes in monetary policy (e.g., the Fed fails to respond to a weakening economy) and active changes (e.g., the Fed tightens policy too much) and therefore provides a complete measure of monetary policy.

cates this is an appropriate lag length and because that many lags are sufficient to whiten the residuals.

To estimate the structural impulse response functions to a Taylor Gap shock, we use a standard recursive decomposition of the covariance matrix for the variable ordering laid out above. This allows the Taylor Gap to have an immediate effect on the all the variables in the system, a reasonable assumption given the data are quarterly. As a robustness check against this ordering of the variables, we also estimate the generalized impulse response functions. This shows the dynamic response of a variable to a shock averaged over all recursive orderings. If the results were sensitive to the ordering, the generalized impulse response function should be significantly different from the structural impulse response function.

Empirical results

Figure 2.18 shows the structural impulse response functions (IRFs) from a standard deviation shock to the Taylor Gap. The figure also reports the generalized impulse response functions (GIRFs). Given the similarity of the IRFs and GIRFs, the results do not appear sensitive to the ordering of the variables.

The positive monetary policy shock causes the Taylor Gap to increase upon impact but only temporarily remains positive before returning to zero. Both US and emerging market economic activity also temporarily increase, with the former persisting for longer. The only surprising result is that the monetary easing has no immediate effect on the trade-weighted dollar and eventually causes it to rise. This result may be explained by Ammer et al. (2016), who find that the effects of stronger US demand and the loosening of foreign financial conditions from US monetary easing may outweigh any downward pressure it creates on the US dollar.

The important question of whether monetary policy affects the demand for safe assets as reflected by changes in the current

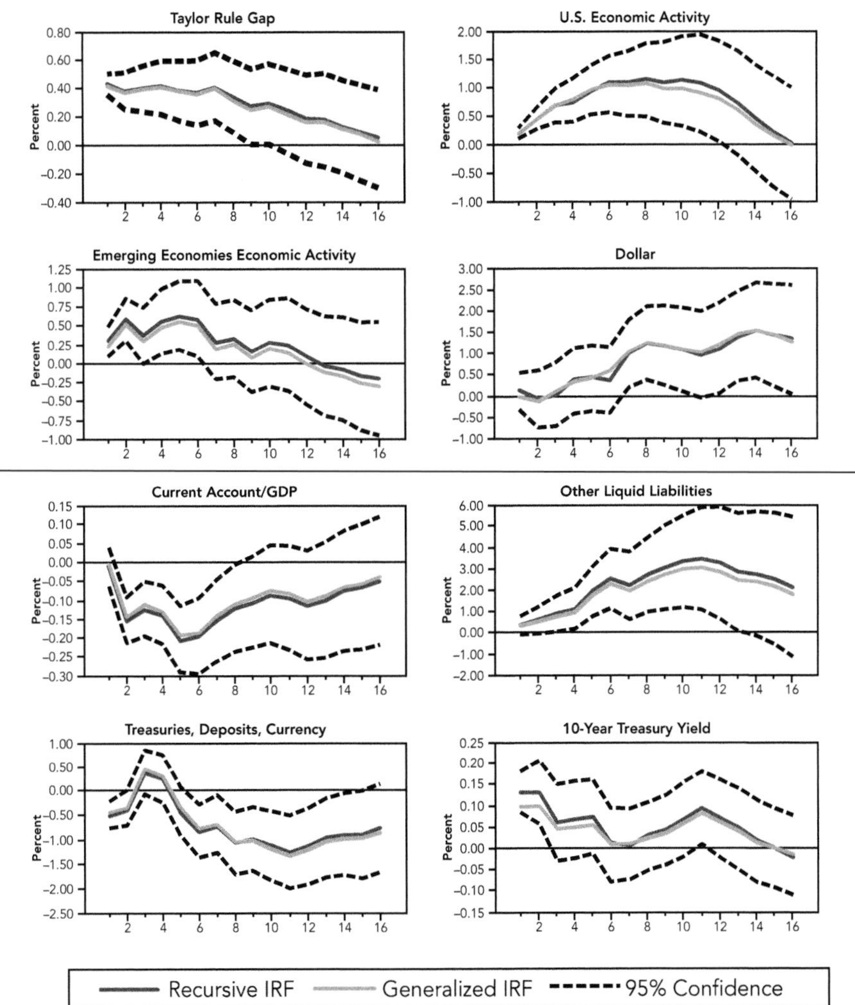

FIGURE 2.18. Impulse Response Function to Standard Deviation Taylor Gap Shock (1999:Q1–2015:Q4)

account balance is answered in the affirmative in the next IRF. The Taylor Gap shock causes the current account to decline in a statistically significant manner for seven quarters. This indicates that monetary easing by the Fed does, in fact, increase the overall demand for US safe assets by foreigners.

The next two IRFs reveal that, while overall demand for US safe assets is raised by the Federal Reserve easing, there is a composition effect as well. The positive shock to the Taylor Gap causes the less safe "other liquid liabilities" category to rise while causing the supersafe Treasuries, deposits, and currency to decline. This composition effect is borne out in the rising ten-year Treasury yield. In other words, the monetary easing causes foreigners to substitute out of the public safe assets into the mostly private safe assets, and this raises (lowers) their yields (prices). Since the VAR is a linear model the opposite would be true, too: tight monetary policy should cause a substitution out of privately produced safe assets into the supersafe government assets.

To see whether these results are not just statistically significant but economically significant, we present the variance decomposition (VDC) of the forecast error in figure 2.19. This shows the percent of the forecast error for each variable that is attributable to the Taylor Gap shock. Of particular interest to us is the VDC of the current account deficit. Figure 2.19 shows that the Taylor Gap shock explains as much as 60% of the forecast error six quarters out. Thereafter, it slowly declines. The Taylor Gap shock also explains about 40% of both the Treasuries, deposits, and currency series and the other liquid liability series ten quarters out. These VDCs indicate that Taylor Gap shocks are both statistically and economically significant to the demand for safe assets provided by the US financial system during both the boom period and the zero-lower-bound period.

As a final check on the effect of the Fed policy on demand for the financial intermediation services provided by the banker to

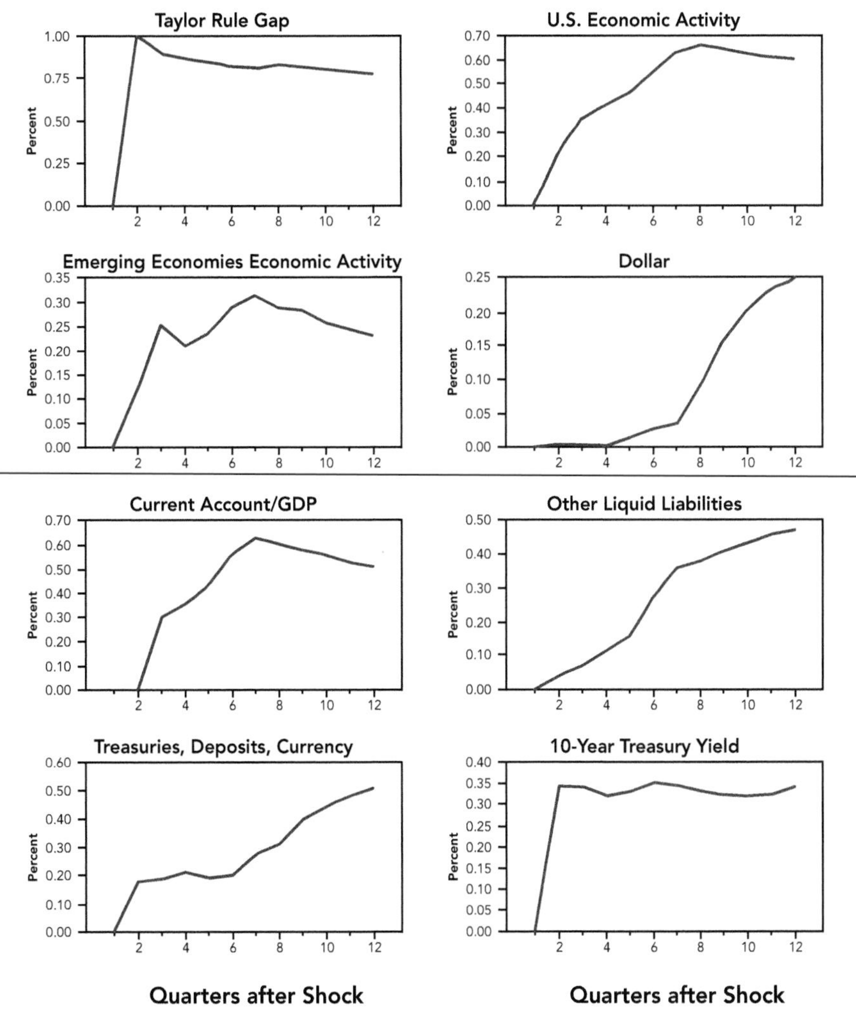

FIGURE 2.19. Percent of Forecast Error Attributable to Standard Deviation Shock to Taylor Gap (1999:Q1–2015:Q4)

the world, we run two counterfactual dynamic forecasts. For the first one, we take the estimated VAR and dynamically forecast it forward starting in 2002:Q1 and run it through 2007:Q4. We run the forecast conditional on the Taylor Gap being zero. We want to see what the estimated VAR predicts would have happened had US monetary policy been neutral between 2002 and 2007. Taylor (2009) sees the Federal Reserve getting off track in 2002, so we pick this as our starting point.

The first column of figure 2.20 shows the outcome of this exercise. There are several interesting results. First, the US current account deficit would have been smaller between 2004 and 2007. At its maximum, the current account as a percent of GDP would have been 1.5 percentage points smaller in 2006:Q1. Starting in 2005, the demand for Treasuries, deposits, and currency would have been higher while the demand for the mostly private other liquid liabilities would have been lower. This increased demand for the government safe assets would have pushed down the ten-year Treasury yield starting in 2005. At its peak in 2006:Q3, it would have been almost 1% lower.

While this is a highly speculative exercise subject to all kinds of criticism, it does suggest the Federal Reserve helped fuel the demand for the AAA-rated private-label assets. The savings glut does, then, seem to be in part a recycling of US monetary policy back into the US economy.

For the second counterfactual exercise, we consider what would have happened had the Taylor Gap been zero beginning in 2008:Q1. In other words, what would have happened had the Fed been able to respond more appropriately to the economic crisis at that time? The first thing to note is the current account deficit would have been persistently smaller starting in 2009. The demand for safe government assets would have been lower starting in 2010, and the demand for the mostly private-label safe assets would have been higher starting in late 2009. Finally, the ten-year Treasury yield

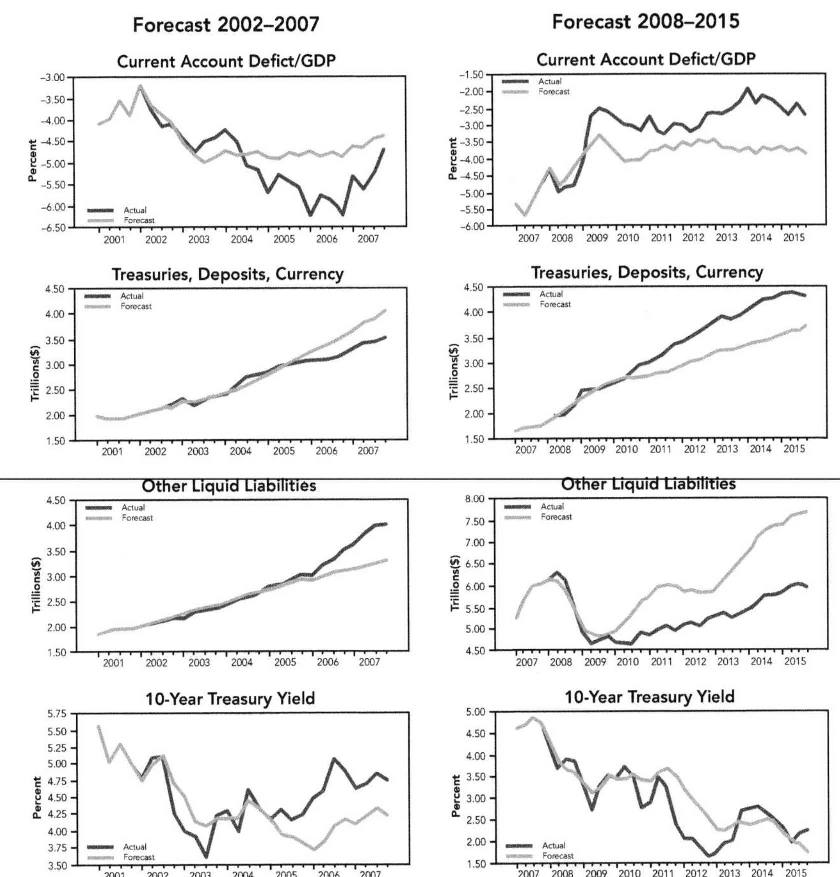

FIGURE 2.20. Forecasted Path Given Neutral Monetary Policy

Note: The conditional dynamic forecasts are made given the Taylor Gap is set equal to zero.

would have been slightly higher starting in 2010 but still would have been trending down.

These results suggest that the effectively tight US monetary policy—due to the zero lower bound—may have prevented a quicker recovery in the safe asset market. That is, had monetary conditions been easier, then a more robust recovery that improved the economic outlook, lowering the demand for supersafe government assets while increasing the demand for privately produced liquid assets, may have materialized.

5. Conclusion

We have shown in this paper that the United States is both a monetary superpower, influencing global monetary conditions, and banker to the world, providing safe assets to the rest of the world. We have also shown how these roles can interact to the detriment of the global economy. During the housing boom the Federal Reserve's accommodative monetary policy got recycled back into the US economy via its banker to the world role and helped fuel the housing boom. Since the crisis in 2008, the Federal Reserve has erred the other way (constrained by the zero lower bound on rates) by effectively being too tight, and this has prevented the US financial system from adequately responding to the safe asset shortage.

As we noted earlier, the safe asset shortage first emerged because of structural reasons in Asia but more recently has intensified thanks to cyclical drivers. This can be seen in figure 2.21, which shows that since the financial crisis most government debt considered safe has seen its yield persistently drop. This global phenomenon has been driven, in our view, by a spate of bad news over the past eight years: the Great Recession, the Eurozone Crisis, China slowdown concerns, political uncertainty, fears of the Federal Reserve tightening too soon, and other issues. These developments, however, have been amplified by a US monetary policy that has been effectively too tight during this time. As we argued via our

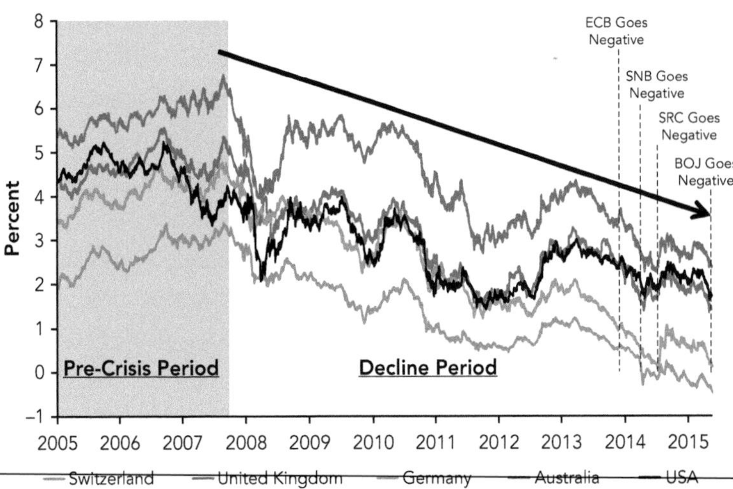

FIGURE 2.21. 10-Year Government Yields on Safe Assets

counterfactual exercises above, this monetary tightness has only increased the demand for supersafe assets.[31]

The safe asset shortage problem is not something with which to be trifled. As recently shown by Caballero et al. (2016), if the safe asset shortage problem is big enough, it will spread across countries and put downward pressure on global rates. This is already happening, as seen in figure 2.21. Moreover, it will keep global aggregate demand growth anemic. We see this, too, with the weak growth in Europe, Japan, and the emerging markets. Safe assets are important because they are the assets that are expected to be liquid and maintain their value. They are, in other words, moneylike and serve as a transaction asset for institutional investors as shown by Gorton (2010). Their shortage, therefore, means a shortage of money and of aggregate demand.

What makes the safe asset shortage problem such a tough challenge is that, if left unchecked, it will push the market-clearing or "natural" interest below zero. When that happens, the safe asset

31. New bank regulations since the crisis may also be increasing the demand for safe assets.

market is not clearing—interest rates are too high, safe asset prices are too low—and problems get worse. Caballero et al. (2016) believe the advanced economies are at that place now. If they are correct, then there are three solutions to safe asset shortage.

The first option is to increase the supply of safe assets to the point that investors are satiated with them. The second is to decrease the demand for safe assets by improving the economic outlook. The third option is to try to break through the zero lower bound and have interest rates reach their market-clearing levels.

The first option seems infeasible as long as the United States maintains its clear competitive advantage in issuing safe assets and political opposition within the United States to a substantial increase in debt issuance remains.[32] The third option is arguably the one being attempted currently, particularly in Europe and Japan. Whether it is feasible is open to question: reaching the market-clearing interest rate may be infeasible given the existence of cash.[33]

This leaves the second option as the most plausible. The best outcome would be a return to more robust levels of global GDP growth, which would boost investment (held back by weak growth expectations) and improve risk appetite, reducing the cyclical demand for safe assets. The structural demand for safe assets would still be with us, but the cyclical uptick in safe asset demand since the crisis could be meaningfully addressed through this option. That is where a more appropriate US monetary policy comes into play.

32. Of course it is partly because US political institutions and voter preferences are opposed to this that the United States enjoys its advantage in issuing safe assets, relative to countries where there is greater debt tolerance.

33. Negative rates have other disadvantages. Concerns have been raised about bank profitability since negative rates are likely to lead to bank spread compression as long as negative rates are difficult to pass on to retail depositors. In addition, negative rates have increased the attractiveness of the euro and yen as funding currencies for global carry strategies, meaning that both have tended to appreciate in "risk off" scenarios, adding a destabilizing degree of procyclicality to domestic financial conditions for these countries, as well as, complicating efforts to maintain weak currencies.

We believe one of the key reasons Federal Reserve policy has been effectively tight over the past eight years is its firm commitment to low inflation, which prevents the Fed from credibly committing to run policy sufficiently loosely to make up for the nominal demand shortfall that followed the deep 2008–2009 recession. All the Fed's tools—the setting of short-term interests, the buying and selling of government bonds, and the management of expectations—were handcuffed by its strict devotion to low inflation. They would never be allowed to generate the spending growth required to put the economy completely back to work. That is why Sumner (2011) and Woodford (2012) have called for nominal gross domestic product (NGDP) level targeting. This approach would anchor long-term inflation expectations but allow for temporary deviations in the inflation rate required to maintain aggregate demand on a stable growth path. Although not a panacea, and subject to some implementation challenges, NGDP level targeting could help solve the cyclical portion of the safe asset problem. At the same time, it would also commit the Federal Reserve to a more rulelike approach to monetary policy. As Taylor (2013) notes, such an approach would make it easier for other central banks to respond to the monetary superpower and therefore bring us closer to an internationally coordinated monetary system.

Are there alternatives to the US dollar that could dethrone the US currency and displace the Fed as monetary superpower? So far, putative competitors such as the euro, yen, or pound sterling have largely fallen by the wayside. However, the rise of the Chinese economy and the increasing international role of the renminbi raise the question of whether the Fed's reign as monetary superpower may be coming to an end. Indeed, one anomaly of the dollar's current dominance is that the largest single contributor (at purchasing power parity GDP) to the dollar bloc is no longer the United States itself, but China.

With the Chinese authorities increasingly pursuing a more flexible Chinese-yuan-to-dollar exchange rate and promoting the use of a number of broader reference baskets for determining the value of the renminbi, China's membership in the dollar bloc is looking more tenuous. Over time it seems likely that the Chinese currency will take on a more important role as a reserve currency in its own right. However, while almost a quarter of China's international trade is settled in renminbi, the currency's international role in asset markets is in its infancy, and overall the renminbi accounts for less than 3% of global cross-border trade and financial transactions and less than 2% of turnover in global foreign exchange markets and about 1% of global official foreign exchange reserves (Prasad 2016). Moreover, China's domestic financial system is still dominated by state-owned banks, the authorities' commitment to liberalization is uncertain, and the path to capital account openness remains beset with risks and obstacles.

Finally, despite well-flagged moves towards greater currency flexibility, the US-dollar-to-renminbi exchange rate is still of central importance to Chinese policymakers: during early 2016 a clear pattern emerged of opportunistic devaluation of the trade-weighted value of the renminbi, with the Chinese authorities allowing the renminbi to weaken alongside the dollar in trade-weighted terms when the latter moved lower, while weakening against the US dollar during periods of general US dollar strength. In our view, China remains part of the dollar bloc—if less securely than before. Hence, the dollar's dominant international role seems unlikely to be seriously challenged in the foreseeable future.

Appendix

Here we show how we estimated our full-employment level of aggregate demand. We begin with the assumption that the output gap—the difference between the actual and full-employment level

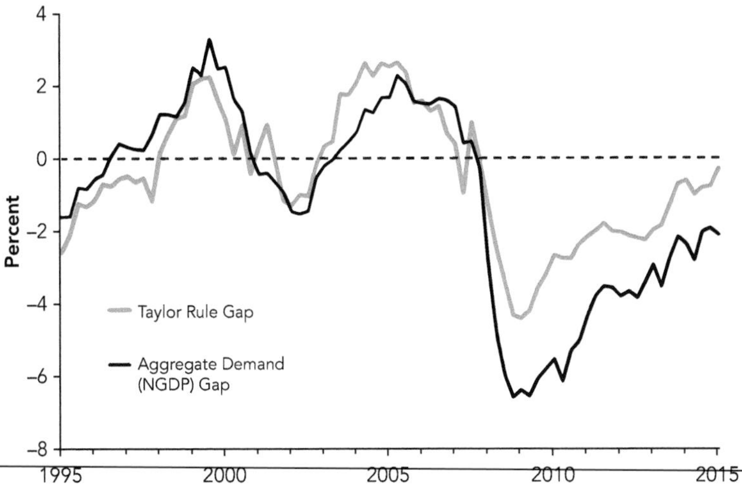

FIGURE 2A.1. The Taylor Rule Gap and the NGDP Gap

of economic activity—is a consequence of there being too much or too little aggregate demand. Since NGDP is a measure of aggregate demand, we can state this relationship as follows:

$$\ln(NGDP_t) - \ln(NGDP_t^{FE}) = \pi_t output\ gap_t, \qquad (1)$$

where $NGDP_t^{FE}$ is the full employment measure of NGDP and π_t is a time-varying parameter. Equation (1) says the output gap is related to the NGDP gap at time *t* via the parameter π_t. Note that equation (1) can be rearranged into the following:

$$\ln(NGDP_t) = \ln(NGDP_t^{FE}) + \pi_t output\ gap_t. \qquad (2)$$

Given sticky prices and the slow changing nature of potential real GDP, we do not expect $NGDP_t^{FE}$ to change quickly. Consequently, we can think of it as a relatively stable NGDP growth path that only gradually changes. This is in line with calls for NGDP level targeting from such folks as Sumner (2011) and Woodford

(2012). Since it is a time-varying growth path, we can estimate it with a rolling regression of the form

$$\ln(NGDP_t) = B_{0,t} + B_{1,t}time_t + B_{2,t}time_t^2 + B_{3,t}output\ gap_t, \quad (3)$$

where the term $B_{0,t} + B_{1,t}time_t + B_{2,t}time_t^2$ represents $NGDP_t^{FE}$. The regression is estimated using quarterly data with a rolling window of 40 observations.

The average of the HP-filtered output gap, the IMF's output gap, the OECD's output gap, and the CBO's output gap measures is taken to get a robust output gap estimate. This average output gap is included with the natural log of NGDP and the two time trends in the rolling regression. The resulting $B_{0,t}$, $B_{1,t}$, and $B_{2,t}$ parameters can then be used to construct $NGDP_t^{FE}$.

References

Ammer, J., M. De Pooter, C. Erceg, and S. Kamin. 2016. International spillovers of monetary policy. *FRB: IFDP Notes,* February 8, 2016. Available at http://federalreserve.gov/econresdata/notes/ifdp-notes/2016/international-spillovers-of-monetary-policy-20160208.html.

Beckworth, D. 2008. Aggregate supply-driven deflation and its implications for macroeconomic stability. *Cato Journal* 28 (3): 363–84.

Beckworth, D., and C. Crowe. 2013. The great liquidity boom and the monetary superpower hypothesis. In *Boom and bust in banking: Causes and Cures of the Great Recession*, ed. Beckworth, 95–127. Oakland, CA: Independent Institute.

Belke, A., and D. Gros. 2005. Asymmetries in transatlantic monetary policy-making: Does the ECB follow the Fed? *Journal of Common Market Studies* 43: 921–46.

Benetrix, A. S., J. C. Shambaugh, and P. R. Lane. 2015. International currency exposures, valuation effects and the global financial crisis. *Journal of International Economics* 96 (S1): S98–S109.

Bloomberg News. 2016. China capital outflow rise to estimated $1 Trillion in 2015. January 25.

Borio, C., and P. Disyatat. 2011. Global imbalances and the financial crisis: Link or no link? BIS Working Paper 346.

Bruno, V., and H. S. Shin. 2014. Crossborder banking and global liquidity. BIS Working Paper 458.

Caballero, R. 2006. On the macroeconomics of asset shortages. NBER Working Paper 12753.

Caballero, R., E. Farhi, and P. Gourinchas. 2008. An equilibrium model of "global imbalances" and low interest rates. *American Economic Review* 98 (1): 358–93.

Caballero, R., E. Farhi, and P. Gourinchas. 2016. Safe asset scarcity and aggregate demand. NBER Working Paper 22044.

Chen, Q., A. Filardo, D. He, and F. Zhu. 2016. Financial crisis, US unconventional monetary policy and international spillovers. *Journal of International Money and Finance* (forthcoming).

Chinn, M., and H. Ito. 2006. What matters for financial development? Capital controls, instituions, and interactions. *Journal of Development Economics* 81 (1): 163–92.

Dasgupta, N., and R. Ham. 2014. US should be mindful of global policy impact: Rajan. *Reuters,* January 31.

Despres, E., C. Kindleberger, and W. Salant. 1966. The dollar and world liquidity: A minority view. *Economist,* 526–29.

Evans-Pritchard, A. 2010. QE2 risk currency wars and the end of dollar hegemony. *Telegraph,* November 1.

Forbes, K. J. 2010. Why do foreigners invest in the United States? *Journal of International Economics* 80: 3–21.

Georgiadis, G. 2016. Determinants of global spillovers from US monetary policy. *Journal of International Money and Finance* (forthcoming).

Ghosh, A., M. Qureshi, and C. Tsangarides. 2014. On the value of words: Inflation and fixed exchange rate regimes. *IMF Economic Review* 62 (2): 288–322.

Goldberg, L. 2011. The international role of the dollar: Does it matter if this changes? *Federal Reserve Bank of New York Staff Reports* no. 522.

Gorton, G. 2010. *Slapped by the invisible hand: The Panic of 2007.* Oxford: Oxford University Press.

Gourinchas, P., and H. Rey. 2007. From world banker to world venture capitalist: US external adjustment and the exorbitant privilege. In *G7 Current Account Imbalances: Sustainability and Adjustment,* ed. R. H. Clarida. Chicago: University of Chicago Press.

Gourinchas, P., N. Gorillot, and H. Rey. 2010. Exhorbitant privilege and exhorbitant duty. Manuscript.

Gray, C. 2013. Responding to the monetary superpower: Investigating the behavioral spillovers of US monetary policy. *Atlantic Economic Journal* 41 (2): 173–84.

Gros, D., T. Mayer, and A. Uribe. 2006. A world out of balance? Special report of the CEPS Macroeconomic Policy Group.

Karaian, J. 2016. There are only two companies left with top-notch AAA credit ratings. *Quartz,* April 27.

Kindleberger, C. 1965. Balance of payments deficits and the international market for liquidity. *Princeton Studies in International Finance.*

Krugman, P. 2007. Will there be a dollar crisis? *Economic Policy* 22: 436–67.

Lane, P., and G. Milesi-Ferretti. 2001. The external wealth of nations: Measures of foreign assets and liabilities for industrial and developing countries. *Journal of International Economics* 55: 263–94.

Lane, P., and G. Milesi-Ferretti. 2007. The external wealth of nations Mark II. *Journal of International Economics* 73: 223–50.

Lastrapes, W. 2004. Estimating and identifying vector autoregressions under diagonality and block exogeneity restrictions. *Economic Letters* 87: 75–81.

Lastrapes, W. 2006. Inflation and distribution of relative prices: The role of productivity and money supply shocks. *Journal of Money, Credit, and Banking* 38: 2159–98.

Mayeda, A. 2015. IMF warns of rising risks as dollar hits emerging markets. *Bloomberg,* April 15.

McCauley, R., P. McQuire, and V. Sushko. 2015. Global dollar credit: Links to US monetary policy and leverage. BIS Working Paper 483.

Mendoza, E. G., V. Quadrini, and J. Rios-Rull. 2009. Financial integration, financial development and global imbalances. *Journal of Political Economy* 117 (3): 371–416.

Mundell, R. 1963. Capital mobility and stabilization policy under fixed and flexible exchange rates. *Canadian Journal of Economic and Political Science* 29 (4): 475–85.

Peterson, K., and M. Derby. 2012. Bernanke: China's dollar peg like being on a gold standard. *Wall Street Journal,* May 20.

Poole, W. 2004. A perspective on US international capital flows. *Federal Reserve of St. Louis Review* 86 (1): 1–7.

Prasad, E. S. 2016. China's efforts to expand the international use of the renminbi. Report prepared for the US-China Economic and Security Review Commission.

Rey, H. 2013. Dilemma not trilemma: The global financial cycle and monetary policy independence. Kansas City Fed Symposium on Global Dimensions of Unconventional Monetary Policy, August 22, 285–333.

Rey, H. 2015. International channels of transmission of monetary policy and the Mundellian Trilemma. IMF Mundell-Fleming Lecture, November 13.

Roubini, N., and B. Setser. 2005. Will the Bretton Woods 2 regime unravel soon? The risk of a hard landing in 2005–2006. Unpublished paper.

Selgin, G., D. Beckworth, and B. Bahadir. 2015. The productivity gap: Monetary policy, the subprime boom, and the post-2001 productivity surge. *Journal of Policy Modeling* 37 (20): 189–207.

Summers, L. 2004. The United States and the global adjustment process. Speech presented at the Third Annual Stavros S. Niarchos Lecture, IIE, Washington, DC, March 23.

Sumner, S. 2011. Re-Targeting the Fed. *National Affairs* 9 (Fall).

Taylor, J. 1999. A historical analysis of monetary policy rules. In *Monetary Policy Rules*, ed. Taylor. Chicago: University of Chicago Press, 319–41.

Taylor, J. 2009. *Getting off track: How government actions and interventions caused, prolonged, and worsened the financial crisis.* Stanford: Hoover Institution Press.

Taylor, J. 2012. Commentary on capital flows and the risk-taking channel of monetary policy. BIS Conference on the Future of Financial Globalization.

Taylor, J. 2013. International monetary coordination and the great deviation. *Journal of Policy Modeling* 35 (3): 463–72.

Theunissen, G., and L. C. McCormick. 2011. Currency wars lose to inflation, emerging markets to win. *Bloomberg*, February 28.

Tille, C. 2003. The impact of exchange rate movements on US foreign debt. *Federal Reserve Bank of New York Current Issues in Economics and Finance* 9 (1).

Wheatley, J., and P. Garnham. 2010. Brazil in "currency war" alert. *Financial Times*, September 27.

Woodford, M. 2012. Methods of policy Accommodation at the zero lower bound. Speech presented at the Kansas City Fed Symposium, September 16.

Yellen, J. 2010. Hong Kong and China and the global recession. Speech reprinted in *FRBSF Economic Letter*, February 28.

DISCUSSION BY CHRISTOPHER ERCEG

This paper by David Beckworth and Christopher Crowe focuses on two related themes. The first is that the Federal Reserve is a monetary superpower that exerts large effects on global interest rates and global output: in the words of the authors, the Fed "to a large extent sets global monetary conditions." The authors support this point both through case studies and also through a structural VAR, with a key empirical result that a more accommodative US monetary policy causes the US current account balance to deteriorate and foreign GDP to rise. The second and closely related theme is how Fed monetary policy affects the demand for safe assets, with particular attention to how the zero bound constraint following the global financial crisis may have exacerbated the global safe asset shortage.

I found this to be a very interesting paper insofar as it examines a wide range of transmission channels through which Fed policy may affect both foreign output and global asset yields. In my discussion, I will begin by focusing on the empirical VAR methodology that the authors use to assess spillovers from Fed policy and then present some complementary evidence suggesting that Fed policy easing (tightening) tends to boost (lower) foreign GDP on balance, rather than exerting "beggar-thy-neighbor" effects. I agree with the authors that the spillovers from Fed policy actions to foreign economies can be quite large for those foreign economies attempting to keep their exchange rates relatively stable against the dollar. However, I will argue that foreign economies with sound fundamentals and a credible monetary policy framework have considerable latitude to adjust their policy rate to achieve domestic stabilization objectives and thus to minimize the potential for undesirable spillovers.

1. The spillover effects of Fed policy

While the authors use both case studies and an empirical VAR to gauge spillovers from Fed policy changes, my discussion will focus more on the latter given that the VAR-based evidence is the more novel contribution of the paper. To briefly recapitulate their methodology, the authors use a structural VAR to estimate the effects of a US monetary policy shock. The authors make two key assumptions to identify monetary policy shocks. First, they measure a monetary policy shock as the gap between the prescription of a modified form of the Taylor (1993) rule (i_t^{tay}) and the realized policy rate (i_t):

$$\tau_t = i_t^{tay} - i_t = r + \gamma_\pi \pi_t + \gamma_x x_t - i_t,$$

where the coefficient γ_x on the output gap x_t is set to unity rather than 0.5 as in the standard (1993) Taylor rule (with the coefficient γ_π on inflation set to 1.5 per usual). They call this monetary policy shock τ_t the "Taylor gap." Thus, rather than estimate the coefficients of the policy reaction function—the typical approach in the literature—the authors simply calibrate the coefficients, and back out the monetary policy shock as a residual.

The second key assumption is that the monetary policy shock is ordered first in the VAR and thus prior to the other variables (which include the industrial production of emerging market economies [EMEs], the trade-weighted dollar, the US current account, and long-term Treasury yields). This contrasts with the usual assumption in the VAR literature using timing restrictions to identify monetary policy shocks, which assumes that policymakers can react contemporaneously—within the same quarter—to domestic output and inflation (and hence orders the policy rate last or at least "further down" in the VAR). I'll return a bit later to discussing some of the consequences of these identifying restrictions, as well as the implications of estimating the model over a sample period (1999:Q1–2015:Q4) in which the zero bound was often binding.

The authors derive some interesting empirical results. First, they show that an expansionary monetary policy shock in their VAR causes the US current account deficit to deteriorate even though the dollar depreciates. Second, the expansionary US monetary policy shock raises EME real activity (i.e., industrial production) persistently. I regard these findings as potentially quite important, because they suggest that exchange rate changes are not the dominant transmission channel in accounting for spillovers from US monetary policy: if they were, the US current account balance would tend to improve in response to US monetary accommodation, and foreign GDP would decline. Given the prominent debates about how unconventional policy stimulus by the Fed and other central banks in recent years may exert "beggar-thy-neighbor" effects on trading partners, my sense is that the authors' countervailing results deserve heightened attention.

The authors' results appear reasonably consistent with my own findings in recent research on US monetary policy spillovers conducted with John Ammer, Michiel De Pooter, and Steven Kamin (2016). In this research, we use a large-scale open economy dynamic stochastic general equilibrium model (SIGMA) to assess how US monetary policy affects foreign activity. One key channel through which a, say, US monetary policy easing affects foreign activity is by causing the dollar to depreciate; a weaker dollar of itself should boost US exports while depressing imports and thus reduce foreign GDP. But US monetary easing also boosts US domestic demand—a second key trade channel that causes US real net exports to deteriorate and, correspondingly, strengthens foreign GDP. Finally, US policy easing reduces foreign bond yields through an array of financial linkages (including through affecting risk premiums on sovereign and private debt). While the trade channels nearly offset—consistent with perhaps a small deterioration in the US trade balance—our analysis suggests that US monetary easing provides a material boost to foreign GDP as the financial channels dominate (that is, although foreign net exports don't respond much because the effects of stronger US activity are offset by an appreciation of foreign currencies, foreign GDP rises because foreign interest rates decline).

I do have significant concerns with the identification assumptions used in the authors' VAR. My main concern is with the authors' choice to order the monetary shock (i.e., the "Taylor gap" τ_t) first in the VAR, consistent with the assumption that it does not respond contemporaneously (within the quarter) to other influences. While this assumption is often used in identifying fiscal shocks in a VAR framework following Blanchard and Perotti (2002)—on the premise that discretionary fiscal policy is not "nimble" enough to respond quickly to changes in economic conditions—this assumption seems less defensible in the case of monetary policy. To the extent that monetary policy responds quickly to economic and financial developments, the VAR under the authors' identification assumption will confound the effects of an "exogenous," say, easing of monetary policy with the effects of a rate cut in response to a deterioration in economic or financial conditions.

In normal times in which monetary policy is unconstrained by the zero lower bound, this identification strategy would tend to bias downward the estimated effects on output (possibly even implying that monetary easing would lower output, if the reaction to current conditions was strong enough); thus, as noted above, most of the literature using timing assumptions has followed Christiano, Eichenbaum, and Evans (1999) in assuming that monetary policy can react to contemporaneous developments. The zero lower bound poses added challenges and shifts the bias towards overstating the pure effects of monetary policy on output: in particular, while their VAR interprets the large negative Taylor Gaps in the Great Recession as exogenous policy tightenings, there is presumably a large endogenous component (as the deterioration in economic and financial conditions itself caused the Taylor Gap to widen).

To address these concerns, it certainly seems worth experimenting with different identifying restrictions and different sample periods in future work. Given the challenges posed by the Great Recession, it would be desirable to extend the estimation sample to earlier periods (say, the early 1980s). It would also seem desirable to utilize sign restrictions, which could allow monetary policy to simultaneously affect financial and even real variables contemporaneously (as in the current paper) without imposing the restriction that monetary policy itself only reacts with a lag.

Notwithstanding these caveats, I like the authors' general approach and think that they have made an important contribution to assessing the empirical channels through which spillovers arise. While there is a voluminous literature estimating financial spillovers abroad from US monetary policy actions, this literature typically adopts a high-frequency-event study methodology that isn't well suited to assessing dynamic effects on macro variables; thus, there is a comparative paucity of empirical research on how US policy actions affect both US trade and foreign GDP, and this paper helps fill this shortfall. In terms of policy implications, I interpret the authors' analysis as suggesting that policy discussions focused mainly on the exchange rate may miss other pivotal channels in accounting for spillovers from monetary policy.

2. Can foreign economies insulate themselves from monetary spillovers?

The accommodative policies of the Fed and other advanced economy central banks following the global financial crisis have often been criticized as having potentially undesirable effects on the rest of the world. An open question is whether foreign economies can insulate themselves from monetary spillovers. This paper—drawing on both VAR-based evidence and a number of case studies—suggests that the answer is probably no: Fed actions create a large wake that rocks even distant coastlines.

I agree with the authors that monetary policy spillovers can indeed be large under certain conditions. Spillovers are likely to be large to those foreign economies that put a high priority on keeping their exchange rate fairly stable against the dollar while also maintaining an open capital account. For these economies, a US monetary easing is stimulative both because it boosts US activity (helping their exports) and because it has a large effect in depressing their domestic bond yields. The induced rise in foreign activity may, of course, be undesirable from the perspective of the foreign economies if business cycle conditions were already strong prior to the easing of US monetary policy. A second group of economies likely to experience relatively large spillovers are those with weaker fundamentals, including lower inflation credibility and substantial dollar-denominated borrowing (Bruno and Shin 2015).

Nevertheless, recent analysis by Bernanke (2013, 2015) and my own research with Ammer, De Pooter, and Kamin (2016) highlight how foreign central banks may have considerable scope to insulate their economies from spillovers under certain conditions, so that spillovers from US monetary policy actions to foreign GDP are much smaller. First, spillovers are smaller if the foreign monetary authority's objectives involve domestic output and inflation, rather than exchange rates or exports. Second, spillovers are smaller if inflation expectations in the foreign economy are well anchored. And finally, spillovers can be mitigated through appropriate communication that helps markets better understand the (foreign) central bank's reaction function.

Applying these considerations to the case studies of monetary policy spillovers in the post-global-financial-crisis period, I would draw three key lessons. First, spillovers to foreign economies depend heavily on the monetary policy choices taken by those economies, rather than being simply determined by US policy. This point was emphasized by former Fed chairman Bernanke in his Mundell-Fleming lecture at the IMF last year. In the context of the 2010–2012 period, rapidly growing EMEs faced a tradeoff between keeping interest rate low—which would reduce upward pressure on their exchange rate—versus raising interest rates and allowing their exchange rates to appreciate by more. While the latter policy was better poised to keep output near potential and inflation near target, it would have hurt the export sector; hence, many EMEs preferred to maintain policies that were in some cases probably too accommodative to stabilize output and inflation and caused some overheating.

The second lesson is that the ability of foreign economies to insulate their GDP from spillovers depends heavily on macroeconomic fundamentals in those economies, including the credibility and transparency of the central bank's inflation target. This lesson seems clearly underscored by the Taper Tantrum experience of 2013. The EMEs with weak fundamentals, including those with high inflation and inflation expectations prior to this shock, experienced very large exchange rate depreciations and had to raise interest rate markedly to keep inflation from ratcheting up further. By contrast, spillovers were much smaller to EMEs with stronger fundamentals and stable nominal anchors, such as Mexico.

The third lesson—also underscored by the Taper Tantrum experience—is that central bank communication about their objectives and reaction functions can mitigate monetary policy spillovers, especially spillovers that arise through financial channels. Thus, although interest rates rose sharply in both the euro area and United Kingdom in the early summer of 2013, communication efforts by the European Central Bank and the Bank of England were effective in pushing rates down in those economies, thus supporting their efforts to achieve their inflation objectives.

3. Conclusion

To conclude, I think this is a very interesting and well-written paper, and it was a pleasure to read. There are a number of implications of the authors' analysis that seem quite important and worth pursuing in follow-up research. Most notably, I think the authors' empirical findings—that US monetary policy easing causes the US current account to deteriorate and foreign GDP to expand—highlights the importance of looking beyond the exchange rate as an international transmission channel. Further empirical analysis of the open economy transmission channels of monetary policy would seem very useful. Finally, I would reiterate that spillovers due to policy actions by major central banks depend crucially on monetary policy—and policy communication—in foreign economies.

References

Ammer, J., M. De Pooter, C. Erceg, and S. Kamin. 2016. International spillovers of monetary policy. IFDP Note: Board of Governors of the Federal Reserve System, February.

Beckworth, David and Christopher Crowe (2016), "The International Impact of the Fed When the US is Banker to the World," edited by Michael Bordo and John B. Taylor, in this volume.

Bernanke, B. 2013. Monetary policy and the global economy. Speech delivered at the Department of Economics and STICERD (Suntory and Toyota International Centres for Economics and Related Disciplines) Public Discussion in association with the Bank of England, London School of Economics, London, March 25.

Bernanke, B. 2015. Monetary policy and the global economy. Mundell-Fleming lecture presented at the 16th Jacques Polak Annual Research Conference, International Monetary Fund, Washington, November 5.

Blanchard, O., and R. Perotti. 2002. An empirical characterization of the dynamic effects of changes in government spending on output. *Quarterly Journal of Economics* 117 (4): 1328–29.

Bruno, V., and H. S. Shin. 2015. Capital flows and the risk-taking channel of monetary policy. *Journal of Monetary Economics* 71:119–32.

Christiano, L., M. Eichenbaum, and C. Evans. 1999. Monetary policy Shocks: What have we learned and to what end? In *Handbook of macroeconomics*, vol. 1A, ed. John B. Taylor and Michael Woodford. Amsterdam: Elsevier Press.

Taylor, J. B. 1993. Discretion versus policy rules in practice." *Carnegie-Rochester Conference Series on Public Policy* 39: 195–214.

GENERAL DISCUSSION

DAVID BECKWORTH: I'll first speak to the VAR and let Chris Crowe answer some of the other questions. On the VAR, we thought about this issue, and Chris Erceg described it absolutely correctly. The way we ordered it is consequential. With that said, one thing we're trying to get at is that you have this identification problem with the VAR. If we have quarterly data, and one of the drawbacks with this identification procedure is if you order it last, you're going to force monetary policy to have a long, delayed effect. It may, in fact, have an immediate effect, for example, on the dollar. So that was one of our motivations. But it doesn't address the problem you brought up. I would note that the Taylor Gap itself has, of course, embedded in it GDP, inflation, and the neutral interest rate. To some extent, then, the Taylor Gap is going to capture some of those endogenous changes to the economy. It doesn't completely resolve your critique, though. We did estimate and generalize impulse response functions, did a robustness check, and they were similar. So I do think it's useful for us to go back and maybe report those, also different orderings, just to show that our growth results are robust. So I think that that's a great point.

CHRISTOPHER CROWE: I thought the point Chris Erceg made about focusing on our bringing out how it's not beggar-thy-neighbor is really interesting. I agree with that 100%. I think, in general, these effects on US aggregate demand are going to be more important for EM economies than any negative effect from a weaker dollar. As I understand it, the current state of the literature is that these particularly trade effects via exchange rate changes have been pretty small recently. Exchange rates seem to matter more for inflation than for output. I think that the argument that a US monetary loosening is basically good from an output point of view for the rest of the world seems to me fairly uncontroversial, which is maybe why we didn't emphasize it as much as we should have done. But I think it is interesting. I think it's also interesting when you think about the central bank valuation channel as well from exchange rates, because we have these huge gross positions on the international investment position. These effects from exchange rate moves can be pretty big, so you have the US dollar appreciating post . . . around 2009, that probably amounted to a sort of wealth transfer to the rest of the world of about 15% of US GDP. And so from my point of view, it's actually even more surprising that these effects are not as big. So maybe we should have emphasized this more.

And maybe one other thing; it's kind of related to the VAR stuff, and it's not so much related to this paper, but I have done other work where I've shown that the sample period is incredibly important. So you're able to identify shocks correctly, and you look at sort of conventional VAR-type identification schemes, which worked well in the past, and you sort of look at a more recent period, even precrisis but sort of 2000s or 1990s, and drop the seventies and eighties. You often find these conventional VAR identification schemes give you very odd-looking results. So I think probably experimenting with different sample sizes would be pretty important for robustness, but I would do it with trepidation, with the expectation that the result could be all over the place.

RICHARD CLARIDA: I have three quick points. Point one: I think this paper has a lot of virtues. One is that having toiled with this data for decades, I think I would strongly urge you, if you've got the RA talent, to regularly update charts one through sixteen, and that will save the rest of us a lot of time. You have a vested interest in keeping it up to date because those are hard to put together in the right way, and you've done a great job.

And point two, more substantively, is I want to piggyback on something Chris Erceg said, which I think is important in all of these discussions, that when we look at Fed cycles, we can always identify EM countries that get hit. But we need to discipline ourselves. You rarely hear people talking about Australia or Canada or even Chile. There are a lot of countries that do quite well in these episodes where the Fed is hiking or easing. They have open economies, but they tend to have very credible exchange rates. They also have a lot of commodity exposure. So I think when making broad statements about the effect of US policy, you've got to look at the whole universe of countries, and a lot of countries actually don't enter the headlines. I think there's sample selection bias in a lot of these episodes.

And then the third point is on VAR identification. I think sign restrictions—as with the approach of Harald Uhlig right here—are really the way to go in a lot of these VAR exercises. There's no perfect identification scheme, but I think exclusion through timing is probably going to be enough in this case, so I urge you to use the sign restriction approach. Nice job.

DAVID BECKWORTH: Those are good points, and we will definitely look at sign restrictions as well when we tinker around with our VAR.

DAVID PAPELL: I've heard Fed policy since 2008 called many things, but "tight" is not one of them. What is the source of tight in this paper? There are two aspects. The first is the Taylor rule. If you'll use the original Taylor rule, which is the rule in John Taylor's 1993 paper, you're going to get something very different from what you get with what you call the Taylor 1999 rule. If you read John's 1999 paper, what you're calling the Taylor 1999 rule is the rule that John describes as the rule that others have used—particularly researchers from the Federal Reserve Board. So call it the Fed rule, call it the Rudebusch rule, call it the Yellen rule, call it the Taylor rule with a doubled coefficient on the output gap. But don't call it the Taylor 1999 rule.

The second aspect is that, by using the federal funds rate since 2009 as the measure of US monetary policy, you are implicitly assuming that unconventional monetary policy has had absolutely no effect on the economy. Forget QE1, QE2, QE3, and forward guidance because all that you are measuring is the fact that the federal funds rate was between zero and 0.025%. I think you really need to use a measure of the shadow federal funds rate. Cynthia Wu and Dora Xia have one that's on the Atlanta Fed website, and Michael Bauer and Glen Rudebusch of the San Francisco Fed have alternatives. But you need to get more stimulative effects than just reducing the federal funds rate to 0.025 or else you're assuming that the Fed did nothing else.

Now what happens if you do both of these things? The Taylor rule deviations switch from positive numbers from 2009 to now to large negative numbers throughout most of that period. And so my question on this is, If you flip the sign of the Taylor rule deviations over this large part of the sample, will it change your results? And if it doesn't, then I would worry about why.

DAVID BECKWORTH: I think we can have reasonable disagreements as to whether policy was purposefully tight. I'm not claiming that. But if you look at things like nominal demand, it collapsed in 2008 and never returned to a kind-of precrisis path. Output gaps, likewise, have been persistently negative. I know they aren't perfectly measured. Estimates of neutral rates have been very negative. All those are signs that monetary policy was effectively too tight. Again, not that Fed policy could easily have avoided this outcome. But we're seeing an effective stance of monetary policy.

On the QE point, we did tinker around with the shadow federal funds rate from the Atlanta Fed. But we were concerned when we were doing it that it would be like double counting.

Because the Taylor rule has the ouput gap, it is already reflecting the effect of QE policies, to the extent they mattered. And if we have that, and we also use a shadow federal funds rate, which has kind of baked into it QE results, we believe it would be a case of double counting. So you're right. The federal funds rate doesn't change much. But the Taylor rule does. And that's reflecting the efforts of QE. That's reflecting the efforts of unconventional monetary policy.

HARALD UHLIG: I learned a lot from the paper. It's quite insightful. And my attention was drawn to the VARs naturally, and I sympathize with the struggle you are facing. As Richard Clarida said, there's no golden approach here, but there's just so many issues. I mean, sign restrictions, yeah, sure, I'd like to see those. There's also other ways of identifying monetary policy shocks. People have used these high-frequency measures, for example, FOMC dates, to try to tease out monetary policy shocks. You could just use those as an additional external series in the VAR as a constructive suggestion.

The VAR itself: there's a question of how far you want to go in really thinking about this, right? I mean, you've written the piece already. There's some nice results. Maybe you want to let it go. I highly sympathize with that. But there's just a long list of things one really ought to look into. So for one, the Taylor Gap, for example . . . I guess the output gap and inflation, they are contemporaneous in their Taylor Gap formula? So it strikes me as sort of a structure variable in some ways, where you fix the coefficient that the interest rate has on the innovation and the output gap and the inflation rate. That's one way of thinking about it. And then try to get the output reaction, and then the inflation reaction from what's above and beyond that. The problem with that is, you don't even have the output gap and inflation rate in the VAR, right? So at a minimum, I would like to see the inflation rate included in the VAR, in particular, since we know that many of the interest-rate-based VAR identifications of monetary policies run into this price puzzle, where price moves in the opposite direction. Since you're doing it structurally, using this Taylor Gap identification, it's possible that you don't get the price puzzle. That will be very, very nice. Right? But if you don't show me what prices do, what inflation does, I'm really not convinced that you got monetary policy in there.

The other issue is the output gap. The output gap is an average of a bunch of things. One of the things that you throw in there, for example, is what is HP-filtered out. Now the HP filter is two sided. So in essence, you're throwing in a variable that includes future variables already. So in the VAR context, that's really problematic. If you could find some way of constructing the output gap just based on present-past data, that would be avoided.

Also—and Christopher Erceg mentioned this—once you run into the zero lower bound, you really have to wonder whether a linear model is a good thing to use at all. At that point, in some ways the Taylor Gap becomes very, very predictable. You know the Taylor rule is way below zero. You know you're stuck at zero. You know the Taylor Gap has to be positive. And so you're treating this in the VAR as if agents are constantly surprised that the Fed yet again chose zero rather than going to –3%. It's hard knowing what to do with the zero lower bound. But there are all kinds of flags raised here. So the question is, What do you do with them? Do you want to go beyond what you have, or do you just want to list these flags as stuff for others to do? But it is interesting. It raises a lot of questions.

CHRISTOPHER CROWE: This issue of using high-frequency measures is something I've actually done in other work, for example, looking at using fed funds futures and identifying policy shocks that way, and it worked pretty well. I guess one of the reasons why we didn't use this even though I'm one of the people who's worked on it was just that the Fed's stuck at the zero lower bound. So it's probably reasonable to expect there won't be much news on every FOMC date in terms of the fed funds futures rate because we know that policy is not going anywhere. And so we come back to the issue of what to do at the zero lower bound. I guess the answer, as in a lot of times when you do empirical work and you sort of run into an intractable problem, is kind of a kitchen sink approach, where you just run a battery of robustness checks and hope that it all stands up to those. And that's maybe something we can do. We didn't do it yet for timing reasons, but it's probably something we should look at. And I guess on the HP filter, we could use a one-sided HP filter to estimate the output gap. What I would say, I suppose, is it's only one of the measures which we use. We can average over several, right? My guess is that the empirical size of it is probably not huge. That would be my prior. Also, I think we should look at inflation. In other work I did, when we were able to recover the decent impulse response functions for output, I still found the price puzzle. The price puzzle seems to be pretty pervasive. Maybe it's just real. Heretical thought.

SEBASTIAN EDWARDS: I want to comment on something Chris Erceg said referring to Mexico. And the point is related also to the previous discussion, and that is how some countries are able to withstand monetary shocks from the Fed. And what Chris said is if they have strong fundamentals, they can withstand in a much better way, which is a noncontroversial proposition. And then you brought in the case of Mexico in 2013, but what makes this more interesting is that Mexico had equally strong fundamentals in 2015 and 2016, and the Mexican peso went just through the floor, and it depreciated about 40%, to the surprise of everyone. And Agustin Carstens had to go out and not only raise interest rates to match but to overmatch the Fed but also intervene in the actual foreign exchange market. So there you have the same strong fundamentals with an overreaction over a period of two years, which adds an additional sort of a puzzle into this discussion.

And I want to make another comment. I think that this paper has two parts to it—the second part, which is the one most of the discussants have been focusing on, has to do with the VAR analysis, which is very interesting. But I found more interesting the first part about the undersupply of safe assets. I think that we have lost that part of the paper in the discussion, and I would like to urge everyone here to come back to this question. I think that an obvious solution to the shortage of safe assets is to increase the supply of safe assets. So let me throw out a proposition here, thinking about class A and class B shares. Would it be possible—I don't know what the answer is—would it be possible for the United States to issue two types of securities—class A and class B securities? These would be similar to what the British used to do by issuing those overseas passports that lots of people wanted to have, although they were not very useful. But there was a big demand for those. And I think that a question dealing with the safe asset supply is the notion that we would have—as we do in the equity market these two types of shares that have different voting rights—two types of securities that maybe would make easier the political problem of issuing more safe asset debt in the United States.

DAVID BECKWORTH: Sebastian, some people have proposed a sovereign wealth fund for the United States, which could do effectively the same thing. Sovereign wealth funds are based on a country's comparative advantage, if it's oil, put the wealth in that; if ours is issuing safe stores of value, use that. But again, there's all kinds of issues, as you know, that come up with that as well. But it is an interesting discussion for sure.

CHRISTOPHER ERCEG: Sebastian Edwards raises an interesting point about Mexico: while Mexico seemed to weather the Taper

Tantrum quite well, the experience of the past several months—in which the Bank of Mexico has raised its policy rate by 75 basis points amidst a continued depreciation of the peso—may suggest that Mexico is experiencing more sizeable monetary policy spillovers. However, my sense is that much of the large depreciation of the peso that Sebastian noted isn't due to monetary policy spillovers but rather to the enormous fall in global commodity prices that has occurred since mid-2014 and that has weighed heavily on the currencies of all commodity-producers. Thus, Mexico's depreciation of over 30% is commensurate with that of Canada and that of Norway, both of which are economies with very well-anchored inflation expectations. Moreover, while the Bank of Mexico has raised its policy rate in recent months, it's important to keep in mind that the policy rate started at a historic low and that the rise from 3% to 3.75% has barely made it positive in real terms. These policy rate adjustments seem quite modest relative to the large hikes in policy rates in the more vulnerable emerging market economies that occurred during the Taper Tantrum. The upshot is that I agree that monetary policy spillovers remain consequential, but, nonetheless, I don't think Mexico's recent experience looks all that different from other commodity-producing economies with stable monetary policy frameworks.

CHRISTOPHER CROWE: I would just like to add that my sense is that having credible policies in a sort of stable policy framework can help to insulate you from having financial crises and big economic dislocations. But it doesn't insulate you from having big exchange rate movements. And it doesn't insulate your central bank from having to pay close attention to what the Fed's doing.

MICHAEL MELVIN: I was really taken by one of your conclusions, that hitting the zero lower bound pushes investors to safe assets. That certainly wasn't the intention of the policy, I think, because the policy suppressed risk premia, and investors searching for yield moved their portfolio compositions considerably. It seems to me that the evidence is pretty clear that, when you hit the zero interest rate, there's a big shift in investor demand toward risky assets. I mean, look at the yields on high yield bonds, for instance. So that was a very surprising conclusion to me, and I would like to hear some more elaboration on that.

DAVID BECKWORTH: We're not claiming this is a conscious effort by the Fed to have tight policy. The zero lower bound is a consequence of this collapse in demand; it's where the Fed found itself as it followed the natural interest rate down, and it got stuck at zero. The demand for safe assets is a consequence of the crisis itself. The zero lower bound is also a consequence of it. The Fed followed the natural interest rate down as far as it could. It couldn't go any farther, so policy effectively became tight. We didn't have a quick recovery. We mentioned in the paper there's a spate of other shocks, and the Eurozone keeps rearing its ugly head, concerns about China—all these things kept the demand for treasuries elevated. This is focusing on the emerging markets. Let me be very clear here, too, that according to the time series that we show, the demand just shot through the roof for Treasury notes and bonds and declined in all the other categories. I don't have an answer for the junk yield story.

CHRISTOPHER CROWE: I guess precrisis our story is that Fed policy was arguably too loose. The US current account deteriorated. There was a recycling of the current account surpluses in the rest of the world back into the United States, into what looks ex-post like fairly dodgy kinds of assets. I had to take a long flight over from London, so I had to watch a number of films, including *The Big Short.* And in retrospect, it's kind of crazy the stuff people were buying. But, you know, people were buying it. And they seemed safe, or they were packaged as safe. And so I guess that shows up in the data. You have this big surge precrisis in less safe so-called safe assets, and then the big drop. And then the big increase in Treasuries. So it certainly seems to be there in the data. Now whether it's understandable in terms of micro aspects of investor behavior is perhaps something we should look at in more detail.

ROBERT HALL: This paper embodies what I would call a Caballero view of the global capital markets—that there's a shortage of safe assets. And then a complement to that is the notion that the United States provides an intermediation service. I've worked on a different view. It comes to sort of the same thing. I view low world interest rates as a natural market outcome resulting from heterogeneity in risk aversion. The United States has risk tolerant investors, a lot of them very well off and presumptively risk tolerant. The rest of the world—China especially—is quite risk averse. And that's enough to give—easily—the market outcome, which is very low interest rates. The risk averse investors want to own safe bonds. Their demand drives down the yield of safe bonds. And that makes one think that interest rates will remain low. Interest rates aren't low for cyclical reasons. They're low because that's what happens when we borrow a lot of money and pay it back later, and therefore cushion risk averse investors against bad outcomes.

I'm very taken by this idea that we ought to be thinking about whether we can reduce the demand for safe assets, which would raise world interest rates and solve a lot of problems. And it seems like the best way to do that is to make the financial system more stable. Of course, the Fed is only one of the players in pushing for a stable financial system. But we certainly learned in 2008 how unstable, and therefore unsafe, the US economy was, and we really need to change that.

CHRISTOPHER CROWE: I guess my answer would be: yes. I agree. Certainly to the last part. Greater financial stability is part of the story, and more confidence in the growth potential for the economy would help, too, I think.

CHAPTER THREE

A Journey Down the Slippery Slope to the European Crisis

A Theorist's Guide

Varadarajan V. Chari, Alessandro Dovis, and Patrick J. Kehoe

ABSTRACT

We offer a theoretically based narrative that attempts to account for both the formation of the European Monetary Union and the challenges it has faced. Lack of commitment to policy plays a central role in this narrative.

This paper is an attempt to develop a consistent intellectual framework to think about the forces that led to the formation of the European Monetary Union and the challenges it has faced. This intellectual framework has been more fully developed in a series of academic papers by Chari and Kehoe and by Chari, Dovis, and Kehoe. Here we summarize the main points discussed in those papers. The central driving force of those papers, and the force reprised here, is that governments and government agencies such as central banks lack commitment to future policies. This lack of commitment can make it desirable to set up institutions like the European Monetary Union, and precisely the same lack of commitment can create challenges for such unions.

We develop three themes in this paper. First, forming a monetary union can be desirable if central banks lack commitment, even when the monetary authority in the union cannot also commit. Second,

The authors thank Harald Uhlig and participants at the International Monetary Stability Conference for useful comments and the NSF for supporting this research. The views expressed herein are those of the authors and not necessarily those of the Federal Reserve Bank of Minneapolis or the Federal Reserve System.

absent commitment by the union's monetary authority, monetary unions create externalities in other policies, including fiscal policy and bank supervision policy. Third, addressing these externalities requires union-wide cooperation in these other policy areas.

These themes allow us to develop a coherent and seamless narrative that ties together the forces that led to the formation of the European Monetary Union and the forces that led to the challenges the union has faced. We draw on Chari, Dovis, and Kehoe (2016) to show that if benevolent central banks lack commitment, monetary unions can be a useful commitment device. We show that inflation rates in unions are less volatile than they would be with flexible exchange rates. This feature of our model is broadly consistent with the experience of the European Monetary Union. After the breakdown of the Bretton Woods system, European economies faced stubbornly high and variable inflation rates. Viewed through the lens of our theory, the founders of the union perceived these outcomes as arising in part due to the inability of central bankers to commit to their policies and saw that forming a union can be desirable. Indeed, inflation rates in Europe since the union was formed have been low and stable.

We draw on Chari and Kehoe (2007, 2008) to show that when the monetary authority in a union cannot commit to its policies, externalities arise in other policy areas. To understand these externalities, consider the optimal inflation rate chosen by a benevolent monetary authority in a union when it has no commitment. This choice balances the costs of ex-post inflation against the gains of reducing the real value of outstanding nominal debt. This balancing act implies that the ex-post inflation rate is higher when the stock of nominal debt is greater. Governments of individual countries in a union have incentives to issue more debt than they would with flexible exchange rates, because in a union the cost of ex-post inflation is partly borne by other member countries. All countries are better off if they can restrict each others' fiscal policies.

From the perspective of the theory, the founders understood that commitment by the newly formed European Central Bank could not be taken as a given and that externalities, especially in fiscal policy, were likely to arise. The Maastricht Treaty and the Stability and Growth Pact imposed restrictions on fiscal policies, in particular on deficits and the level of government debt relative to output, in individual countries to address the externalities. After Germany and France violated the deficit limits in the early 2000s, it became more likely that the restrictions would not be enforced, and the stage was set for excessive deficits and debt issue by members of the union.

From our perspective, the founders seemed to underestimate the externalities in banking policy. Consider a situation in which a financial crisis is under way. If the monetary authority lacks commitment, it will engage in bailouts of bank debt holders financed by inflation. If debt holders of banks see bailouts of their debt as likely in the event of a banking crisis, bank equity holders have strong incentives to take on socially excessive risk, and financial crises are more likely to occur. Individual countries have weaker incentives to supervise risk-taking by banks if they perceive that the bailout will be conducted by the union as a whole. These factors, in our view, contributed to the severity of the recent European debt and financial crisis. The European Central Bank's expression of resolve "to do whatever it takes" may well have ameliorated the crisis, but it may also have reinforced beliefs by the public that future bailouts are now more likely. Such reinforcement of beliefs may well make future crises more likely.

A key aspect of the theories described so far is that the central bank is a Good Samaritan, in the sense that it is benevolent. A benevolent central bank that lacks commitment has strong incentives to engage in inflationary bailouts of governments of distressed countries in financial crises, even if the inflation imposes costs on residents of less distressed countries. In this paper, we develop a simple model intended to illustrate the idea that the mere presence of a Good Samaritan may induce governments of less distressed countries to engage in bailouts in the form of debt forgiveness or fiscally financed transfers. Indeed, such fiscal bailouts may be large enough that the Good Samaritan ends up not engaging in any inflationary bailouts at all. Anticipations of such fiscal bailouts induce governments of countries in a union to borrow inefficiently large amounts from residents of other member countries in the union. In this sense, the mere presence of the Good Samaritan introduces externalities in other policy areas. The Good Samaritan may well end up seeming not to change its policies at all.

Bulow and Rogoff (2015) argue that Greece received substantially more funds during its crisis from the troika consisting of the European Monetary Union, the European Commission, and the International Monetary Fund than essentially any emerging market economy did from external sources during their crises. Our theory is consistent with this feature of the data. Viewed through the lens of our model, the troika rationally acted to forestall the European Central Bank from acting on its own. We view this consistency with the data as an attractive feature of our theoretical work.

Our perspective leads to policy implications for redesigning the European Monetary Union. Some economists advocate that the union should simply be dissolved. This advocacy misses the essential point that the founders of the union, with good reason, thought that forming a monetary union would help solve the problems of high and variable inflation. Indeed, arguably, the union has been successful in this regard. Others (see, for example, Baldwin and Giavazzi [2016] in a volume for the Centre for Economic Policy Research [CEPR]) have advocated policies that maintain the union but alter some of its practices. Sixteen economists who wrote policy papers for the CEPR volume advocate for a variety of institutional changes. Our reading is that the vast majority are pessimistic about the prospects of setting binding limits on fiscal policy, agree that bank regulation should be conducted in substantial part at the union-wide level, and argue that Europe needs a lender of last resort with substantially greater resources and more latitude to act than the European Central Bank currently possesses.

We too are pessimistic about the prospects for binding limits on fiscal policy, though, for reasons outlined below, we think constraints on the maturity structure of debt, while leaving the aggregate amount of debt unconstrained, are desirable and, perhaps, enforceable. We agree that a common supervisory framework for bank supervision is desirable. We are skeptical that enlarging the bailout powers of the union by creating a giant lender of last resort is a desirable policy. In our view, a strong supervisory system can reduce the probability of financial crises more effectively, and the moral hazard problems created by expectations of bailouts will likely be enhanced by a bailout authority with increased access to bailout funds.

1. The journey begins

When are monetary unions desirable? The traditional criterion for the desirability of forming a union weighs the benefits, from increased trade and financial integration associated with a union, against the costs from the loss of independence in monetary policy. The classic analyses of Friedman (1953) and Mundell (1961) point out that, when each country pursues an independent monetary policy, each country can tailor its policies to its own idiosyncratic shocks. When policy is set in common, it cannot be tailored to every country's idiosyncratic shocks. The implicit assumption in these analyses is that the monetary authority can commit to its policies. Thus, the classic analyses imply that, in terms of monetary policy alone, monetary unions only have costs and no benefits.

1.1. Monetary unions can confer commitment benefits

In Chari, Dovis, and Kehoe (2016), we revisit the classic analyses using simplified versions of standard sticky price models. We assume that both in a union and under flexible exchange rates, monetary policy is influenced by all countries in the union. Specifically, we assume that policy is chosen either cooperatively or by majority rule. When countries have commitment, forming a union is costly and a flexible exchange rate regime is preferred by all member countries. Thus, this analysis confirms the key message of the classic analyses. The reason that forming a union is costly is that, with sticky prices, it is optimal for policy to react to idiosyncratic shocks. With a union, it is impossible to have monetary policy react to every country's idiosyncratic shocks. Interestingly, it turns out that monetary policy should respond only to a subset of shocks, labeled *Mundellian shocks.*

Without commitment to monetary policy, policymakers have incentives to deviate from the commitment plan to generate surprise inflation. These incentives are particularly strong when shocks, labeled *temptation shocks,* affect the economy. Private agents anticipate that the monetary authority will react to such shocks and alter their price-setting behavior. In equilibrium, it turns out that inflation is higher and more variable than it would be under commitment, but the reactions of private agents lead output to be just as variable as under commitment. Since monetary policy in the union cannot react to every country's idiosyncratic shocks, the monetary authority in the union ends up reacting to neither idiosyncratic Mundellian shocks nor idiosyncratic temptation shocks. Forming a union is, in this sense, a commitment device. A union has costs because policy does not react to Mundellian shocks, and it has benefits because it does not react to temptation shocks either. Thus, forming a union is desirable if temptation shocks are sufficiently large relative to Mundellian shocks.

We emphasize that, in making this argument, we assume that the monetary authority in the union faces exactly the same commitment problem as do policymakers in individual countries. The monetary authority in the union does react to aggregate shocks that affect all member countries. In particular, it does react to aggregate temptation shocks. The reason that the monetary authority does not react to idiosyncratic shocks is that, while some countries would like to see a positive surprise inflation, other countries would like to see a negative surprise inflation. When policy is set cooperatively or by majority rule, the desires of these countries on optimal policy offset each other and the union ends up not reacting to idiosyncratic shocks affecting its members.

From this perspective, forming the European Monetary Union was a sensible response by policymakers in Europe to the volatile inflation rates they experienced in the wake of the collapse of the Bretton Woods system. One measure of this success is that inflation rates in Europe became less volatile after the union was formed. The standard deviation of inflation in the 19 years prior to the formation of the union was 3.7%, and it's been 1.2% in the years since. Of course, the union cannot be credited or blamed entirely for this observation. Other factors were surely at play. Nevertheless, it is comforting that this observation is consistent with the theory laid out in Chari, Dovis, and Kehoe (2016).

1.2. Monetary unions can create externalities in other policy areas

Chari and Kehoe (2007, 2008) argued that if the monetary authority in a union cannot commit to its policies, then externalities can be created in other policy areas. One area we highlighted is fiscal policy. The basic idea in those papers is that the monetary authority's incentives to engender surprise inflation are stronger when the outstanding stock of nominal debt is larger. Such surprise inflation reduces the real amount of debt and reduces the distorting taxes needed to service or retire the debt. Surprise inflation, ex-post, can be welfare enhancing for the residents of the country. A monetary authority without commitment will balance the costs of surprise inflation against the costs of distorting taxes needed to service or retire the debt. When the stock of existing nominal debt is larger, the ex-post optimal inflation rate is higher.

Private lenders understand these incentives. If the fiscal authorities issue a lot of debt in the first place, the nominal interest rate rises in anticipation of the future inflation, and real rates are not affected. The fiscal authorities understand these incentives on the part of the monetary authority, too. With flexible exchange rates, they see that if they issue a lot of debt, future inflation will be higher. The costs of this inflation will be borne by the residents of the country. The fiscal authority appropriately balances the tax-smoothing gains of debt issue against the costs of resulting inflation.

In a union, however, a free-rider problem arises. If an individual country increases its current debt issue, in the future the benevolent monetary authority has a stronger incentive to engender inflation. With a union, part of the cost of the future inflation is borne by other member countries. Thus, in a union, debt issue is inefficiently larger than it would be with flexible exchange rates. As with other classic free-rider problems, all countries would gain if they could set fiscal policy cooperatively. Also, as with other classic free-rider problems, an individual country would like restraints on the fiscal policies of other countries while being permitted to have an unrestricted policy for itself.

When paired with our results on optimal currency areas, we see that lack of commitment can create benefits to forming a union in terms of monetary policy but can lead to spillovers which lead to poor outcomes in terms of other policies. These spillovers make cooperative arrangements in other policy areas valuable. The theory provides one rationale for the limits on fiscal policy that were enshrined in the Maastricht Treaty and the Stability and Growth Pact. Arguably, the founders of the European Monetary Union understood these economic issues very well. They saw that, by using the commitment device of forming a union, they would gain in terms of reduced volatility of inflation. They understood, furthermore, that this lack of commitment created externalities, and they enshrined restrictions on the fiscal policies of member countries to limit those externalities. We may be giving them too much credit, but certainly their attempts to address these problems are consistent with the theoretical framework outlined here.

The theory also explains why some countries were tempted to violate the constraints if they could get away with such violations. The founders did not, however, understand that there might be incentives to bail out banks, and that is something we turn to next.

Chari and Kehoe (2008) showed that exactly the same kinds of free-riding problems in fiscal policy show up when it comes to supervisory policy of banks. The basic argument here is very similar. In the event of a run, or in the event of a financial crisis, central banks ex-post have an incentive to bail out bank debtors. Anticipations of such bailouts imply that debtors have reduced incentives to monitor the riskiness of bank portfolios. The interest rate on debt becomes less sensitive to the riskiness of bank portfolios. Owners and managers of banks have increased incentive to make their portfolios riskier. Note that this incentive remains even if policymakers bail out only debt holders and do not rescue equity holders at all. This well-known moral hazard problem goes back at least to Kareken and Wallace (1978). One way to address this moral hazard problem is to supervise and regulate bank portfolios closely. In a monetary union, national supervisors have weak incentives to engage in close monitoring and supervision because part of the costs will be borne by other countries, and the same kind of free-rider problem emerges in bank supervisory policy as in fiscal policy.

1.3. Bailouts and the Good Samaritan problem

In Chari and Kehoe (2008), we assumed that bailouts are financed by the central bank. Here we develop a simple model in which lack of commitment by the monetary authority can induce members of a union to voluntarily engage in tax-financed bailouts. These bailouts act to forestall inflationary bailouts by a monetary authority. The point of this model is that when a benevolent monetary authority lacks commitment, it will act to redistribute resources if it finds it optimal to do so. In this sense, the monetary authority is a Good Samaritan without commitment. This threat that the monetary authority will act induces fiscal authorities to bail out unlucky countries by forgiving debt or making their own transfers to prevent the monetary authority from acting. In our model, it turns out that in equilibrium the monetary authority never responds.

Expectations of such bailouts create a free-rider problem by inducing governments to issue too much debt relative to an environment with commitment by the monetary authority. At the end of the day, these bailouts have to be paid for by countries who turn out to be lucky. Thus, the excessive debt issue, from an ex-ante perspective, only has costs and no benefits. All countries are better off if they could restrain each other from issuing too much debt. Furthermore, policies which make it easier for the monetary authority to engage in inflationary bailouts worsen the free-rider problem.

1.3.1. Environment

Consider a two-period model with a continuum of identical countries labeled by i. In period 1 each country receives an endowment y_1 and needs to issue debt to finance a public good of size g. This public good yields a utility in period 1 of $w(g)$. We assume that the government must finance this public good by issuing debt that matures in period 2.

The endowment in period 2 is random and is determined both by exogenous uncertainty and the taxes needed to repay the debt. The exogenous uncertainty is described by a random variable which can take on one of two values, denoted s_L and s_H. The probabilities of these shocks are given by μ_L and μ_H respectively. By the law of large numbers, the fraction of countries with state s is μ_s. We refer to countries with realizations of s_H as "lucky" countries and countries with realizations of s_L as "unlucky" countries.

After the endowment is realized, the government in, say, country i decides whether or not to repay its debts to foreigners. If it chooses to repay its debt, it must raise revenues through distorting taxes. We model the tax distortions as directly reducing output. Specifically, the endowment is given by $y_s(\tau)$, where τ denotes the tax revenues needed to pay off debt. We assume that $y_H(\tau) > y_L(\tau)$. We have in mind that taxes are particularly distorting in low output times and less distorting in high output times. For simplicity, we model these differentially distorting effects by simply assuming that taxes are not distorting at all in good times. Specifically, we assume that in the lucky state, s_H, y_H is independent of τ and, in the unlucky state, s_L, y_L is a decreasing and concave function of τ.

We follow the sovereign default literature in assuming that defaults have direct costs. In particular, if the country defaults on foreign debt b, then its endowment is reduced by $y_s(0)\kappa(b)$, where s denotes the exogenous state and κ is an increasing function.

Households are risk neutral and discount period 2 consumption at a rate β. We assume for simplicity that households will hold only foreign debt. (This assumption emerges as a result in a more elaborate model in which governments can default in a discriminatory fashion on domestic and foreign debt holders and in which defaulting on foreign debt is costly, but defaulting on domestic debt is costless. Then domestic households hold no domestic debt.) The budget constraint for the representative household in country i in period 1 is

$$c_{1i} + \int_j Q_j b_{ij} dj = \omega_1,$$

where b_{ij} denotes the amount of country j debt held by country i households, Q_j denotes the price of debt issued by country j, and ω_1 denotes the endowment of households in period 1. The price Q_j of debt is determined by country j's default decision, which, in turn, will depend on the amount of debt issued by country j.

If country i does not default, then the budget constraint in the second period in state s is

$$c_{2i}(s) = \int_j \delta_j b_{ij} dj + y_s(\tau_i) - \tau_i,$$

where $\delta_j = 0$ denotes a default by country j and $\delta_j = 1$ denotes a repayment.

If country i does default, then the period 2 budget constraint is

$$c_{2i}(s) = \int_j \delta_j b_{ij} dj + y_s(0) - y_s(0)\kappa(B_i),$$

where B_i denotes the amount of debt issued by country i.

1.3.2. Characterizing equilibria without a monetary authority

Here we assume that the monetary authority is not present or, equivalently, that it can commit to its policies. Consider the default decision in the second period. Since taxes are undistorting for lucky countries and distorting for unlucky countries, unlucky countries have stronger incentives to default. Indeed, in our model only unlucky countries will threaten to default. In this economy, as in most sovereign default models, lenders have an incentive to renegotiate their contracts ex-post when faced with the prospect of a default. Such renegotiation can make the borrower better off by avoiding the output costs of default and can ensure that lenders receive some repayment rather than none. Individual lenders have incentives to hold out in such renegotiation, creating a collective action problem. We think of this collective action problem as being solved by transfers, or forced debt forgiveness, by governments. Let $T = (T_H, T_L)$ denote the vector of transfers to lucky and unlucky countries. Obviously, T_H will be negative and T_L will be positive in equilibrium.

Specifically, the timing of actions in period 2 is as follows. After the state is realized, lucky countries make a take-it-or-leave-it offer $T_L \geq 0$ to each unlucky country. If the offer is accepted by a particular country, it cannot default. If the offer is rejected, the country may default. We assume that the offer T_L does not depend on the amount of debt issued by an individual country. In a related bailout paper, Chari and Kehoe (2016) provide a rationale for this assumption. The basic idea is that monitoring the ex-post debt levels of individual countries is costly and often imperfect and, in equilibrium, unnecessary. So, the best decision of the countries making the offer is to make a take-it-or-leave-it offer rather than engaging in the messy task of determining whether an individual country has deviated from the equilibrium. Note that the prices of debt issued will depend on the amount of debt issued by a given country. This asymmetry seems natural to us because private agents have stronger incentives to monitor the amount of debt than do governments.

Given the vector of inherited debts for each country, B_i, an *equilibrium of the offer game* consists of offers T_L, T_H for each unlucky and lucky country such that the countries optimally decide whether or not to accept the offer and whether or not to default if they reject the offer, the lucky countries choose their offer, and markets clear in that

$$\mu_L T_L + \mu_H T_H = 0. \tag{1}$$

We now characterize the equilibrium of the offer game. Consider the problem of an unlucky country i which has received the transfer offer T_L. Since T_L is nonnegative, the country will reject the offer only if it plans to default. Thus, the decision on whether to accept the offer can be combined with the default decision. Thus, country i solves

$$\begin{aligned} V_L(B_i, \{b_{ij}\}, T) = \max_{\delta_i} \; & y_L(\delta_i(B_i - T_L)) \\ & + \int \delta_j b_{ij} dj - \delta_i(B_i - T_L) - (1 - \delta_i) y_L \kappa(B_i). \end{aligned} \tag{2}$$

The solution to this problem is to accept the offer and not default by setting $\delta_i = 1$ if and only if

$$y_L((B_i - T_L)) - (B_i - T_L) \geq y_L(0) - y_L \kappa(B_i). \tag{3}$$

Let B_L^* be the critical value such that, absent transfers, country i does not default, that is, B_L^* is given by

$$y_L(B_L^*) - B_L^* = y_L(0) - y_L \kappa(B_L^*).$$

Let $T_L^*(B_i)$ denote the minimum offer that is accepted. If $B_i \geq B_L^*$, this minimum accepted offer is set so that the government is indifferent between repaying and defaulting, in that (3) holds with equality. If $B_i < B_L^*$, the minimum accepted offer is 0. Note from (3) that if $T_L \geq T_L^*(B_i)$, the country gladly accepts and does not default. Thus, $T_L^*(B_i)$ is the minimum offer the unlucky country will accept. Also, note that countries do not need their debts to be completely forgiven to induce them not to default. That is, $T_L^*(B_i) \leq B_i$. To see this result, note that (3) holds with strict inequality at $T_L^*(B_i) = B_i$.

Note, for later, that since $T_L^*(B_i)$ is defined by (3) with equality, when $B_i \geq B_L^*$, it follows that $B_i - T_L^*(B_i)$ is increasing in B_i. We assume that

$$(y'_L - 1 + y_L\kappa') \leq 0. \tag{4}$$

This assumption implies that T_L^* is increasing in B_i.

Next, consider the offer decision of the lucky countries. In the equilibrium of the two-period model, all countries will choose the same level of debt. The lucky countries take the debt levels of the representative unlucky country, denoted by B, as given and choose their offer. If $B < B_L^*$, the representative unlucky country will not default, regardless of the offer, and the optimal offer is 0. If $B \geq B_L^*$, the representative unlucky country will default unless it receives an offer of at least $T_L^*(B)$. Since $T_L^*(B) \leq B$, the offer that maximizes the payoff of the lucky countries, $B - T_L$, is to set the transfer to the lowest acceptable level, namely, $T_L^*(B)$:

$$\begin{aligned} V_H(B_i, \{b_{ij}\}, T) = \max_{\delta_i} \; & y_H + \int \delta_j b_{ij} dj - \delta_i B_i \\ & + T_H - (1 - \delta_i) y_H \kappa(B_i). \end{aligned} \tag{5}$$

As long as T_H is negative, this country sets $\delta_i = 1$ if and only if

$$B_i \leq y_H \kappa(B_i). \tag{6}$$

Let B_H^* denote the value of B_i such that (6) holds with equality. Thus, if $B_i \leq B_H^*$, lucky countries do not default.

We summarize this characterization in the following lemma.

Lemma: Suppose that the debt level of the representative country satisfies $B \leq B_H^*$. Then lucky countries do not default. All unlucky countries receive an offer of $T_L^*(B)$, if $B \geq B_L^*$, and an offer of 0 otherwise. An individual unlucky country accepts the transfer if its debt level $B_i \leq B$ and rejects the transfer and defaults if $B_i > B$.

This lemma immediately implies that, if the representative country has a debt level $B \leq B_H^*$, private lenders anticipate no default in period 2 by lucky countries. If an individual unlucky country has a debt level $B_i \leq B$, private lenders anticipate bailouts and no default. Thus, if $B_i \leq B$, the price of debt $Q_i = \beta$. If an individual country has a debt level $B_i > B$, private lenders anticipate default in the unlucky state, and the price of debt is given by $Q_i = \beta\mu_H$.

Next, we turn to the decision on how much government spending to finance in period 1 and how much debt to issue given the pricing function. We assume that this decision satisfies $B_i \leq B_H^*$. It is straightforward to provide sufficient conditions on $w(g)$ for this assumption to be satisfied.

Taking as given the debt issues by other countries, and therefore the representative debt level B, the payoffs of a country i if it chooses a debt level $B_i \leq B$, ignoring irrelevant constants, are given by

$$w(\beta B_i) - \beta\mu_H B_i - \beta\mu_L y_L(B_i - T_L^*(B)) - (B_i - T_L^*(B)), \quad (7)$$

noting that the price of debt is β. Its payoffs if it chooses a debt level $B_i > B$ are given by

$$w(\beta\mu_H B_i) - \beta\mu_H B_i - \beta\mu_L(y_L(0) - y_L\kappa(B_i)), \quad (8)$$

noting that the price of debt is, in this case, $\beta\mu_H$.

Country i's problem is to choose a debt level, B_i, that maximizes its payoffs, given the representative debt level B. Let $B_i(B)$ denote the best response function that solves this problem.

An *equilibrium for the two-period model* consists of a best response function $B_i(B)$ that maximizes each country's payoffs given the future transfer vector T and satisfies the fixed point condition, $B_i(B) = B$, and a transfer vector T that is an equilibrium of the offer game.

Next, we claim that in any equilibrium, the best response function $B_i(B)$ must maximize (7). The argument is by contradiction. Suppose this best response function maximized (7). Note that the maximized value of debt is independent of B and is the same for all countries. In the second period, given the level of inherited debt associated with solving (7), lucky countries would find it optimal to engage in bailouts. Thus, the price of the debt cannot be $\beta\mu_H$ and must be β.

Suppose next that in period 1, government consumption is sufficiently valuable in that

$$w'(\beta B_L^*) \geq \mu_H + \mu_L[1 - y_L'(B_L^*)]. \tag{9}$$

That is, the government would like to issue more debt than B_L^* if it could commit itself to not defaulting. Then it turns out that the two-period model has a continuum of equilibria. Any value of B which satisfies the first-order condition associated with maximizing (7) subject to $B_i \leq B$ is part of an equilibrium. The first-order condition is given by

$$w'(\beta B) \geq \mu_H + \mu_L[1 - y_L'(B)]. \tag{10}$$

Of particular interest is the *maximal debt equilibrium* in which the level of debt B_{max} is such that (10) holds with equality at B_{max}. We summarize this discussion in the following proposition.

Proposition 1 (Multiplicity of equilibria): Any debt level B that satisfies (10) is part of an equilibrium.

In what follows, we focus on the maximal debt equilibrium.

1.3.3. Characterizing equilibrium with a benevolent monetary authority

Now we introduce a monetary authority that lacks commitment. With this authority, the timing in period 2 is that shocks are realized, then the lucky countries make offers to the unlucky countries, and then the monetary authority chooses a transfer R_H and R_L to the unlucky countries. We require that these transfers must satisfy the resource constraint

$$\mu_H R_H + \mu_L R_L = 0.$$

We assume that the monetary transfer imposes a cost of τ_m per unit of transfer to the lucky country. One interpretation is that the monetary authority taxes lucky countries R_H each and makes transfers R_L to unlucky countries, and that these transfers impose an extra cost of τ_m on lucky countries. An alternative interpretation is that a monetary transfer of R_L raises inflation in all countries and imposes a cost $(1 + \tau_m)R_H$ on each lucky country. The assumption that monetary transfers are distorting is meant to capture the idea that, at the margin, inflation is more distorting than a fiscal transfer. Inflation is more distorting if fiscal transfers are a form of debt forgiveness. Such forgiveness often does not impose additional ex-post distortions.

The problem for the monetary authority given B and transfers T is to choose R to maximize the sum of utilities of residents in all countries. Ignoring irrelevant constants, and substituting in from the resource constraint, this problem reduces to

$$\max_R \left[\mu_H(1 + \tau_m)R_H + \mu_L \left(y_L \left(B - T_L + \frac{\mu_H}{\mu_L} R_H \right) - \frac{\mu_H}{\mu_L} R_H \right) \right].$$

The first-order condition for this problem is

$$\tau_m = -y_L'(B - (T_L + R_L)).$$

This first-order condition yields a striking result. Given the level of debt, B, fiscal transfers completely crowd out monetary transfers.

Lemma (Complete crowding out): For each level of B, total transfers to the unlucky countries $R_L + T_L$ are independent of T_L. Furthermore, the total amount repaid to the foreigners, $B - (T_L + R_L)$, is independent of B.

Now consider the union transfer problem. Since the transfer made by the monetary authority is distorting and the direct transfer is not, it is optimal for the lucky countries to make a transfer $\overline{T}_L(B)$ such that $\overline{T}_L(B)$ satisfies

$$\tau_m = -y_L'(B - \overline{T}_L(B)).$$

Suppose that τ_m is sufficiently small in that

$$-y_L'(B_{\max} - T_{Lnd}) > \tau_m, \tag{11}$$

then $R_L > 0$ at $(B_{\max}, T_{\max})$. This assumption implies that at the maximal debt equilibrium, the monetary authority will intervene.

Now we can consider the period 1 problem of choosing the optimal level of debt issue assuming that τ_m is sufficiently small. The first-order condition for the period 1 debt issue decision is

$$w'(\beta B) - \mu_H - \mu_L[1 - y_L'(B - \overline{T}_L(B))] \geq 0.$$

We have the following proposition.

Proposition 2. Under the assumption that τ_m is sufficiently small so that the monetary authority will intervene at the no-monetary-authority equilibrium outcome, in that (11) is satisfied, the model with a benevolent monetary authority has an equilibrium in which the level of debt satisfies

$$w'(\beta B) = \mu_H + \mu_L[1 + \tau_m]$$

$$\tau_m = -y_L'(B - \overline{T}_L(B)).$$

In this equilibrium, the level of debt issued by all countries is higher than in the equilibrium without the monetary authority.

This theory offers one rationale for Bulow and Rogoff's finding that Greece received larger transfers (including debt forgiveness) during its foreign debt crisis than did other economies during their foreign debt crises.

Note that if τ_m falls, debt issue rises. In this sense, making it easier for the monetary authority to respond worsens the debt overissue problem.

We have shown that lack of commitment by the monetary authority leads countries to issue too much debt. In equilibrium, the monetary authority does not respond. The threat that it might do so induces lucky countries to be more willing to bail out unlucky countries. This increased willingness worsens the debt overissue problem.

It is straightforward to extend the framework here to analyze how anticipation of bailouts of bank debtors by fiscal authorities aggravates the moral hazard problem of bank risk, and to show that a Good Samaritan monetary authority worsens this problem even further. An interesting feature of such a model is that the Good Samaritan may well never have to actually engage in inflationary bailouts.

2. Down the slippery slope

The theoretical framework developed here is consistent with key observations regarding the European Monetary Union. It was formed to help solve commitment problems. Unions can create externalities, particularly in fiscal policy and bank supervision. Constraints on fiscal policy are desirable and were imposed, along with penalties for violating them. These constraints were violated, but no penalties were imposed. Governments had strong incentives to run deficits, anticipating bailouts by the union, if economic circumstances turned sour. Banks had incentives to take on excessive risk.

These forces made a financial crisis more likely. A crisis did occur. As in our Good Samaritan model, fiscal authorities in Northern European economies ended up bearing a disproportionate share of the bailout burden during the crisis, and, as in that model, ex-post they rationally decided that such bailouts were preferred to actions by the European Central Bank. Also, as in that model, a benevolent monetary authority announced that it would "do whatever it takes" in a crisis. That is, indeed, the rational response given that a crisis was well under way.

In this sense, the framework developed here offers a coherent narrative for both the formation of the European Monetary Union and the challenges it has faced. We have argued that both the formation and the challenges arise fundamentally from lack of commitment.

3. The road ahead

Given that this theoretical framework is arguably consistent with broad features of the European experience, we now use it to think about policy, in the sense of redesigning European institutions. We address three kinds of policy questions. The first is, How big should the role of the European Central Bank or the European stability mechanism be as effectively lenders of last resort—How big should the bailout fund be? The second is, What's the extent to which bank regulations should be centralized? And the third is, What constraints on fiscal policy are desirable?

Interestingly enough, a volume of papers issued by the Centre for Economic Policy Research (CEPR) has collected the views of leading economists in Europe on these and other policy questions. Our reading is that, first, the vast majority of economists who have written these papers think the European Monetary Union needs a lender of last resort with even larger resources than it currently has. Second, essentially all of them agree that bank regulations should be centralized. Third, given the historical experience, they are generally pessimistic about enforcing constraints on fiscal policy.

On the lender of last resort, for reasons we have outlined, the remedy may exacerbate the problems that it is intended to solve.

On bank regulation, the externalities are real and centralization is desirable. The devil is in the details.

In terms of constraints on fiscal policies, we do offer one suggestion. The sovereign default literature suggests that excessive amounts of short-term debt can exacerbate rollover crises (see Cole and Kehoe [2000]). Without a monetary union, countries balance this additional cost of short-term debt against other benefits, as outlined, for example, in Bocola and Dovis (2016), in determining the optimal maturity structure of debt. In a union, externalities could arise for reasons similar to those discussed here. If the authorities in a union lack commitment, they may find it optimal to engage in bailouts during a rollover crisis. Expectations of such bailouts can induce individual countries to be less concerned about rollover crises than they would be if they were not part of a monetary union. This reduced concern may lead individual countries to tilt the maturity structure of debt toward short-term instruments to a greater extent than they would if they were not part of a monetary union. Given these externalities from lack of commitment, constraints on the maturity structure of debt are then desirable. Such constraints might well be enforceable even when constraints on the aggregate amount of debt are not.

References

Baldwin, R., and F. Giavazzi, eds. 2016. *How to fix Europe's monetary union: Views of leading economists.* Available at http://voxeu.org/content/how-fix-europe-s-monetary-union-views-leading-economists.

Bocola, L., and A. Dovis. 2016. Self-Fulfilling Debt Crises: A Quantitative Analysis. Working paper, University of Pennsylvania.

Bulow, J., and K. Rogoff. 2015. *The modern Greek tragedy.* Available at http://voxeu.org/article/modern-greek-tragedy.

Chari, V. V., A. Dovis, and P. Kehoe. 2016. Rethinking optimal currency areas. Working paper, Federal Reserve Bank of Minneapolis.

Chari, V. V., and P. Kehoe. 2007. On the need for fiscal constraints in a monetary union. *Journal of Monetary Economics* 54 (8): 2399–2408.

Chari, V. V., and P. Kehoe. 2008. Time inconsistency and free-riding in a monetary union. *Journal of Money, Credit and Banking* 40 (7): 1329–1356.

Chari, V. V., and P. Kehoe. 2016. Bailouts, time inconsistency, and optimal regulation: A macroeconomic view. *American Economic Review* (forthcoming).

Cole, H. L., and T. J. Kehoe. 2000. Self-fulfilling debt crises. *Review of Economic Studies* 67 (1): 91–116.

Friedman, M. 1953. The case for flexible exchange rates. In *Essays in positive economics*. Chicago: University of Chicago Press.

Friedman, M. 1973. Monetary policy in developing countries. In *Nations and households in economic growth: Essays in honor of Moses Abramovitz*, ed. P. A. David and M. W. Reder, 265–278. New York: Academic Press.

Kareken, J. H., and N. Wallace. 1978. Deposit insurance and bank regulation: A partial-equilibrium exposition. *Journal of Business* 51 (3): 413–438.

Mundell, R. A. 1961. A theory of optimum currency areas. *American Economic Review* 51 (4): 657–665.

DISCUSSION BY HARALD UHLIG

1. Introduction

This is an intriguing paper. According to the authors, it seeks to "develop a coherent and seamless narrative" and "a consistent intellectual framework to think about the forces that led to the formation of the European Monetary Union (EMU) and the challenges it has faced." This, of course, is a tall objective. Building on beautiful prior work of these authors or a subset, it emphasizes issues of commitment and issues of monetary-fiscal interaction. In essence, a monetary union can be an excellent commitment device, if national central banks are otherwise weak, even if the central bank in the monetary union also lacks commitment. Absent such commitment, there are externalities in fiscal policies and bank supervision policies, the solution of which requires union-wide cooperation. These are excellent and interesting points, and the authors are right in making them a central focus of their analysis.

The themes emphasized by the authors certainly resonate with me. This is a good point to shamelessly cite my own research within this context. The authors emphasize that externalities of fiscal choices imply the necessity to impose constraints on the latter. Beetsma and Uhlig (1999) likewise emphasize this point in their analysis of the Stability and Growth Pact. The authors argue that the failure of the Maastricht Treaty is a failure of bank regulation. Likewise, I consider the issue of bank regulation and its issues for sovereign default risk to be central in a monetary union (see Uhlig 2013). In Roch and Uhlig (2016) we find that central bank interventions and guarantees lead to higher debt levels, just as the au-

I have an ongoing consulting relationship with a Federal Reserve Bank, the Bundesbank, and the ECB.

thors here do. Finally, Uhlig (2016) agrees with the authors that an ECB intervention is likely to precipitate fiscal bailouts.

Despite the authors' intentions, though, it needs to be recognized that the European Monetary Union exists for reasons beyond the purely economic advantages and the role of commitment problems. A brief history of the European Monetary Union would start with the initial dominance of the Bundesbank in the late 1980s and in the system of European central banks and currencies, outside the control of other affected countries. That dominance was not always appreciated. Thus, as a price to be paid by Germany for German reunification, a European Central Bank was created, effectively replacing the leadership position of the Bundesbank, within the context of a single currency, and creating a degree of control by all countries over this central portion of European macroeconomic policy. Put differently, EMU can be thought of as providing an avenue to commit the Bundesbank to the desires of all other countries, that is, to commit to a strong national central bank. The European Monetary Union was also a piece within the agenda of the visionaries who dreamt of a "United States of Europe." The question at the time was not so much whether this was a desirable objective (there was wide agreement about that), but rather whether monetary union should come as the last step ("crowning theory") or as an early step to push other developments forward ("locomotive theory"). Is the framework by Chari, Dovis, and Kehoe suitable for answering such questions as, Why does German chancellor Merkel seeks to keep Greece in the EMU? Is a breakup of the Eurozone into northern and southern portions, with the North introducing a new Euro or "NEuro," a good or a bad idea, and why? Finally, what is different about EMU versus the United States, and what is similar? Put differently, what would be bad about introducing a separate currency in California? Once one begins thinking more about these questions, one realizes that monetary unions exist for more, and probably more important, reasons than as costly commitment devices for weak national central banks. There are important questions and analyses about the EMU to be pursued beyond the framework offered by the authors here.

Furthermore, there may not be a strong case that the EMU was truly instrumental as a commitment device for weak national banks. Examine figure 3.1. It compares the inflationary developments in the Eurozone countries to those of the United States. The general patterns look remarkably similar (though perhaps not on the same time scale): initially high inflation was gradually declining to lower and stable inflation rates. There was the introduction of a European Monetary Union some time within the sample for the EMU countries, but obviously not for the United States. The juxtaposition of this position does not strongly suggest a special role for the introduction of the European Monetary Union, though I shall concede that I tend to rather believe that it did. It may be worth investigating this matter more and with a more open mind.

All these remarks are not meant to take away from this truly fine paper, but rather they are meant to put its contributions and insights into some perspective.

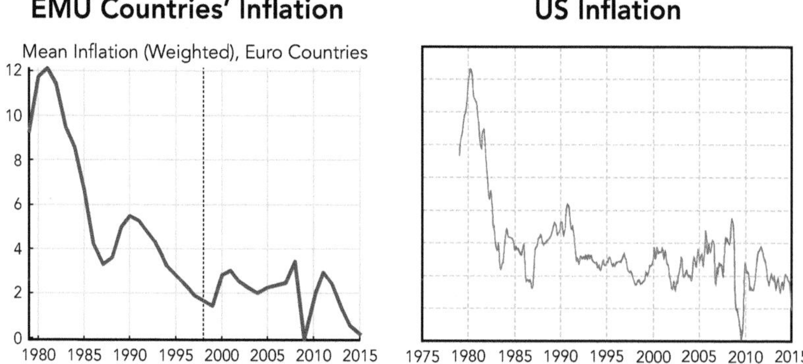

FIGURE 3.1. Inflation in Europe vs inflation in the United States.

2. The model

Let me therefore reflect on the theoretical framework that the authors provide. After all, that is what they consider to be their key contribution. Allow me to present a simplified version of their model. I shall do so by building up from an even simpler structure towards a version of the structure that these authors employ.

For the simpler structure, consider two countries, N or "North" and S or "South." There are two periods and one consumption good each period. Suppose S borrows some amount B from N in period $t = 1$, where B is chosen by S. For the resources thus obtained, S experiences period-1 utility $w(B)$. In period 2, S has some income y and two choices. It may either pay some amount x to N, where x is chosen by N. Or it may choose to not pay that amount, experiencing instead a debt-level-dependent resource loss of $\kappa(B)$ for some given function $\kappa(\cdot)$. The latter choice may best be thought of as S defaulting on N and the demanded repayment x, with $\kappa(B)$ the resulting damage to the economy from default. S then experiences linear utility in the resources c_2 remaining, after either paying x or $\kappa(B)$. Overall, the utility of S is

$$U = w(B) + c, \text{ where } c = y - x \text{ or } c = y - \kappa(B).$$

For N, we just need to know that they prefer more resources to fewer resources. Figure 3.2 provides an overview of what is going on. Let us solve for the resulting choices by proceeding backwards in time. First, in period 2, N will choose x to equal $\kappa(B)$: it is basically a take-it-or-leave-it (TIOLI) offer by N to S for avoiding the cost $\kappa(B)$, and N will choose that it be as large as possible subject to the participation constraint that $x \leq \kappa(B)$. We can therefore write the utility for South as

$$U = w(B) + y - \kappa(B)$$

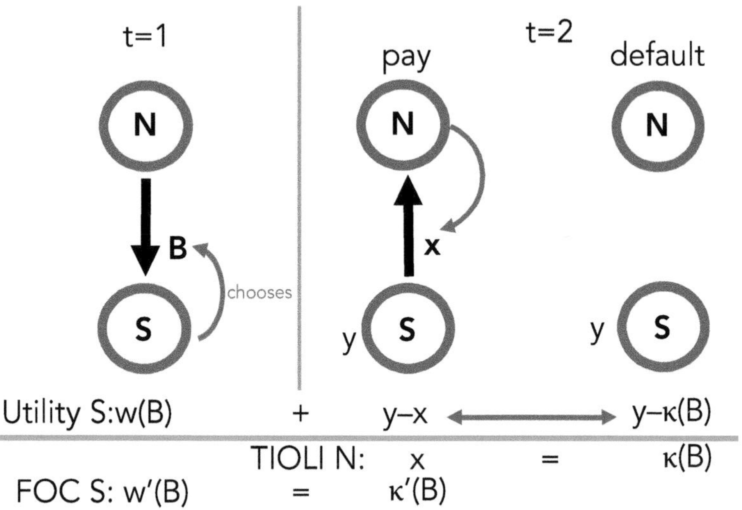

FIGURE 3.2. A simpler structure: one country, one choice of repayment.

regardless of the choice. The first-order condition

$$w'(B) = \kappa'(B) \tag{1}$$

then determines B.

There is an equivalent way of rewriting this simpler structure (see figure 3.3). Replace x by the difference between a full repayment from S to N of the initial debt B, and a transfer T to the South,

$$x = B - T.$$

We still obtain the same first-order condition (1). The only difference is notation. The participation constraint from the TIOLI offer by N now is

$$B - T = \kappa(B).$$

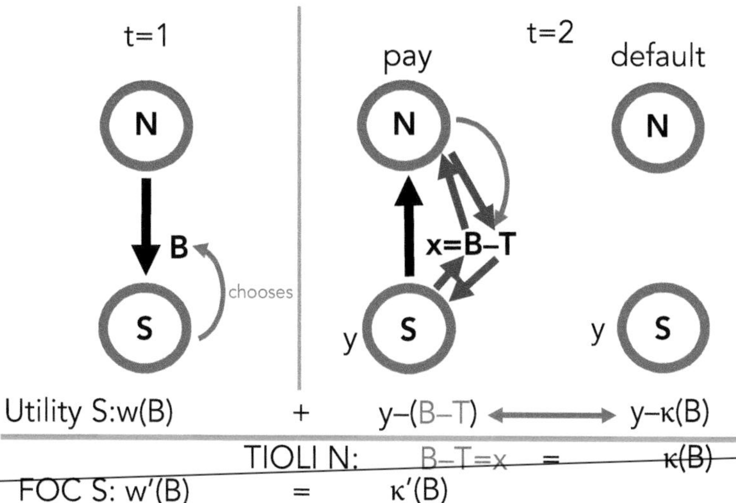

FIGURE 3.3. A simpler structure: one country, one choice of repayment, expressed with debt repayments and transfers.

That should not surprise. The interpretation is interesting, though. One can think of T as debt relief provided to the South. That debt relief is chosen by N as small as possible, subject to the constraint of S not defaulting. For that interpretation, one may wish to impose that $T \geq 0$.

The authors, though, pursue a somewhat different structure. They assume that there are many identical southern countries: perhaps many northern countries, too, though that is of less relevance. Additionally they assume that N commits to the same level of transfers $T \geq 0$ to all southern countries in such a way that the TIOLI indifference condition is satisfied for all other countries, choosing some level of debt $\overline{B}$. Consider then a particular southern country S, which now takes the variables chosen by N and all other southern countries as given (see figure 3.4). In effect, the aggregate choice $\overline{B}$ now imposes an upper limit of debt in period 2, given the

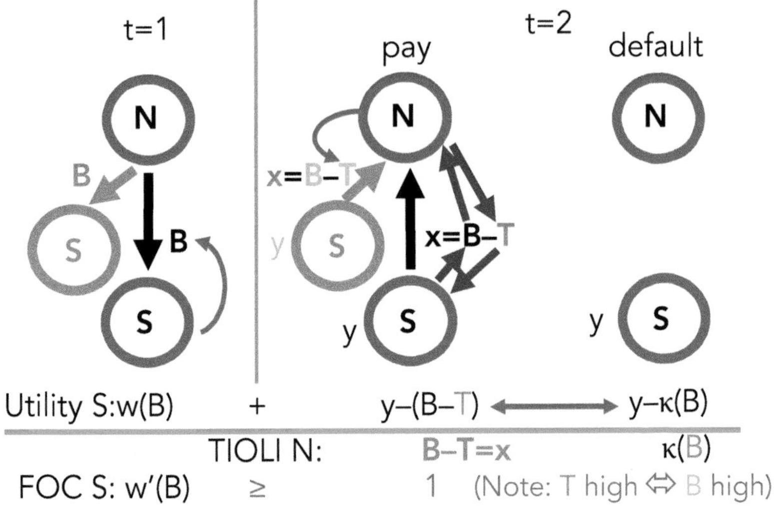

FIGURE 3.4. The model: many southern countries, holding transfers fixed across them. Note the multiplicity of equilibria.

choice of $\overline{T}$ as fixed across all countries. Since $\overline{T}$ is now treated as fixed by S, the first-order condition (1) is no longer correct. It is replaced instead by

$$w'(B) \geq 1. \tag{2}$$

S needs to compare the benefit of obtaining an additional unit of resource in period 1 to the costs of exactly repaying that unit in period 2. It is clear that it cannot be the case that $w'(B) < 1$: in that case, S would simply borrow a bit less, improving its overall situation. Since the same logic applies to all other southern countries, too, the aggregate choice $\overline{B} = B$ cannot be too high. However, it can be the case that $w'(B) > 1$. In that case, S desires to increase its debt level beyond the imposed limit B. But if it were to borrow more, it would end up defaulting in period 2, given the fixed transfer $T = \overline{T}$: thus N does not allow S to proceed with these higher debt levels. One way of reading this is that N first fixes $T = \overline{T}$. Given $\overline{T}$, the TIOLI condition then determines $B = \overline{B}$. There are obviously lots of pairs (B,T), resulting in the same value $x = B - T$, even when one imposes (2). Thus, one can easily see that the model has multiple solutions or equilibria, without further considerations of the choice problem for N. For N, note that they cannot possibly obtain more than $x = \kappa(B)$. If $\kappa'(B) < 1$, as is reasonable, and if N only cares about total consumption, then N would rather prefer lower to higher levels of T and thus B. Any such analysis needs more assumptions about N, though.

Thus, let us introduce some more elements here. Let N fix $\overline{T}$ as the maximal bailout payment to private lenders (banks) from the North, who at the same time decide on the resources B to be lent to S. Suppose that N is desperate to avoid default by a positive fraction of private lenders, while lenders care about total resources (and perhaps a bit more about second period resources). If lenders expect some level $\overline{T}$, then their lending B will satisfy $B - \kappa(B) \leq T$, and equality, with $\kappa'(B) < 1$ and a slight preference for period 2 consumption. Conversely, if the government of N sees private lenders all lending some amount B, it will pick transfers T satisfying $B - T = \kappa(B)$ in order to avoid defaults. This generates a multipilicity of equilibria.

Finally then, introduce a central bank as a Good Samaritan (see figure 3.5). To proceed, let me drop the notational distinction between $\overline{T}$ and T. The central bank chooses the final, overall level of common transfers $T^* \geq 0$ to the southern countries, unless N chooses an even higher level. Given that choice, N then picks T provided directly by N, with $T^* - T$ provided indirectly by the central bank, if that amount is nonnegative. These indirect transfers are assumed to be less efficient than if N had chosen that higher level of transfers in the first place: it is assumed that these additional transfers result in costs $(T^* - T)(1 + \tau)$ for some $\tau > 0$ rather than $T^* - T$ for the North, for a total cost of

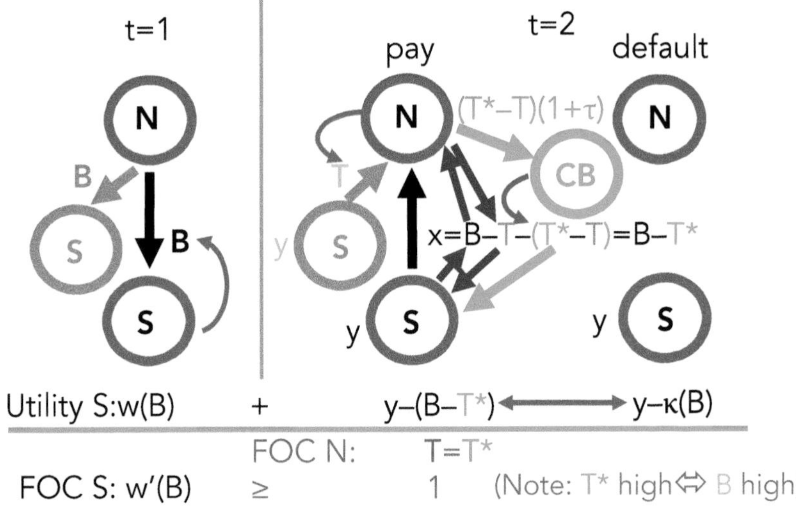

FIGURE 3.5. The model: introducing the common central bank as a Good Samaritan.

$$\begin{aligned} costs &= \max\{T^* - T; 0\}(1 + \tau) + T \\ &= \max\{T^*; T\} + \tau \max\{T^* - T; 0\}. \end{aligned} \tag{3}$$

Despite the presence of a central bank, note that there is no "money" here. Everything is expressed in real terms, and the central bank is an additional fiscal player, with its own set of tools and objectives. However, one should think of $T^* - T$ as additional transfers resulting effectively from the various policies of leniency by the European Central Bank, per their Long-term Refinancing Operations or Outright Monetary Transactions (OMT) policies or their emergency lending procedures. This does strike me as a reasonable simplification, cutting to the essence of the final fiscal consequences, and the authors ought to be applauded for that.

As far as the South is concerned, the discussion for figure 4 applies here as well, using $\max\{T^*;T\}$ in place of T. There still is the first-order condition $w'(B) \geq 1$. With the additional elements of private credit markets and coordination, there still is the multiplicity of equilibria. What is new here now, compared to figure 4, is that we get some action regarding the choice of T by N. Since N cannot do anything about T^*, they can only seek to minimize the costs of equation (3). Among all T in the range $T \in [0, T^*]$, the solution is then rather obviously to set $T = T^*$. Put differently, the implicit threat of the common central bank to bail out the South leads the North to do it already, so that the common central bank will not carry out that bailout itself.

I think that this is really a beautiful insight. It reminds me of the self-congratulation of Draghi and the ECB leadership, that its announcement of the OMT program brought down yields in Europe, without ever purchasing anything. Draghi called it the most successful program ever. This analysis here shows that indeed the announcement of T^* alone may avoid a default on certain debt levels B, on which we otherwise might see defaults. But the analysis also shows that this comes at considerable costs to taxpayers in the North, who will now have to pony up the level T^* forced upon them by the central bank. If the northern countries weren't willing to go there, had it not been for the intervention by the central bank, then there is little to congratulate the ECB and Draghi for, other than playing Robin Hood, stealing from the North to give to the South, without ever having to come out of the woods themselves.

The North could decide to be even more generous from the start in terms of these transfers, but it has to be at least as generous as the level envisioned by the central bank. These higher transfer levels then result in higher debt levels B, as discussed for figure 4. With $\kappa'(B) < 1$, getting dragged there by the central bank, it appears, is bad for the North but good for the South. In the extreme case that $\kappa'(B) = 0$, an increase of T^* by one unit increases B by one unit and thus an additional unit of resources for the South in the first period, courtesy of the North, without changing anything about the total repayment $x = B - T = \kappa(B) \equiv \bar{\kappa}$ in the second period.

One can view the readiness of the central bank to provide these funds as resulting from some lack of commitment. Therefore the authors find that lack of commitment by the common central bank or perhaps merely the presence of such a common central bank leads to overall higher debt levels in the southern countries.

3. Some remarks regarading the assumptions

This is a beautiful analysis indeed. With this presentation, it is not hard to notice that the authors made some crucial choices that surely deserve further debate. First, is it reasonable to assume that indeed the same transfer shall be given to all countries, regardless of their debt choice? I strongly believe that the answer to this question is no. The bailout of Greece and the transfers to Greece appear to be chosen to keep Greece in the union, at considerable protest on their side against the imposed "austerity" conditions, in order to keep other countries in check and in order to avoid paying transfers to these countries as well. It seems to me that this is a rather crucial difference between their model and a more refined analysis of the political game played in the European Monetary Union. Second, suppose the North has a linear utility for overall resources, summed across both periods. Then lending any positive amounts to the South in period 1 is a bad deal, unless $T^* = 0$: for any value $T^* > 0$, the North receives less resources in the second period than in the first. So, why does N allow any lending to S in period 1? At best, one may wish to interpret this as a failed bank regulation, when adding the elements of private creditors and coordination.

Conversely, it may be a bit extreme that the North can be bothered to only provide just that amount of transfers ex-post that would avoid a default by the South. In these political debates, there are many other matters at stake, too, though fine: perhaps this particular assumption is not too far off. As far as the transfers by the common central bank are concerned, note that bailouts in particular by the European Central Bank are very clearly ruled out by the Maastricht Treaty. I guess the authors take the perspective that many of the provisions of the Maastricht Treaty are nothing more than black ink on a sheet of paper, and I am sympathetic to that. Others, in particular officials at the ECB, may strongly disagree with the notion that they have found lavish ways to circumvent these treaty provisions, though. Note, though, that the central bank actually never ends up making these transfers: it is just the threat of making them that forces the North to cough up these high transfers in the first place.

Finally, given that the North somehow has to come up with the transfer resources, it is not a priori obvious that doing it via the various programs of the ECB is particularly ineffective, thus justifying the positive tax rate $\tau > 0$ in the analysis above. It may well be that monetary means turn out to be a cheaper way to finance fiscal transfers, in which case the North would end up choosing $T = 0$, leaving it all to the central banks. One may then wish to treat the Maastricht Treaty violation arguments more seriously, and the resulting analysis would then look quite a bit different.

4. Conclusions

This is an intriguing paper on an important topic. Many themes and insights resonate, as I can credibly testify, given my own work. However, a number of key assumptions and details need a good defense: I still consider myself a skeptic on a number of them. Further, the model leaves out some key considerations, despite the claims of the authors to the contrary. It is always good to make sure that one is solving the relevant problem for the situation at hand. The authors make a good step in that direction and provide an important contribution, but the reader is advised to devote thought to the question as to whether the authors have indeed succeeded in picking the central issue.

Because these critiques of some details should not take away from the overall assessment that this is a fine analysis indeed. I particularly enjoyed the point that the implicit threat of the common central bank to bail out the South leads the North to do it already, so that the common central bank will not carry out that bailout itself. It may be worth restating what was stated in the text already. The beautiful insights of the analysis offered here provide an important perspective on the self-congratulation of Draghi and the ECB leadership that its announcement of the OMT program brought down yields in Europe without ever purchasing anything. Draghi called it the most successful program ever. The analysis here shows that indeed the announcement of T^* alone may avoid a deafult on certain debt levels B, on which we otherwise might see defaults. But the analysis also shows that this comes at considerable costs to taxpayers in the North, who will now have to pony up the level T^* forced upon them by the central bank. If the northern countries weren't willing to go there, had it not been for the intervention by the central bank, then there is little to congratulate the ECB and Draghi for other than playing Robin Hood, stealing from the North to give to the South, without ever having to come out of the woods themselves. Should the ECB be allowed to play that role? It seems to me that this should be a crucial part of the debate on the future architecture of the European Monetary System. The analysis here offers an important guide to that debate.

References

Beetsma, R., and H. Uhlig. 1999. An analysis of the Stability and Growth Pact. *Economic Journal,* October: 546–571.

Roch, F., and H. Uhlig. 2016. The dynamics of sovereign debt crises and bailouts. Draft, University of Chicago.

Uhlig, H. 2013. Sovereign default risk and banks in a monetary union. *German Economic Review* 15 (1): 23–41.

Uhlig, H. 2016. The risk of sovereign default and the conundrum of the common central bank. Draft, University of Chicago.

GENERAL DISCUSSION

GEORGE SHULTZ: I found this a fascinating discussion because it seems to me it fits into a broader framework. I'd like to state that framework and then see if you might comment on how the economic part fits it. It seems to me that the overriding problem of governance all over the world in this new age is the problem of how you govern over diversity in an age of transparency. With the information and communication age, people know what's going on pretty fast, and they communicate. They've all got cell phones, and they organize, and we've seen this over and over. Diversity is everywhere, so the trick is knowing how to govern over it so it can express itself but at the same time fit into a pattern, and economics plays a large part in this process. Take Europe: it's been a civilized place for a long time, but you have to start with the fact that these countries are *very* different from each other. Italians are not like Finns, and they never will be, and we shouldn't even want them to be, yet they are part of a similar economy. So what are the things that allow diversity to be expressed comfortably and at the same time be put into a framework that's going to enlarge it and make it better? I would say the open borders to trade and to movement have been very much in that vein. I was in a discussion in Berlin about three months before the euro was introduced, and everybody was saying, "What a dumb idea." Marty Feldstein took it apart at the seams, and most of the hard things that have happened, he predicted. So to a certain extent, it's an attempt to govern over diversity in a way that doesn't fit.

V. V. CHARI: I think you're dead on, on this. So I'd point to a slightly different aspect of diversity that shows up in some of the models that we wrote down, which is not necessarily diversity in terms of ex-ante heterogeneity, but diversity in terms of how different countries, regions, people are going to be affected by different circumstances—different shocks so to speak, using our lingo—to a different extent. And in those kinds of situations when people, even if in an ex-ante sense they're not that different, if they're exposed to different shocks, different circumstances, then Good Samaritans at the end of the day—I want to emphasize this—at the situation where they are confronted they will and they should attempt to try and narrow those differences. But the problem that I'm highlighting is those attempts, ex-post, to narrow those differences across people to create adverse economic incentives. So you're challenging question is, What do we do about this? The Germanic response, if you will, is just, "Nonsense! Commit to it, and do it." And I also think that it may also be an unwise policy prescription in the following sense: that in order for commitment to be valuable, it is not enough that you the policymaker are committed to a particular policy rule. It is critically important that people and markets *believe* that you are. The worst possible outcome is when private agents don't believe that you are committed, take on, for example, excessive risk, and then you take a moralistic position that says, "I won't do the bailouts." That is in some sense worse than going ahead and remedying the problem. So that's why what I've tried to argue throughout is that all of these kinds of things call for ex-ante, if you will, restraints and restrictions on a variety of policies, whether it's banks, whether it's governments, a variety of different ways, just as a way of addressing this problem.

GEORGE SHULTZ: Let me use as a contrast the emergence of North America. It's very different from Europe. There's no Brussels; there's no bureaucracy. But after NAFTA, it has kind of emerged. There are a million Canadians living in California, and people don't even know it. Our US imports from Mexico are 40% US content. People aren't aware of the way in which this has become a kind of integrated production process. And probably it works because nobody's trying to run it. It's just happening as people respond to the incentives that are there.

KEN SINGLETON: I fully agree with Harald's comment about how EMU is more a political matter, part of the seventy-year transformation of Europe, instead of being motivated by economics. A better example of the model that you have, particularly with the large number assumption, is another monetary union, a much bigger one, and a much more durable one. That's the United States. The Federal Reserve is a hundred years old. Now that seems to fit your model in many ways better than the EU, particularly because the EMU has a couple of big players and a lot of small guys. Do you see anything in the past hundred years in the US that is predicted by your model?

V. V. CHARI: I tried as far as possible to keep myself within the confines of the academic papers that I have written. But let me offer a speculative observation. As I said earlier, the worst thing in the world that happens is people take on a lot of risk, a lot of exposure, and then believing that you're not committed, and then you think you're committed, and you don't do this. One, some admittedly very controversial—but I like—interpretation of what Friedman and Schwartz's account of the Great Depression, which I think contains the essence of the truth of the matter, is that had the Federal Reserve done what JP Morgan did in 1907, which is suspend convertibility. In effect, that is a bailout, if you will. Or, had we had deposit insurance, which is another form of bailout, the consequences of the Great Depression, the associate decline in the aggregate money stock, which is primarily not in the base—it was in the banking system—would have been much less severe. The climb out would have been much less severe. So that's one example of something I see in recent history, if you will. And most obviously, as far as the recent financial crisis is concerned, the markets were right. Investors in large financial enterprises, if you take their cumulative ex-post return after the financial crisis, you got a modestly higher rate of return on average from that portfolio than you would have on Treasury bills. In other words, they were effectively bailed out. And so those are examples I can see in my analysis.

I just want to say a couple of things, and then maybe we'll have lunch or something? I agree. Monetary unions are more than costly commitment devices. And political scientists may be exactly right, it may be part of some other broader drive. I'm not an expert in those areas. I want to focus on one aspect. And it's a quantitative question, How big is it? I don't want to say that it is zero. Because people who have looked at ECB policy after the forming of the union have shown it is not the Bundesbank. That is, ECB policy seems to react to Euro-wide conditions, not merely to German conditions. Furthermore, it's not the case that Germany had dramatically low inflation rates before. Inflation rates in Germany have fallen.

Finally, this is related to an observation of Harald's. So I did—I should have put it up on the slides—I did compare US inflation to Japanese inflation. It's true the standard deviation fell. But it did fall by a lot more in Europe. So that's worthwhile remembering.

One last comment about the United States: if you think about a monetary union as a costly commitment device, I think that the formation of the United States, the Constitution of the United States in 1789, is what this paper at some level is also about. The Federalist Papers are very clear about the conflicts that were going on. They thought that having effectively 13 different monetary policies was a terrible idea, even though they understood the advantages of flexible exchange rates. You see it throughout the Federalist Papers. So the United States went through exactly the same kind of struggle and set it up for those kinds of reasons. And I agree, there may have been other motivations in Europe, but there were other motivations in the United States also. And so people. . . . And Marty Feldstein is right, that forming the European Union is going to have costs. Right? But except I don't think he emphasized the key aspects of the costs that I have emphasized. Because there's a free-rider problem in a monetary union: individual countries have incentives to issue excessive debt. Individual countries have incentives to pursue excessively lax supervisory policies. Those are real. Those are important. You can't evade those. And so you have to confront them, and you have to design policies in such a way that you put yourself at a smaller threat of suffering a serious crisis. That reality is something we cannot escape.

SEBASTIAN EDWARDS: Great paper. Great discussion. I liked all those little circles, different colors. That was a great rendition of the model. So, Chari, at the heart of your presentation is what we've emphasized throughout this discussion. Monetary unions have costly commitment devices. So I want to ask you, does your model have anything to say about ways of getting the commitment in a less costly way? And what I have in mind is dollarization, just giving up your currency, which is something of course, Argentina considered in 2001. John Taylor and I wrote about those subjects. And it's an issue that has gone away in Latin America, but I can assure you that within our lifetime it's going to come back. To what extent can your model deal with that issue, which is, give up your currency? And what are the costs in that case?

V. V. CHARI: Dollarization is very different from a monetary union in one important respect. With dollarization or with euroization, you are ceding all control over monetary policy to an outsider. With a monetary union, the way most monetary unions are structured, you have a voice at the table. That makes a big difference.

SEBASTIAN EDWARDS: Do you think that Portugal is really heard at the ECB? When the Portuguese speak, do people pay attention?

V. V. CHARI: They do have a weighted majority voting scheme. I prefer to think about these as the way any parliament works, which is that people engage in some amount of horse trading. So the question is, is Germany's vote—and I think the population of Portugal is about ten million, the population of Germany is 80 million, so my guess is that Germany has probably eight times the weight in the deliberations. But I wouldn't argue that Portugal has zero. And that's what our model is meant to capture.

MICHAEL HUTCHISON: Chari emphasized the slippery slope, and that Germany and France, by violating the Stability and Growth Pact, may have started it. But in my view, it started much earlier. And that was with the entry criteria and the interpretation of the Maastricht Treaty—the interpretation of the criteria went from "static" to "dynamic." No longer did countries have to meet the debt level target, but rather simply be on a dynamic trajectory to approach that level. So I think in some sense that was really the beginning of the problem. Rather than North/South EMU, you started with one collective EMU with very different economies. So I'd like to ask you this: Who would be in the EMU if you the EC had rigorously enforced the Maastricht Treaty? Of all the weak countries, only Ireland would be an EMU member. Conceptualize a situation where the weaker countries, Portugal, Greece in particular, weren't in EMU. Would they be facing a financial crisis today? Would this not be simply another Greek financial crisis? They've had many. This is one more. The only difference is, it's harder for them to get out of it, and default becomes a European issue as opposed to just a Greek issue.

V. V. CHARI: Let me start with the last observation, because that's, I think, the key to all this. Sovereign governments borrow all the time, and default a decent fraction of the time. This happens to

Ecuador, Argentina, over and over again. And in every one of these cases, they bear the primary cost of the default; they bear the primary benefits of the borrower. What I've tried to highlight is once you are in a union, and you can imagine exiting, as Harald Uhlig emphasized, exit can be costly, not just because of default but it could also be costly because default requires that you exit the union. In all of these situations, part of the cost of the bailout, if you will, of the renegotiation, is going to be borne by someone else—by the Netherlands, by France, by Germany. If they're going to bear part of the cost, then that exacerbates my incentives. All right? And so that's why, to answer your question more directly, I don't know, but my guess is Greece would probably have been in trouble given the kinds of shocks that they were subject to. But lenders would have been much more reluctant ex-ante to lend to Greece as much as they did, in part because lenders were anticipating—an anticipation that turned out to be not too far off—at the end of the day, the private lenders were not quite made whole. They took a haircut. But they didn't take a huge haircut. A lot of that haircut got shifted over when the debt got shifted over to the SM and to other kinds of mechanism. And that's exactly what, I would argue, lenders were anticipating. And given those anticipations, Greece did the smart thing for Greece, which is: let's have a party. And they had a party. And the party had unfortunate consequences. That's part of the risks they ran into. I want to argue that everybody in this game was pursuing what they saw as their rational self-interests. Nobody was fooled into anything like that. They were surprised in the sense that the shocks hit. But they weren't surprised in the sense that they didn't think that these were positive probability events.

CHAPTER FOUR

The Fundamental Structure of the International Monetary System

Pierre-Olivier Gourinchas

ABSTRACT

A fundamental function of the International Monetary System is to allocate scarce safe assets across countries. The system is fundamentally asymmetric. Net global safe asset producers are at the center. They enjoy an external premium and face a slack external adjustment constraint. This fundamental characteristic is largely independent of formal exchange rate arrangements (fixed or flexible exchange rates). Global imbalances mutate at the zero lower bound (ZLB) from benign to malign. Away from the ZLB, safe asset scarcity propagates low equilibrium real interest rates via current account surpluses. At the ZLB, safe asset scarcity propagates recessions via current account surpluses. Away from the ZLB, net safe asset suppliers enjoy a premium. At the ZLB, they must absorb a larger share of the global recession.

In a stabilized world, a recession in one part of the world economy is balanced by expanded lending by the depressed country. This finances balance-of-payments deficits of other countries, and enables investment to be maintained. Britain operated such a mechanism in the years before 1914; it was unable to do so after 1929. [Neither the United States] nor France proved able or willing to maintain the system with loans. . . . One reason was that potential borrowers had lost their credit-worthiness. Default, currency depreciation, political coups, but especially falling prices made most countries unattractive risks for loans.

—Charles Kindleberger, *The World in Depression, 1929–1939*

These remarks were originally published in shorter form in the *NBER Reporter* 2016, no. 1, available at http://nber.org/reporter/2016number1/gourinchas.html. Most of the research described in this article was done in collaboration with Ricardo Caballero (MIT) and Emmanuel Farhi (Harvard) or Hélène Rey (London Business School).

Anyone looking at recent financial headlines could be forgiven for thinking that the international monetary system is under heavy strains. The People's Bank of China faces severe private capital outflows, a result of the yuan's appreciation in tandem with the US dollar and the slowing down of the Chinese economy. The Bank of Japan is battling persistent deflation by trying to depreciate the yen. The European Central Bank has clearly telegraphed that it, too, would welcome further depreciation of the euro. In the United States, notwithstanding a modest "lift-off" in December 2015, the Federal Reserve is confronted with a global slowdown and a rising dollar. Policy discussions explicitly mention the possibility of negative policy rates in the future. Talks of "currency wars" abound. To understand the current environment, it is helpful to step back and consider the international monetary system circa 1960, during the Bretton Woods era.

The international monetary system then . . .

Back in those days, the international monetary system was relatively simple. Market economies pegged their currency against the US dollar. In turn, the United States maintained the value of its dollar at $35 per ounce of gold. With the assistance of the International Monetary Fund, countries could obtain liquidity to deal with "temporary" imbalances, but it was incumbent upon them to implement a fiscal and monetary policy mix that would be consistent with a stable dollar parity or, infrequently, to request an adjustment in their exchange rate.

The United States faced no such constraint. The requirement to maintain the $35 an ounce parity had only minimal bite on US monetary authorities, as long as foreign central banks were willing, or could be convinced, to support the dollar. By design, then, the system was asymmetric, with the United States at its center, a situation that reflected the country's economic and political strengths in the immediate aftermath of World War II.[1]

Not everyone was happy about this state of affairs. Some objected to the special role of the dollar. In 1965, France famously requested the conversion of its dollar reserves into gold, while its minister of finance complained loudly about the United States' "exorbitant privilege" (Aron 1965).[2] The Bretton Woods regime allowed the United States to acquire valuable foreign assets, so the argument went, because the dollar reserves required to maintain the dollar parity of foreign countries amounted to automatic low-interest, dollar-denominated loans to the United States (Rueff 1961, 126–127, 262, 267–268).

Others worried about the long-term sustainability of the system. As the world economy grew rapidly in the 1950s and 1960s, so did the global demand for liquidity and the stock of dollar assets held abroad. With unchanged global gold supplies, something had to give. This is the celebrated "Triffin dilemma" (1960). In 1968, Triffin's predictions came to pass: faced with a run on gold reserves, the US authorities suspended dollar-gold convertibility. Shortly thereafter, the Bretton Woods system of fixed but adjustable parities was consigned to the dustbin of history. The era of floating rates began.

The international monetary system outside the ZLB: Exorbitant privilege, safe assets, and exorbitant duty

Under the new regime, countries were free to adjust their monetary policy independently. Mundell's "trilemma" required either that market forces determine the value of their currency or that

1. For a discussion of the original Bretton Woods negotiations and especially the exchanges between J. M. Keynes, on the UK delegation, and H. D. White, from the US Treasury, see Steil (2013).

2. For a historical perspective on the exorbitant privilege, see also Eichengreen (2012).

capital controls be imposed (Mundell, 1963). In principle, this environment should be more symmetrical: no more "exorbitant privilege" for the United States since other countries would not be forced to hold low-interest dollar reserves to maintain the value of their dollar exchange rate; no asymmetry in external adjustment between the United States and the rest of the world since exchange rates would now adjust freely; and no Triffin dilemma since dollar liquidity would be decoupled from gold supply.

Yet, recent research illustrates that the era of floating rates shares many of the same structural features as the Bretton Woods regime. Consider the question of the "exorbitant privilege," defined as the excess return on US gross external assets relative to US gross external liabilities. Hélène Rey and I set out to measure this excess return using disaggregated data on the US net international investment position and its balance of payment. These calculations are often imprecise, given the coarseness of the historical data, but they all point in the same direction: the United States earns a significant excess return which has *increased* since the end of Bretton Woods from 0.8% per annum between 1952 and 1972 to between 2.0% and 3.8% per annum since 1973 (Gourinchas and Rey 2007a).[3]

A large share of these excess returns arises because of the changing composition of the US external balance sheet over time: as financial globalization proceeded, US investors concentrated their foreign holdings in risky and/or illiquid securities such as portfolio equity or direct investment, while foreign investors concentrated their US asset purchases in portfolio debt, especially Treasuries and bonds issued by government-affiliated agencies, and cross-border loans (see figure 4.1).[4] The "exorbitant privilege" should be properly understood as a risk premium.

3. See also Gourinchas and Rey (2014). For a more conservative estimate on a shorter time period, see Curcuru et al. (2008).

4. Recent work on the structure of global banking flows helps nuance this picture. For instance, Shin (2012) shows that prior to the financial crisis, foreign banks borrowed dollars

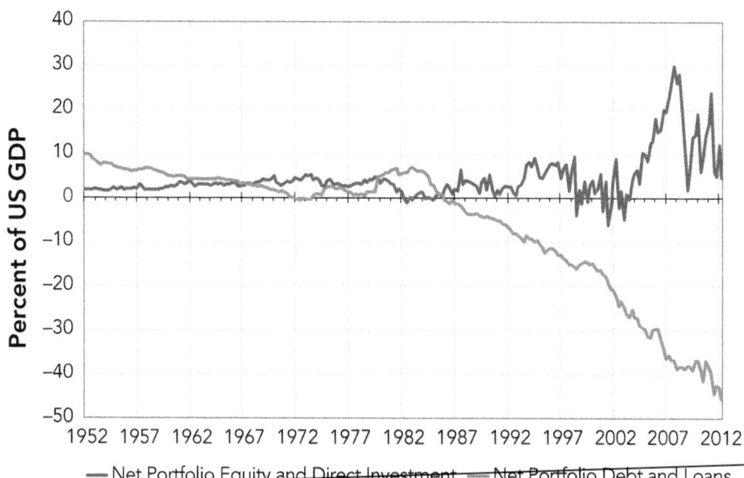

FIGURE 4.1. US External Leverage.

Note: The figure reports US net portfolio equity and direct investment (as a percent of US GDP) and US net portfolio debt and other assets (as a percent of US GDP). Starting in the 1970s, the United States builds a large short position in "safer" assets (portfolio debt and loans) and a large long position in riskier investments (portfolio equity and direct investment).

Source: P-O. Gourinchas and H. Rey, "External Adjustment, Global Imbalances and Valuation Effects," NBER Working Paper No. 19240, July 2013, and Chapter 10 in Handbook of International Economics, Volume 4, 2014, pp. 585–645.

These large and growing US excess returns have first order implications for the sustainability of US trade deficits and the interpretation of current account deficits. As an illustration of the orders of magnitude involved, suppose that the United States has a balanced net international investment position with gross assets and liabilities of 100% of GDP. An excess return of 2% per annum implies that, on average, the United States can run a trade deficit of 2% of GDP while leaving its net international investment position unchanged. More generally, since a large part of realized returns takes the form of valuation gains—due to changes in asset

from US money market funds and invested into riskier US assets such as mortgage-backed securities.

prices and exchange rates—the current account, which excludes nonproduced income such as capital gains, will provide an increasingly distorted picture of the change in a country's external position.[5]

Consider next the question of external adjustment. The United States still faces a very different process then most other countries. For instance, Hélène Rey and I found that a deterioration of the US trade balance or of its net international investment position is often followed by a predictable depreciation of the US dollar against other currencies. This depreciation may subsequently improve the US trade balance, along the usual channels, but it also improves the return on US financial assets held abroad, thereby making the United States relatively richer (Gourinchas and Rey 2007b).[6] Most other countries don't seem to enjoy a similar advantage.[7] These findings help us understand why markets have taken a somewhat benign view of the United States' persistent current account deficits since the 1980s (see figure 4.2).

What accounts for this risk premium? In my work with Ricardo Caballero and Emmanuel Farhi, we argued that it reflects a superior capacity of the United States to supply "safe assets"—assets that deliver stable returns even in global downturns. To illustrate the argument, consider a world consisting of only two regions, the United States (U) and the rest of the world (R). The regions may vary in their capacity to produce safe assets because of differences in the soundness of their fiscal policy or in their levels of financial development. They may also differ in their demand for these assets, because of demographic differences, financial frictions, and/or differences in preferences for saving (Caballero et al. 2008).[8]

5. See for instance Obstfeld (2012) and also Gourinchas and Rey (2014) for a range of countries.

6. See also Corsetti and Konstantinou (2012).

7. However, Rogoff and Tashiro (2015) find positive excess returns for Japan between 2001 and 2013.

8. See also Bernanke (2005) and Mendoza et al. (2009).

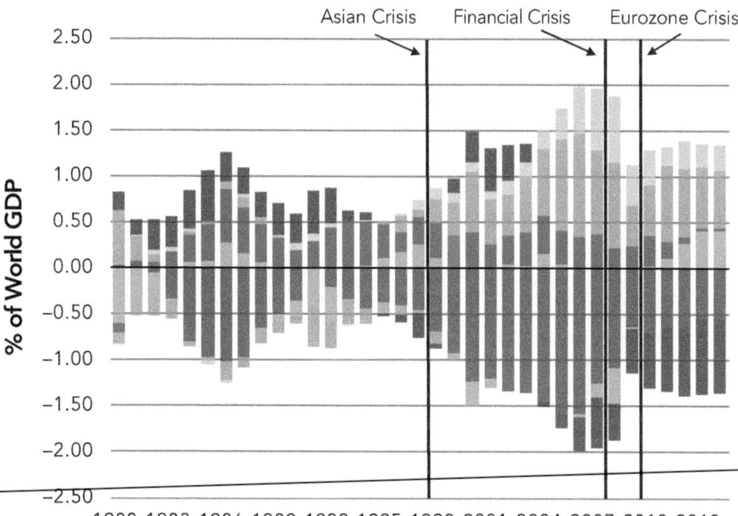

FIGURE 4.2. Global Imbalances.

Note: The graph shows current account balances as a fraction of world GDP. We observe the buildup of global imbalances in the early 2000s, until the financial crisis of 2008. Since then, global imbalances have receded but not disappeared. Notably, deficits subsided in the United States, and surpluses emerged in Europe. Oil Producers: Bahrain, Canada, Iran, Iraq, Kuwait, Libya, Mexico, Nigeria, Norway, Oman, Russia, Saudi Arabia, United Arab Emirates, Venezuela; Emerging Asia ex-China: India, Indonesia, Korea, Malaysia, Philippines, Singapore, Taiwan, Thailand, Vietnam.
Source: World Economic Outlook Database, April 2015 and author's calculations.

Suppose U is a natural *net* supplier of these assets. If the two countries were forced to live in financial autarky, unable to borrow from, or lend to, one another, the price of safe assets would be higher in R, and their return lower. If the two countries integrate financially, capital will flow from R to U, as R investors are eager to purchase U's safe assets. From the perspective of U, two things happen: it runs a current account deficit (foreign capital flows in), and interest rates decrease. By the same logic, suppose R's risky assets offer a higher autarky return. Then U would also want to invest in these risky assets. The pattern of cross-border *gross* financial flows and positions would resemble the one we observe in the data with the United States investing in foreign risky assets, issuing safe assets, and earning a risk premium.[9]

This line of research successfully accounts for the simultaneous deterioration in US current account imbalances (figure 4.2), the secular decline in real interest rates (figure 4.3), and the increased leverage of the US external portfolio since the 1980s (figure 4.1). These trends reflect a combination of shocks such as the collapse of the Japanese equity and housing bubble of the early 1990s and the Asian financial crisis of 1997, and trends such as the integration of China into the world economy with low initial levels of financial development and rapidly aging populations in Japan, Germany, and China.[10]

The flip side of the "exorbitant privilege" is an increased vulnerability of the United States' external portfolio to global shocks, which Hélène Rey and I dubbed the "exorbitant duty" (Gourinchas et al. 2010). Indeed, we estimate that, at the peak of the global financial crisis, US valuation losses, corresponding to the valuation gains of the rest of the world, amounted to roughly 14% of US GDP.[11] We then build a model in which the United States has more risk-absorbing capacity than the rest of the world. The model replicates the external portfolio structure of the United States, long on risky assets and short on safe ones, the "exorbitant privilege" as well as the "exorbitant duty." The model has one key implication: willingly or not, global suppliers of safe-haven assets must bear more exposure to global risks. These findings carry important lessons for regional safe-asset providers such as Germany or Switzerland, or for

9. The implications in terms of overall current account surplus or deficit are more complex when both risky and safe assets are traded and depend on the relative scarcities in safe and risky assets. See Caballero et al. (2016).

10. On China, see Song et al. (2011) and Coeurdacier et al. (2015).

11. Gourinchas et al. (2012) explores the geographic distribution of valuation gains and losses during the financial crisis and finds that losses are concentrated in the United States, the Eurozone, and China.

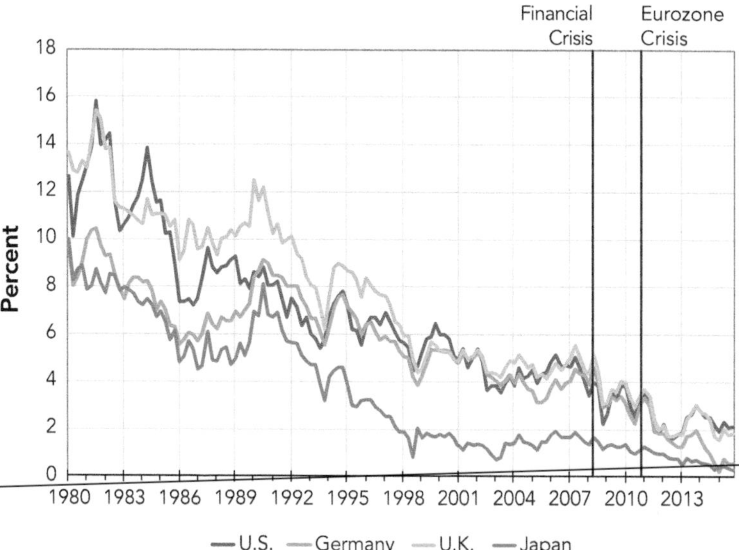

FIGURE 4.3. Global Interest Rates.

Note: The figure reports the yield on ten-year government securities for the United States, Germany, the United Kingdom, and Japan. Following the global financial crisis, long-term yields in many advanced economies declined to historically low levels, while policy rates remained at the ZLB.

Source: Global Financial Database.

future safe-asset providers, be they the Eurozone or China: lower funding costs come with a commensurate increase in the global exposure of their external balance sheet.

The international monetary system at the ZLB: Capital flows and currency wars

With the global financial crisis and its aftermath, we have entered a new phase in the relationship between safe-asset imbalances and capital flows. The crisis triggered a sharp contraction in safe-asset supply and a surge in global safe-asset demand as households and the nonfinancial corporate sector attempted to deleverage. These shocks depressed further equilibrium real interest rates, pushing policy rates throughout the developed world to the ZLB.[12]

In recent theoretical work, Caballero et al. (2015) argue that the safe-asset scarcity *mutates* at the ZLB, from a *benign* phenomenon that depresses risk-free rates to a *malign* one where interest rates cannot equilibrate asset markets any longer, leading to a global recession.[13]

The fundamental reason is that the decline in output generically reduces asset demand more than asset supply. To understand why, observe that by definition the supply of true safe assets does not change with a decline in output, hence the recession disproportionately affects safe-asset demand. Equilibrium in the asset market is restored by making savers poorer. Our analysis predicts the emergence of potentially persistent global liquidity traps, a situation that characterizes most of the advanced economies today.

Our theoretical model features nominal rigidities, so that the ZLB matters, and a non-Ricardian setting, so that heterogeneity in asset supply and demand affects interest rates. We use this framework to address two questions.

First, we ask: What is the role of capital flows at the ZLB? We find that, everything else equal, at the ZLB capital flows propagate recessions from one country to another. Countries with more severe safe-asset scarcities under financial autarky will experience milder recessions when integrated, and run current account surpluses. Current account surpluses help spread liquidity traps globally.

Second, we ask: What is the role of exchange rates? Here, our theoretical analysis delivers an important result: within a range,

12. Most estimates of the natural rate of interest rate such as Laubach and Williams (2015) or Hamilton et al. (2015) are consistent with a substantial decline in the natural real interest rate. Strictly speaking, the ZLB should be defined as the lowest admissible nominal interest rate. As demonstrated by various central banks in recent months, this lowest admissible nominal interest rate may well be negative.

13. A related analysis is Eggertsson et al. (2015).

the nominal exchange rate becomes indeterminate. The fundamental reason is that exchange rates are indeterminate when countries follow pure interest rate targets, as is the case at the ZLB (Kareken and Wallace 1981). In our environment, this indeterminacy has real consequences: different values of the nominal exchange rate translate into different values of the real exchange rate and therefore affect the relative demand for domestic versus foreign goods. Our theoretical framework provides a powerful way to think about the current lively debate on currency wars. By pursuing policies that lead to a more depreciated exchange rate, a country can shift the burden of the global recession onto its trading partners, a *beggar-thy-neighbor* policy.[14]

Our analysis also uncovers a new and important dimension of the "exorbitant duty" faced by safe-asset net suppliers. In a ZLB environment, such nations either have more appreciated currencies, as a result of investors' flight to safety, or lower funding costs, because their currencies are expected to appreciate in case of global shocks. The first effect tends to worsen the size of the ZLB recession for these countries. The second indicates that they are more likely to hit the ZLB in the first place and experience a recession. Either way, safe-asset suppliers shoulder a larger share of the burden. Yet, because issuance of safe assets anywhere, public or private, is beneficial everywhere, the global provision of safe assets may remain inadequate.

Because our model is non-Ricardian, there is an important role for debt policy. Issuing additional debt (or a balanced budget increase in government spending, or even helicopter drops of money, which are equivalent to debt policy at the ZLB) can potentially address the net shortage of assets and stimulate the economy in all countries, alleviating a global liquidity trap. They are both as-

14. Outside the ZLB, this type of beggar-thy-neighbor policy is unnecessary since each country can reach potential output via traditional monetary policy while letting its currency fluctuate.

sociated with large Keynesian multipliers, which exceed one in the case of government spending. Yet, they also worsen the current account and net foreign asset position of the country undertaking the policy stimulus.

Our baseline model abstracted away from risk, focusing instead on the supply of "stores of value." Yet the distinction between safe and risky assets is an important one. There is substantial evidence that the relevant asset shortage is a *safe* asset shortage, rather than a *general* shortage of stores of value. For instance, while real returns on *safe* assets have *declined* (see figure 4.3), estimates of the real returns on productive capital in the United States indicate that they are currently high, not low.[15] Similarly, current estimates of the equity risk premium indicate that it is at an all-time high (figure 4.4). How, it is sometimes argued, can the expected risk premium be so high given that price/earnings ratios have recovered from their decline during the crisis, and are high by historical norms?[16] The answer is that price/earnings ratios are high precisely because risk-free interest rates are at historical lows.

The evidence, I would argue, is consistent with a world where investors' desire to hold safe assets has increased—some of which is undoubtedly the result of investor mandates and increased regulation of the financial sector—while the supply of safe stores of value has declined globally.[17]

To model differences in the net supply of safe asset, we allow heterogeneity in risk aversion within and across countries, and in

15. See Gomme et al. (2015). These authors find that pre- and post-tax real returns on business capital and all capital have not been declining. In fact, they are now at the highest level over the past three decades. Their estimated real after-tax return to business capital is 8%.

16. For instance, the Standard and Poor's 500 price/earnings ratio is close to 25, well below its maximum of 124 in May 2009, but also higher than its historical average of 15.6.

17. The supply of US safe assets may well have increased. For instance, US marketable debt is now in excess of 100% of GDP, up from 64% in 2006. Yet, what matters is the global supply of safe assets. Eichengreen (2016) estimates that the global supply of international liquid assets has declined from 60% of global GDP in 2009 to 30% now.

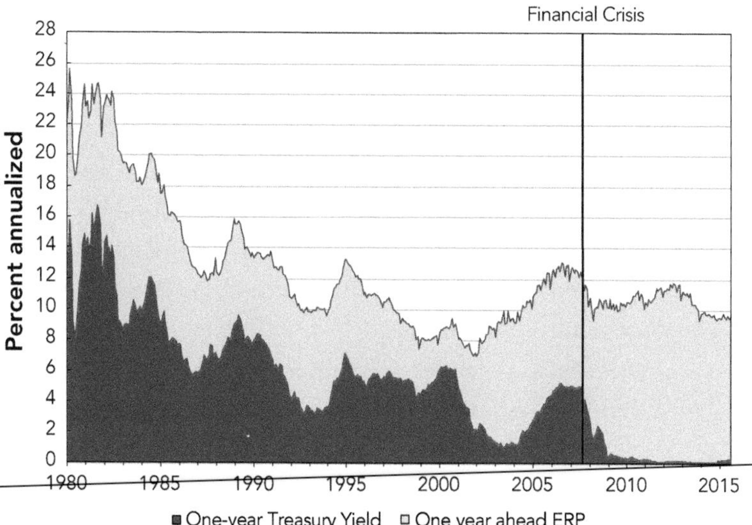

FIGURE 4.4. US Interest Rate and Expected Risk Premium.

Note: The graph shows the one-year US Treasury yield and the one-year expected risk premium (ERP), calculated as the first principal component of twenty models of the one-year-ahead equity risk premium. The figure shows that the equity risk premium has increased, especially since the global financial crisis.
Source: One-year Treasury yield: Federal Reserve H.15; ERP: Duarte and Rosa (2015).

the ability to produce safe assets. By introducing risk and heterogeneity, we are able to account for the increase in the expected risk premium (figure 4.4) and to rationalize the "exorbitant privilege." In the model, the expected risk premium rises because the decline in output makes all savers poorer, reducing the demand for risky and safe assets altogether. Further, net safe-asset issuers run a permanent current account deficit, financed by the excess return of their (riskier) external assets on their (safer) external liabilities. Moreover, the model gives rise to a risk premium in the uncovered interest rate parity: because the currency of safe-asset net issuers is expected to appreciate in bad times, they face lower interest rates, which makes them more likely to enter the ZLB, even if the rest of the world is able to avoid it.

Conclusion

This recent research illustrates that the *fundamental* structure of the international monetary system may largely transcend formal exchange-rate arrangements, with US dollar assets at the center. Going forward, this raises a number of important questions which current research is exploring. First, a recent and influential line of work is questioning whether floating exchange rates provide much insulation against foreign shocks, a central tenet of Mundell's trilemma (Rey 2013; Farhi and Werning 2014).[18] If they don't, monetary authorities may find that they are even more dependent on the monetary policy "at the center," as was the case during Bretton Woods.

Second, our results point to a modern—and more sinister—version of the Triffin dilemma. As the world economy grows faster than that of the United States, so does the global demand for safe assets relative to its supply (Farhi et al. 2011).[19] This depresses global interest rates and could push the global economy into a persistent ZLB environment, a form of "secular stagnation" (Summers 2015).

One likely response would be the endogenous emergence of alternatives to dollar-denominated safe assets produced either by the private sector or by other countries. This raises the difficult question of how different safe assets can coexist and compete in equilibrium and suggests that the safety of an asset is an equilibrium outcome, one that depends not only on the underlying fundamental characteristics of the asset itself but also on the coordination decisions of investors (Gourinchas and Jeanne 2012).[20]

Finally, a body of empirical evidence suggests that environments with low interest rates may fuel leverage boom and bust cycles. The vulnerability of emerging and advanced economies alike to these

18. See also Bernanke (2016).
19. See also Obstfeld (2014).
20. See also He et al. (2015).

crises has been amply demonstrated in the past. At the country level, the empirical evidence suggests that self-insurance via official reserve (safe-asset) accumulation is an effective line of defense against leveraged booms (Gourinchas and Obstfeld 2012). But what is optimal at the level of an individual country may be inefficient at a global level if it fuels further the safe-asset scarcity and depresses global interest rates. This question is central to current discussions on global safety nets.

References

Aron, R. 1965. Le figaro. In *Les Articles du Figaro,* vol. II, 1994. Paris: Editions de Fallois, 1475.

Bernanke, B. 2005. The global saving glut and the US current account deficit. Sandridge Lecture, Virginia Association of Economics, Richmond, Virginia, Federal Reserve Board, March.

Bernanke, B. 2016. Federal Reserve policy in an international context. Mundell-Fleming lecture. *IMF Economic Review* (forthcoming).

Caballero, R., E. Farhi, and P. Gourinchas. 2008. An equilibrium model of "global imbalances" and low interest rates. *American Economic Review* 98, no. 1 (March): 358–93.

Caballero, R., E. Farhi, and P. Gourinchas. 2015. Global imbalances and currency wars at the ZLB. NBER Working Paper no. 21670 (October).

Caballero, R., E. Farhi, and P. Gourinchas. 2016. Safe asset scarcity and aggregate demand. *American Economic Review Papers & Proceedings* (May).

Cochrane, J. Comments on "The fundamental structure of the international monetary system", this volume.

Coeurdacier, N., S. Guibaud, and K. Jin. 2015. Credit constraints and growth in a global economy. *American Economic Review* 105 (9): 2838–81.

Corsetti, G., and P. Konstantinou. 2012. What drives US foreign borrowing? Evidence on the external adjustment to transitory and permanent shocks. *American Economic Review* 102 (2): 1062–92.

Curcuru, S., T. Dvorak, and F. Warnock. 2008. Cross-border return differentials. *Quarterly Journal of Economics* 123 (4): 1495–1530.

Duarte, F., and C. Rosa. 2015. The equity risk premium: A review of models. Staff reports 714, Federal Reserve Bank of New York (February).

Eggertsson, G., N. Mehrotra, S. Singh, and L. Summers. 2015. A contagious malady? Open economy dimensions of secular stagnation. Mimeo. Brown University (November).

Eichengreen, B. 2012. Exorbitant privilege: The rise and fall of the dollar. Oxford: Oxford University Press.

Eichengreen, B. 2016. Financial scarcity amid plenty. *Project Syndicate*, June 14.

Farhi, E., P. Gourinchas, and H. Rey. 2011. Reforming the international monetary system. CEPR e-book.

Farhi, E., and I. Werning. 2014. Dilemma not trilemma? Capital controls and exchange rates with volatile capital flows. *IMF Economic Review* 62 (4): 569–605.

Gomme, P., B. Ravikumar, and P. Rupert. 2015. Secular stagnation and returns on capital. St Louis Federal Reserve Bank Economic Synopses no. 19.

Gourinchas, P., and O. Jeanne. 2012. Global safe assets. BIS Working Paper 399 (December).

Gourinchas, P., and M. Obstfeld. 2012. Stories of the twentieth century for the twenty-first. *American Economic Journal: Macroeconomics* 4 (1): 226–65.

Gourinchas, P., and H. Rey. 2007a. From world banker to world venture capitalist: US external adjustment and the exorbitant privilege. In *G7 Current Account Imbalances: Sustainability and Adjustment,* ed. R. Clarida. Chicago: University of Chicago Press.

Gourinchas, P., and H. Rey. 2007b. International financial adjustment. *Journal of Political Economy* 115 (4): 665–703.

Gourinchas, P., and H. Rey. 2014. External adjustment, global imbalances and valuation effects. In vol. 4 of *Handbook of International Economics,* ed. G. Gopinath, E. Helpman, and K. Rogoff, 585–645, Elsevier, Amsterdam.

Gourinchas, P., H. Rey, and N. Govillot. 2010. Exorbitant privilege and exorbitant duty. Mimeo. University of California–Berkeley (May).

Gourinchas, P., H. Rey, and K. Truempler. 2012. The financial crisis and the geography of wealth transfers. *Journal of International Economics* 88 (2): 266–83.

Hamilton, J., E. Harris, J. Hatzius, and K. West. The equilibrium real funds rate: Past, present and future. NBER Working Paper no. 21476 (August).

He, Z., A. Krishnamurthy, and K. Millbradt. A model of the reserve asset. Mimeo. Stanford GSB (November).

Kareken, J., and N. Wallace. 1981. On the indeterminacy of equilibrium exchange rates. *Quarterly Journal of Economics* 96 (2): 207–222.

Kindleberger, C. 1973. *The world in depression 1929–1939.* Fortieth-anniversary ed., Berkeley: University of California Press.

Laubach, T., and J. Williams. 2015. Measuring the natural rate of interest. Federal Reserve Bank of San Francisco Working Paper 2015–16 (October).

Mendoza, E., V. Quadrini, and J. Rios-Rull. 2009. Financial integration, financial deepness and global imbalances. *Journal of Political Economy* 117 (3): 371–410.

Mundell, R. 1963. Capital mobility and stabilization policy under fixed and flexible exchange rates. *Canadian Journal of Economic and Political Science* 29 (4): 475–85.

Obstfeld, M. 2012. Does the current account still matter? *American Economic Review* 102 (3): 1–23.

Obstfeld, M. 2014. The international monetary system: Living with asymmetry. In *Globalization in an age of crisis: Multilateral economic cooperation in the twenty-first century,* ed. R. Feenstra and A. Taylor, Chicago University Press, Chicago, 301–342

Rey, H. 2013. Dilemma not trilemma: The global financial cycle and monetary policy independence. Proceedings of the Economic Policy Symposium, Jackson Hole, Federal Reserve Bank of Kansas City.

Rogoff, K., and T. Tashiro. 2015. Japan's exorbitant privilege. *Journal of the Japanese and International Economies* 35 (March): 43–61.

Rueff, J. 1961. The West is risking a credit collapse. *Fortune,* June.

Shin, H. 2012. Global banking glut and loan risk premium. *IMF Economic Review* 60 (2): 155–92.

Song, Z., K. Storesletten, and F. Zilibotti. 2011. Growing like China. *American Economic Review* 101 (1): 196–233.

Steil, B. 2013. *The battle of Bretton Woods.* Princeton: Princeton University Press.

Summers, L. 2015. Have we entered an age of secular stagnation? *IMF Economic Review* 63 (1): 277–80.

Triffin, R. 1960. *Gold and the dollar crisis: The future of convertibility.* New Haven, CT: Yale University Press.

DISCUSSION BY JOHN H. COCHRANE

My comments refer both to the underlying academic paper presented at the conference, as well as the excellent and less technical discussion of similar points included in this volume. My exact comments at the conference, relating only to the preceding paper and with funny slides, are available on my webpage [http://faculty.chicagobooth.edu/john.cochrane/research/Papers/Gourinchas_comments.pdf].

These are great papers. I'm going to sound a bit critical, but I want you to know praise is coming at the end.

Twenty years ago, international economists were puzzled that capital and trade flows seemed *too small,* as characterized by the Feldstein-Horioka and home bias puzzles. Briefly, countries that wanted to save more seemed to do it at home, rather than abroad, and countries that wanted to invest more seemed to do it from domestic savings rather than borrowing abroad.

Then, the world started to look a bit more like our models, but international economists changed their minds. Now, they think capital and trade flows are *too large,* "global imbalances" and "savings gluts" needing strong policy remediation.

I seem to live in a different world. Let me summarize some key issues and differences between my world and this paper's world.

Why are interest rates so low?

In the world of these papers, low interest rates and "global imbalances" come from an inability to "produce safe stores of value"

This is entirely a financial friction. Real investment opportunities are unchanged. Economies can't "produce" enough *pieces of paper.* In the model, there is a binding limit on how much of an investment project that firms can pledge to back financial assets, and government debt is financed only by taxing the young.

In my world, real interest rates are low because real investment opportunities are bad—the marginal product of capital is low. Exchange rates move when people in places with lower productivity and interest rates invest in places with higher productivity and interest rates, driving exchange rates up due to shipping and adjustment costs.

(Just why marginal products of capital are low isn't relevant for today. I think it's policy-induced sclerosis. It could also be Bob Gordon's theory that we've run out of good ideas, or the view that modern technology just doesn't need much capital. We had a discussion at the conference over the fact that corporate profits are high, but what matters in my model is the marginal product of new capital, marginal Q, and the fact that investment is low, new business formation is low, and expected returns are low, are all consistent with that view, even if existing businesses are making money.)

Why is growth so low?

In Pierre-Olivier's world, it's all the zero lower bound: "Away from the ZLB, . . . a shock that creates an asset shortage . . . results in an endogenous reduction in real interest rates," and output gaps are all zero. "At the ZLB, . . . global output endogenously declines" instead. That output fall is all "gap," and none "potential."

In my world, low real interest rates mean low growth rates, and it's "potential" not "demand." In my world, the ZLB isn't a big, long-run problem.

Is the ZLB a problem?

If we need a negative real rate, why does inflation not solve the problem? The model turns off inflation, first by assumption, then using the standard (and in my view fragile[21]) new-Keynesian tricks to rule out the high-inflation equilibrium. In my world, inflation can adjust, and the zero bound is therefore not a first-order problem.

My first graph (figure 4.5) shows inflation and interest rates. The United States has had about two percent inflation, and negative two percent real rates since the recession ended. So, negative two is not enough?

I have a more general frustration. Zero bound models claim that a negative "natural" real rate is the driving cause of all our problems, the zero bound is the single relevant wedge or distorted price in the entire global economy—more than taxes, regulations, wage restrictions, social programs, or any other obvious wedge we see looking out the window. Yet, there is no independent quantitative measurement of this negative natural rate, beyond fitting the same models and naming the residuals.

The graph also shows that the behavior of inflation is identical in and out of the zero bound. *In the model* the ZLB is indeed a big "tipping point." Dynamics are all different at the ZLB. In the data, as in my world, the Consumer Price Index and bond prices post-ZLB look just like they did before. You'll see this in many of my graphs.

My second graph (figure 4.6) presents the exchange rate and the trade balance. You can see the big blips in fall 2008 and similar blips in many of my graphs. I do think that many parts of this model—"Financial Frictions," a "flight to quality," a huge demand for US Treasuries—are important to understanding the crisis period.[22]

But that's over. This paper is about now, and it's hard to see a big difference. The exchange rate, which we will talk about in a

---

21. See John H. Cochrane, 2015, "The New-Keynesian Liquidity Trap," http://faculty.chicagobooth.edu/john.cochrane/research.papers/zero_bound_2.pdf

22. In writing, see John H. Cochrane, 2011, "Understanding fiscal and monetary policy in the great recession: Some unpleasant fiscal arithmetic." *European Economic Review* 55: 2–30, http://faculty.chicagobooth.edu/john.cochrane?research/papers/understanding_policy_EER.pdf

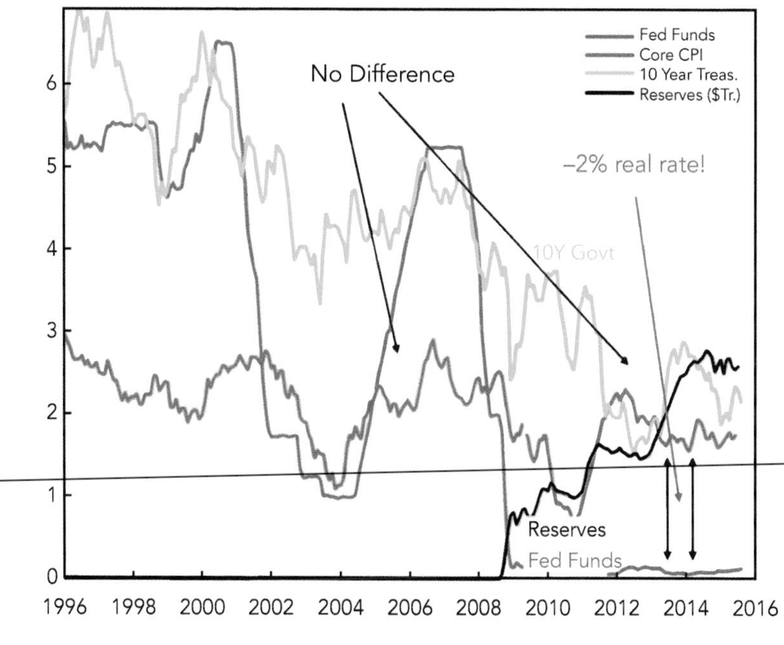

FIGURE 4.5.

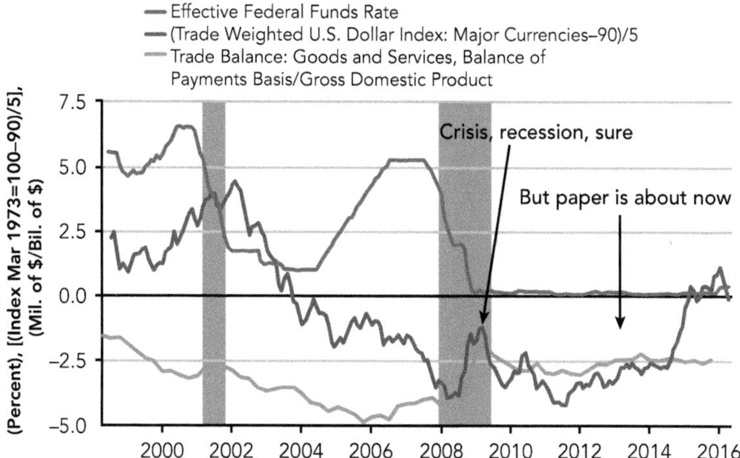

FIGURE 4.6.

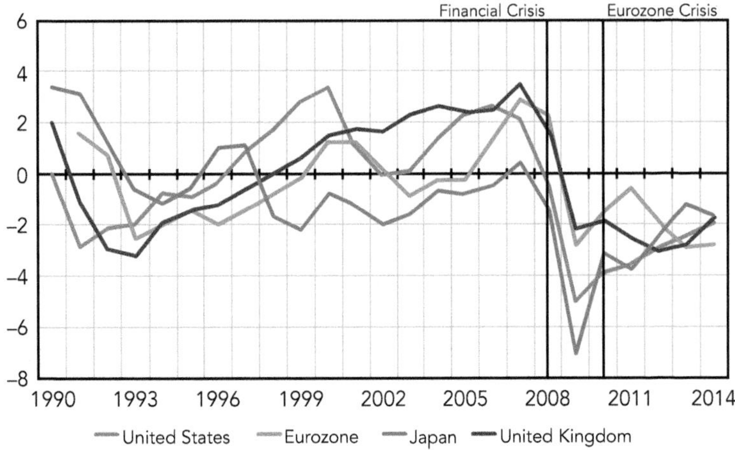

FIGURE 4.7. Output Gaps (percent).

minute, also is no more volatile now than it was out of the zero-bound regime.

The paper offers one piece of evidence for different behavior at the zero bound—"persistent increases in output gaps" as shown in figure 4.7.

First, in my world, this is reverse causality; low growth implies low interest rates.

Second, the model says that output should become more volatile and more correlated across countries at the zero bound "tipping point." Again, outside the immediate crisis period, it's hard to see anything.

More generally, is our disappointing output all "gap" from unchanged potential? Yes, in the model. But even measured gaps are falling—and it's "potential" that's doing the adjusting, not actual output. Low potential growth is our problem, not gaps.

Unemployment is back to normal. It's eight years since the financial crisis, and seven since the trough. Just how long can we keep saying "insufficient demand"?

Exchange rates

This is an international paper, so what about exchange rates? Pierre-Olivier's model is about indeterminacies, not standard supply and demand: "The . . . model has a critical degree of indeterminacy when at the ZLB."

In forward-looking models such as these, an interest rate peg, such as zero, can nail down expected inflation. But unexpected inflation can then be anything—there are the multiple equilibria. In a frictionless model, unexpected inflation also means unexpected exchange rate changes. With nominal rigidities, indeterminacies result in real fluctuations, too.

So the model predicts this extra multiple-equilibrium volatility in exchange rates, output, and trade balances at the bound. The data don't show any increase in volatility or signs of such indeterminacy.

The indeterminacy "creates fertile grounds for . . . beggar-thy-neighbor devaluations achieved by direct interventions in exchange rate markets." I was puzzled by this, reading the paper. If interventions can "change" exchange rates, why don't they "determine" rates? Pierre-Olivier explained in the talk that this is somewhat "outside the model," which makes sense.

"If agents coordinate" is, I think, the clue. In zero-bound multiple-equilibrium models, the central bank is reduced to talk, trying to "coordinate expectations" one way or another because it can't actually *do* anything. There is lots of talk therapy or "forward guidance" recommended in related policy advice. It's like a DJ calling, "put your left foot out, now put your right foot out" to get us all to dance the same way.

In my world, the value of government debt is the present value of primary surpluses that will retire that debt. Then inflation and exchange rate innovations are *determined* by innovations to the present value of fiscal surpluses. (My world includes price stickiness, but I'm keeping it simple for a discussion.) Exchange rates are *volatile*, just as stock prices are volatile, and hard for pundits to explain ex-post. That volatility, however, has little to do with the zero bound, as in the data.

We have some agreement here. The section in the paper on "helicopter drops" points out, as in my equations, that if you can increase B without increasing G-T, you could get some inflation going, if you wanted to, which I don't.

Safe-asset shortages

Next, I will address "safe-asset shortages." The modeling problem is that normal investors are always happy to take a little more risk for a little more return. So, the paper adds infinitely risk averse agents.

The result: normally, we think of it as a good thing that the United States can issue at lower rates than other countries. But with "safe-asset scarcity," that rate can get pushed to zero, where all the bad things are supposed to happen.

I'm skeptical, both of facts and theory requiring the sudden appearance of infinitely risk averse agents.

Safe asset shortage? 100 to 200% debt to GDP ratios, rapidly growing, are not enough? Plus government-guaranteed mortgage-backed securities, repurchase agreements, bank deposits, and so on?

A "safe-asset shortage" means a high risk premium for risky assets, because few people are willing to hold them. (Low prices, high expected returns over risk-free rates, and "risk premium" are all synonyms.) The paper provides this evidence in this picture.

The claim is astounding—that risk premiums be as high as they were in the depths of the crisis.

Every other estimate goes the other way. For example, figure 4.8 shows the Standard and Poor's 500 price/earnings ratio, which reliably forecasts returns. It took a big dip in the crisis. But

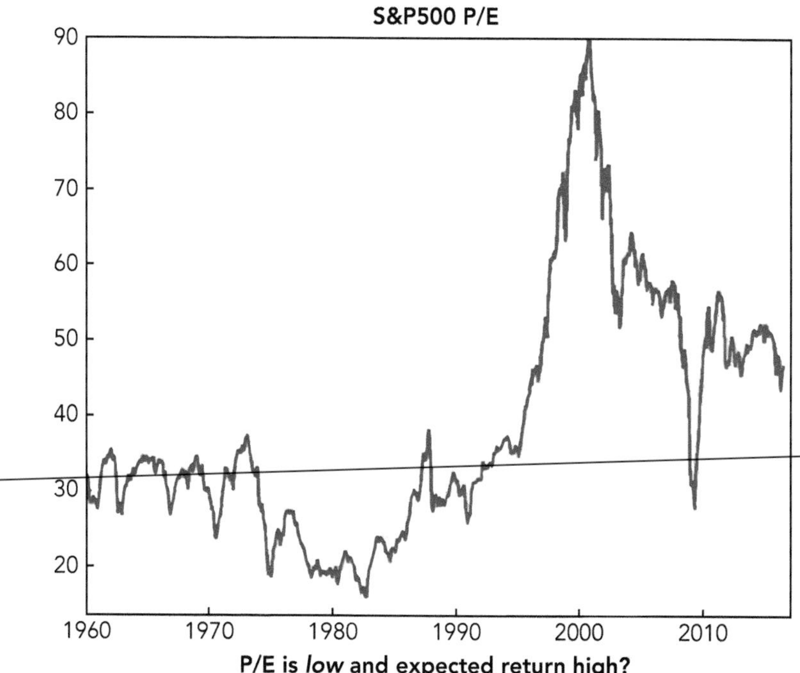

FIGURE 4.8.

now it's right back, and high by historical norms. House prices are now *low,* reflecting high-risk premiums (especially in Berkeley and Palo Alto)?

The same policy and pundit world is loudly complaining about "reach for yield," "Fed-inspired bubbles" in stocks and houses—low risk premiums. Yes, that is completely inconsistent with the same world complaining about "safe-asset shortage." Well, maybe the pundit world isn't right about everything.

Our worlds differ sharply on policy implications. In my world, central banks have done their jobs, killing inflation and bringing about Milton Friedman's optimal quantity of money. They can't raise productivity; that's the job of "structural reform." They should stop trying to fix things beyond their control.

Pierre-Olivier's view is an explicit invitation to international macroeconomic dirigisme, exchange rate interventions, deliberate fiscal inflation, "managing expectations," and "managing" capital flows—denying your and my right to buy things abroad. You know which view is popular in central banks and international institutions!

Summary

To summarize, I have a very simple view of today's world. Low productivity drives low interest rates and low growth. Nominal interest pegs, including zero, are determinate and stable. Prices are not infinitely sticky, so inflation can soak up slow moves in real rates. Exchange rates are volatile because they respond to the present value of fiscal surpluses, as well as to standard real interest differentials.

To be clear, I *am* sympathetic to the basic ingredients—financial frictions, a flight to US Treasury debt, a binding zero bound, inadequate "demand"—in the fall of 2008. But it's not groundhog day, forever 2008. At some point, financial crisis theory must give way to not-enough-growth theory.

As I promised to say at the start, this is a *great* paper. Three of the best minds in international macroeconomics have found ways to formalize all the blather we hear from the international policy community, "global imbalances," "savings gluts," "managing expectations," "flight to quality," "safeasset shortage," "ZLB contagion," and so on. As an economist, I am awed by their ability to write down a coherent model that captures these (to me) goofy ideas.

This being a policy conference, not a theory conference, I won't go over the clever ways they formalized these ideas. But this is why math and modeling is important in economics. Without it, we don't know what the chatter can possibly mean, nor whether it makes any sense.

To our media guests: you may think that economics works like regular science, where the equations come first, then tests in the data, then popular exposition with colorful language ("black holes!"), then, maybe, policy. No, we work backwards: first central banks feel their way to the policies they want to try, then colorful words like "global imbalances" are coined to describe their intuition about why, then theorists come up with equations that maybe make sense of the words, and finally we start testing theories in data. That second to last step is vital. Without it, we have no idea whether the colorful language makes any sense at all. Math in economics is vital.

Only with an explicit model can we begin to have a discussion. This model is great because I can read each ingredient—unpledgeable capital, taxes that fall only on the young, infinitely risk-averse agents—as *necessary,* not just *sufficient* to generate the policy blather. So I read this paper as a brilliant *negative* result. It shows just how extreme the implicit assumptions are behind the policy blather. It shows just how empty the idea is that our policymakers understand any of this stuff at a scientific, empirically tested level and should take strong actions to offset the supposed problems these buzzwords allude to.

Bottom line: you have in front of you two utterly different worldviews. Each set of models is reasonably internally consistent. The question is, which model applies to which planet?

GENERAL DISCUSSION

LEE OHANIAN: So in your paper and the other safe-asset-shortage papers, it seems that there is no ability for society to create more safe assets. So oftentimes in economics, if society wants more of a certain commodity, we find a way to produce that. Maybe not right away, but over time. What economic forces are you thinking about that prevent society from creating more safe assets? Are there things that we haven't thought about yet? Are there some fundamental restrictions that would have an analog in the model you have?

PIERRE-OLIVIER GOURINCHAS: You are correct. In the world we describe, there is a premium for issuing safe assets, so that should spur the creation of "private safe assets." But that supposes that the private sector can indeed generate these safe assets, and in sufficient quantities. Here counterparty risk and agency problems are important, and this is the main reason I think that the private sector is often unable to create truly safe assets, or at least in sufficient enough quantities, compared to the ability of some, not all, but some, public institutions. The question is: What ensures that something is safe? Counterparty risk is important: the likelihood that some private institution, financial or nonfinancial—think about JP Morgan, Facebook, or Apple, or General Motors—will be there and able to honor its obligations in the next 15 to 20 years is high, but it's less than one. The likelihood that the Greek government will be able to honor its promises in the next three years is certainly much less than one. I would argue that the same probability for the US Treasury is one. Now, as we've seen in the last crisis, there are strong incentives for the private sector to produce assets that look safe. Bernanke called them "private-label safe assets". But as the crisis illustrated, they were really not that safe in the end. So yes: there is an important difference, arising from counterparty risks and agency problems, between true safe-asset providers, who are few and often public institutions backed by the power of taxation, and private institutions.

JOHN COCHRANE: The real question is, What do you mean by a demand for special safe assets? In fact, most estimates of risk premiums are quite low right now. Well, what's so special about safe assets?

PIERRE-OLIVIER GOURINCHAS: Real interest rates are at historical lows. Someone is willing to lend to the Japanese government and earn a negative rate. Someone lends to the US government and earns a negative rate. Estimates of risk premiums are not that low, as we show in our paper. They are in fact quite high.

JOHN COCHRANE: Stock price dividend ratios are high. Interest rate spreads are low. Credit spreads are low.

PIERRE-OLIVIER GOURINCHAS: The dividend price ratio is high precisely because risk-free rates are low.

JOHN COCHRANE: But it's not about the level of rates. The issue is risk premiums. I agree about the level. People want to save. There's not much to invest it in. Inflation is low. Sure, the level of all rates is low.

ROBERT HALL: So one thing I keep track of quite carefully and accurately is the marginal product of capital. And I'm sorry to say, John, that it's just remarkably high. And this has been discussed a lot in the financial press, too, that the earnings of capital, physical capital, which presumably reflect the marginal product, have remained astonishingly high and stable. So I think the whole declining-marginal-product-of-capital hypothesis can be crossed off.

But I think I agree with this question. First of all, there are supersafe assets, and there are pretty-safe assets. But privately creating pretty-safe assets through over-collateralization, which is an extremely powerful tool in spite of any abuses that occurred in 2006, is an amazingly impressive way for private, pretty-safe assets to be created. And there's been an explosion and there continues to be an explosion of over-collateralization to satisfy demand. So the idea that there's a shortage and unsatisfied demand, I think, is crazy. We have a market equilibrium, which cannot be described as having a shortage, but it's one in which there's been a growing segment of the world's investors that have high risk aversion, not infinite. A coefficient of relative risk aversion of 2.5 for the risk-averse investors relative to 2.0 for the risk-tolerant investors is enough of a heterogeneity of risk aversion to generate the kind of low interest rates that we have today.

So we should dispense with this idea that there's something called a shortage or that only public instruments can be called "safe." Those are crazy ideas. The right ideas are that we have a world equilibrium, which delivers extremely low real interest rates and with low inflation, therefore, low nominal rates—dangerously low. But it's a market equilibrium. This idea that somehow only the public can do it, I think, is particularly dangerous.

PIERRE-OLIVIER GOURINCHAS: Can I come back to that? I think 2008 is a good example of when we see the tide going out and we see who is swimming without a swimsuit. At that point, what we see in the balance-of-payment data, in particular, is quite striking. All the gross inflows go into US Treasuries. They even come out of agencies at that point. They go to Treasuries and notes. They come out of everything else. And they come out of all the "private label" safe assets. So when the going got tough, private assets just did not cut it. Now perhaps it was because these assets were poorly regulated, or poorly collateralized. And perhaps savers are now looking at these assets suspiciously. But when the shocks are large enough, it is quite natural to expect these assets to fail before public assets do. And the fact that these assets don't necessarily have a backstop also makes them vulnerable to runs.

Now on the notion of the safe-asset shortage, I want to clarify an important point. The term does not describe the equilibrium outcome: in equilibrium, of course, things happen so that demand equals supply. What "safe-asset shortage" refers to is a shift in demand for these assets. If the price can adjust, then it will: interest rate will be low. If the price can't adjust—i.e., interest rates cannot fall enough—then something else will adjust: we argue it is output. And I think we can all agree that there's been a huge increase in the demand for this kind of asset, without a corresponding increase in supply: after all, real interest rates have declined. Some of it goes all the way back to the aftermath of the 1998 Asian financial crisis, and the surge in reserve accumulation by foreign officials, central banks. Some of it comes from the private sector too. A lot of gross demand for safe assets originates within the financial sector itself. In normal times, the financial sector should be a net provider of safe assets. But this masks large gross positions within the financial sector itself. Sight deposit accounts are a safe asset. But financial institutions also demand safe assets for collateral in repurchase-agreement transactions, for instance. Gary Gorton has written extensively on this. In times of crisis, the financial sector itself wants to get its hands on truly safe assets, so the financial sector itself becomes a net demander of safe assets.

And so I think you're right that the private sector produces them in normal times, but then when we get the kind of very large shock that we experienced eight years ago, then this is not sufficient.

ROBERT HALL: Well-rated corporate bonds are a good example. They're heavily over-collateralized. They're treated as safe. It was only a very minor shock in 2008. It's the less well-rated bonds that had a spike in their yields.

SEBASTIAN EDWARDS: Everything that Pierre-Olivier said was about 2007 and 2008. And then you added the shocks, the huge shocks we had eight years ago. So I go back to John Cochrane's point. The crisis is over, man. So I would buy what you're saying for 2008, maybe 2009, but not for 2015. I think that's still something that you have to persuade us about, that there is not enough supply of these safe assets at this very precise moment. So timing is of the essence in this narrative.

VARADARAJAN CHARI: It's interesting as theory. But I think that taken to the next level, it would really help a lot if we would start putting some numbers behind these kinds of things. I want to begin by reiterating a point. John took a larger number. But looking at federal debt held by the public as a percentage of gross domestic product, it's very similar to the picture John had. In the 2000s—this is just public debt—it was roughly 35% of GDP. Now, it's 75% of GDP. And yes, the Fed has bought up a bunch of that stuff, but the Fed has issued reserves, which are just as safe, in exchange for that. So what I want to know is, suppose I put in that kind of an increase—40%. So we're talking six trillion dollars. Same thing for Japan. Same thing for the European Union. Are you going to get the kinds of effects you're talking about? There's just not enough of this stuff? That's one.

The second thing that bothers me a lot is that price rigidity assumptions have to play a critical role. In your model, there has to be a stationary equilibrium in the long run, so to speak, and John's of the view—and I'm sympathetic—that eight years is close enough for macroeconomists to the long run. You'd think that if this was a real problem, the inflation rate now would be minus two percent, not plus two percent. Because the main thing that you guys are focusing on, this very worthwhile thing, is you're trying to account for this so-called secular stagnation. But your view of secular stagnation relies very heavily on the idea that you can't have an equilibrium with minus two percent inflation for five or six years, because that's the steady state in which you get back to the normal market-clearing kind of stuff. You're shutting down a lot of those mechanisms. It's bothering me.

The last thing, just one more thing: I didn't understand the stuff about flows. You said that all the data said the flows were from bonds or from agencies to Treasuries. It can't be a statement about the flows, because the aggregate stock of agency securities didn't change. For every buyer there was a seller. It has to be some statement about prices. So somehow you're saying that the demand for safety went up? That may be right, but it seems to me a lot closer to what Bob Hall was talking about.

PIERRE-OLIVIER GOURINCHAS: Lots of very interesting points here. First on inflation: what I presented today doesn't have any inflation. But we have a whole section in the paper where we bring in inflation. Then the amount of deflation you would get once you're in the liquidity trap (since output is below potential) is something that is controlled by a bunch of things, such as the elasticity of your inflation rate to the output gap. In steady state, what you get is deflation, not inflation. Deflation does not help you: it keeps real rates high and therefore output depressed, which is why you remain stuck. Now, on whether in 2016 events that occurred in 2008 should have receded into the background: that is not clear to me. Clearly, the low real rates and high-risk premium indicate that investors don't view the situation as normalized.

JOHN COCHRANE: I think Chari misspoke. The steady state you want has *in*flation, right? If you need to generate a persistent steady state with negative two percent real, the answer is two percent positive inflation, and it takes a lot of tricks to keep that from being the steady state that emerges.

PIERRE-OLIVIER GOURINCHAS: In the model with inflation there are multiple equilibria. If the inflation target is high enough, there is an equilibrium with sufficiently high inflation and output at potential: there is no trap. If the inflation target is too low, this equilibrium does not exist anymore. But regardless of the inflation target, there is another equilibrium with low inflation (or deflation) and output below potential. In an international environment, there are also asymmetric equilibria where one country is in the trap (and experiences deflation) and the other is not. Now we can disagree about the underlying, dynamic process that may or may not allow us to reach that global liquidity trap equilibrium. I think that's a healthy scientific discussion. But that is maybe beyond the point you were raising.

Now on Chari's point about flows and stock, Chari is absolutely correct: the stock does not change, so prices must adjust and a new equilibrium obtains given the changes in demand. Risk free rates fall and expected risky returns increase. What the financial account gives us is a window into that shift in demand. If all investors were identical, there would be no flows, just an adjustment in prices. But not all investors are identical, so we're going to see international flows. And there was a big domestic actor here that stepped up and made sure that the prices of the agencies wouldn't move too much: the Fed. What the Fed was doing was issuing central bank liabilities, which are very safe. In fact, it is almost the definition of a safe asset: you cannot run against it and its nominal value is fixed. What we see in the balance of payment data is the private sector running for the exits on these supposedly safe assets—even ones with implicit guaranties from the US-government-like agencies.

The real disagreement with the view of the world that John presented is the disagreement about whether the marginal product of capital and the decline in the marginal product of capital is sufficient to generate everything we see. And here, I'm fully siding with Bob Hall. I don't see the evidence in terms of the corporate profitability that would justify that.

JOHN COCHRANE: Since you both said it, can I have one second on that? Bob Hall and I have this discussion all the time. But investment is very low, and real interest rates and expected returns on stocks are really low. So there are two pieces of evidence that the marginal product of capital and marginal *Q* are really low. It makes sense that existing businesses are doing great, but no one wants to invest in new businesses, and we can all discuss obvious reasons why. That's at least a consistent story—if not one that will keep Bob happy—for how you can see high corporate profits, and very low investment, and very low rates of return.

CHAPTER FIVE

Monetary Policy Cooperation and Coordination

An Historical Perspective on the Importance of Rules

Michael D. Bordo and Catherine Schenk

1. Introduction

Events since the financial crisis of 2007–2008 have led to renewed interest in monetary policy cooperation and coordination (Frankel 2015). While the reintroduction of the Federal Reserve's swap lines with major advanced country central banks in September 2008 and coordinated policy rate cuts announced at the G20 Summit in October 2008 attracted praise, claims of 'currency wars' by central bankers from emerging countries following quantitative easing by the Fed and later by the Bank of Japan and the European Central Bank (ECB) have led to calls for monetary policymakers to take coordinated action to reduce the international spillover from their domestic actions (Eichengreen 2013b). An alternative view argues that the externalities from recent monetary policy actions reflects the deviation from rules-based monetary policy (Taylor 2013; Ahrend 2010; Bordo and Landon-Lane 2012). By a rules-based policy what is meant is that the central bank sets its policy instrument (in the United States, the federal funds rate) in a predictable way in reaction to its primary policy goals: the deviation of real growth from potential and the deviation of inflation from its target. In this

Paper prepared for the conference International Monetary Stability: Past, Present and Future. Hoover Institution, Stanford University, May 5, 2016. For helpful comments we thank Owen Humpage, Geoffrey Wood, Forrest Capie, and Harold James.

view, a return to rules-based monetary policy and a rolling back of the "global great deviation" by each country's central bank would lead to a beneficial global outcome without the need for policy coordination.

This paper reviews the issue of monetary policy cooperation and coordination from an historical perspective. We examine the experiences of cooperation and coordination since the late nineteenth century among advanced countries across several exchange rate regimes: the classical gold standard, 1880 to 1914; the interwar gold exchange standard, 1924 to 1936; the Bretton Woods system, 1944 to 1973; and the Managed Float, 1973 to the present. We distinguish between cooperation and coordination, although the distinction in reality is pretty murky. By cooperation we mean the sharing of information and techniques of central banking, the discussion of common problems and occasional/ad hoc emergency lending or other operations between central banks in periods of financial crisis. By coordination we mean policy actions formally agreed upon and taken by groups of policymakers (including finance ministers and central bankers) aimed at achieving beneficial outcomes for the international system as a whole. Such actions may conflict with domestic policy goals. To conserve on space, we limit ourselves to monetary policy actions, including some cases of lender of last resort. We also avoid the vast example of monetary policy cooperation and coordination leading to the creation of the European Monetary Union, and we only tangentially discuss the growing role of the emerging countries, especially China, in the international monetary system.

In this paper we argue that, in monetary regimes that are rules based (in the sense of the modern literature on rules versus discretion), cooperation was most successful and less so in regimes based on discretion or poorly grounded rules. We find less success for more elaborate schemes of coordination.

2. The classical gold standard, 1880 to 1914

The classical gold standard was the original rules-based monetary policy regime (Bordo and Kydland 1995). The basic rule for each monetary authority was to maintain convertibility of its paper currency in terms of gold at the official nominal price (or as a fixed number of ounces of gold). This required subsuming domestic policy goals to the dictates of external balance (except in the case of a banking panic). In fact, monetary authorities with credibility had some limited flexibility to attend to domestic stability goals within the gold points that bounded the official parity (Bordo and Macdonald 2005).

The gold standard was a rule in the modern (Kydland and Prescott 1977) sense. Adhering to the convertibility rule was a credible commitment mechanism to prevent the monetary authorities from following time inconsistent discretionary policies. The gold standard rule was also a contingent rule. Convertibility could be suspended in the event of well understood emergencies such as a major war or a financial crisis not of the domestic authority's own making (Bordo and Kydland 1995). In such circumstances the monetary authority could issue fiat money on the understanding that it would be retired once the war had ended. In the event of a financial crisis, a temporary suspension could allow the authority to provide lender of last resort liquidity.

Central banks in advanced countries before 1914 did consistently follow the convertibility rule. They also were supposed to adhere to the "rules of the game"—rules of thumb that they would use their discount rates to speed up the adjustment to external imbalances. In actual fact some countries did not strictly follow these "rules of the game" but engaged in sterilization and gold policy (policies to widen the gold export point) (Bordo 1981).[1]

1. A prominent example of which was France. See Bazot, Bordo, and Monnet (2016). As discussed in Bloomfield (1959), many other countries also violated the "Rules".

Cooperation during the gold standard was quite limited. To the extent that central banks adhered to the gold standard, they implicitly cooperated. Even the minor violations of the gold points that occurred were never sufficient to threaten the international monetary system. There is evidence that in the face of several large financial crises (for example, 1890 and 1907), the Banque de France, which had very large gold reserves, lent gold on commercial terms to the Bank of England to allow it to avoid suspending convertibility. Some argue that that this cooperation was essential to the survival of the gold standard (Borio and Toniolo 2005; Eichengreen 1992), but the evidence suggests otherwise (Flandreau 1997; Bordo and Schwartz 1999). The Bank of England held a "thin film of gold" because it had a long record of credibility, which ensured that capital flows would be stabilizing. Moreover, in financial crises that did not involve rescue loans, the Bank of England requested a "Treasury Letter" allowing it to temporarily suspend convertibility. When this happened, as in 1825 and 1847, the panic ended.

Several early unsuccessful attempts at international monetary coordination occurred at a number of conferences held to try to standardize gold coins across the major countries. In conferences held in Paris in 1867 and 1878, France tried to convince Great Britain and the United States to change the weights of their standard gold sovereign and gold eagle into that of the five franc gold coin. The idea was that having similar coins across the gold standard would reduce the transactions costs of international trade. The adjustments in weights for each currency were very minor, but the British and American opposition to such an infringement on their monetary sovereignty was overwhelming (Eichengreen 2013a; James 2016). Later in the century, at the height of the Free Silver movement, a number of international conferences were held in the United States to promote global bimetallism. Nothing came out of them.

The gold standard was successful because it was rules based and each member voluntarily adhered to the convertibility rule. Many authors have argued that gold standard adherence was not enough to maintain the gold standard (see Bordo 1984). They argued that it was durable because it was managed by Great Britain, the leading commercial power. London was the center of the global financial system, and it housed the leading financial markets and commodity markets, and many international banks had headquarters there, or at least branches. The traditional view is that the Bank of England could draw "money from the moon" by raising its discount rate. Moreover, it was backed by the safe assets of the British Empire whose sovereign debt was guaranteed by the British government (Ferguson and Schularick 2012). Others argue that France and Germany were also key players in the gold standard and that implicit cooperation between them guaranteed the safety of the system (Tullio and Walters 1996).

Despite its success as a rules-based system, the gold standard collapsed because World War I completely unraveled the global financial system and virtually bankrupted all of the European belligerents. Had the war not happened, it could have lasted longer.

3. The interwar gold exchange standard, 1924 to 1936

After World War I, Great Britain, France, and other countries expressed a strong desire to restore the gold standard. The United States had never left gold; it just imposed an embargo on gold exports for two years after it entered the war in April 1917. All of the belligerents had financed their war efforts with a combination of taxes, debt, and seigniorage. All had large debt overhangs and high inflation. In Great Britain the price level more than doubled, in the United States it inflated somewhat less, in France it tripled, and in Germany it increased considerably more than that. The debt overhang and high inflation meant that it would be difficult for most countries to go back to the gold standard at the prewar parities, and most experts believed that it would take major international cooperation and coordination to restore it. Two important conferences in Brussels (1920) and Genoa (1922) set the stage for the restoration of the gold standard. Because of a predicted gold shortage (the real price of gold had been vastly deflated by the global wartime inflation), it was to be a gold exchange standard under which members would hold both foreign exchange and gold as international reserves. Great Britain and the United States were to be the center countries of the new international monetary system, and they were to hold their international reserves in gold valued at the prewar parities.

Extensive international cooperation was required to stabilize the central European countries that had run hyperinflations. The stabilization packages were imposed by the League of Nations and private sector lenders such as JP Morgan in return for the loans required to build up the reserves needed to restore convertibility, which involved massive disinflation and budget balance. To facilitate Great Britain's return to gold in 1925, the New York Fed established a $200 million line of credit for the Bank of England in New York (Bordo, Humpage, and Schwartz 2015, ch. 2). The Fed also kept its policy looser than would otherwise have been the case (Friedman and Schwartz 1963).

The interwar gold standard was based on the convertibility rule, as was its prewar ancestor, but the rule was more fragile and less credible. One key difference between the gold exchange standard and the classical gold standard was that few countries were perceived to be willing to maintain external balance at the expense of domestic policy goals. Because of the extension of the franchise in most countries, the growth of organized labor, and the fresh responsibilities of governments for the economic and social welfare of their populations after the terrible experience of war, more emphasis was placed on domestic output, employment, and price stability. Central banks began to focus more on stabilizing the business cycle in support of expansionary economic policy targets for employment and growth (Polanyi 1944; Eichengreen 1992). In addition, many of the post–World War I parities were misaligned, reflecting miscalculation of equilibrium exchange rates and political pressures, together with some expectation that if the parity were changed it could be changed again, which expectation meant that a changed parity reduced credibility (Eichengreen 1992, ch. 6). Sterling was pegged to gold at an overvalued (prewar) parity in April 1925 while France went back in 1926 after an 80% devaluation, at a greatly undervalued parity. This meant that the adjustment mechanism of the gold standard was destined to malfunction (Meltzer 2003). The Bank of England had to continually tighten monetary policy to protect its gold reserves in the face of persistent balance of payments deficits, which continually deflated the British economy (Keynes 1925). At the same time, France ran persistent balance of payments surpluses, which should have led to an expansion in the money supply and inflation but instead were continuously sterilized. This meant that France was absorbing a larger and larger amount of the world's gold reserves (Irwin 2013). The United States kept sterilizing its surpluses, joining France in sucking gold from the rest of the world. In addition to the maldistribution of gold, the system was further weakened by failing confidence in sterling as a reserve currency. Declining gold reserves at the Bank of England and Federal Reserve sterilization policies prompted countries to shift their foreign exchange reserves from sterling to dollars (Eichengreen et al. 2017).

Against this background of flawed rules, considerable central bank cooperation was required just to prop up the system. Much of the cooperation was personal; between Montagu Norman, governor of the Bank of England, Benjamin Strong, governor of the Federal Reserve Bank of New York, Hjalmar Schacht, president of the Reichsbank, and Emile Moreau, president of the Banque de France (Clarke 1967; Ahamed 2009; James 2016). Norman and Strong worked tirelessly to get the gold standard working. Once underway, the perennial problem of sterling's weakness came to the fore. It was aggravated by the Banque de France's pro-gold policy of converting sterling bills into gold. In July 1927 Strong organized a clandestine meeting between the four governors at the house of Undersecretary of the Treasury Ogden Mills on Long Island. At this meeting one of the classic monetary policy coordinations of all time was worked out to protect sterling. The New York Fed agreed to cut its discount rate and to conduct expansionary open market operations while the Banque de France (and the Reichsbank) agreed to shift their gold purchases from London to New York. The meeting was organized by Strong, and only one member of the Federal Reserve Board in Washington was present. Sterling was saved for another day, but the fallout from the meeting in the United States kept spreading. In 1931 at the peak of the Great Contraction, Adolph Miller, a governor of the Federal Reserve Board, blamed Strong's actions for fueling the Wall Street boom that burst in October 1929 and for creating the Great Contraction. His criticism was picked up by Parker Willis and Carter Glass and later by Herbert Hoover in his memoirs (Meltzer 2003). The episode eventually led to a major reform in the Banking Act of 1933, which stripped the New York Fed (and any other Federal Reserve bank) of any role in international monetary policy and gave full responsibility to the Federal Reserve Board. Moreover, Strong's actions bailing out Britain on two occasions may have encouraged moral hazard by discouraging the British from learning to adjust (Meltzer 2003). After Strong's death in 1928 and Schacht's departure from the Reichsbank, Norman pushed hard to institutionalize monetary policy cooperation, which came to fruition with the creation of the Bank for International Settlements (BIS) in Basel in 1930.

The initial operational purpose for the BIS was to manage German reparations after the Young Plan, but its more fundamental function was to promote central bank cooperation. It was a venue for sharing information and provided a confidential forum for central bankers to meet on a regular basis as well as providing services for central banks (for example, gold swaps, deposits, and lines of credit) (Toniolo and Clement 2005; Borio and Toniolo 2005). But its early attempts at cooperation were not successful (James 2016). The BIS was involved in two failed attempts in spring and summer of 1931 to rescue the Austrian schilling and the German mark. Its resources were too small, and the rescues did not have the political backing of France.

The architecture of the interwar gold standard emphasized the importance of central banks for the exercise of monetary policy. The delegates at the Genoa International Economic Conference in 1922 explicitly stated that central bank cooperation was a vital aspect of a prospective new gold standard and that this should be institutionalized in a convention or "entente" (Schenk and Straumann 2016; James 2016). Montagu Norman promoted a network of central banks modeled on the Bank of England that could cooperate to deliver "orthodox" policies aimed at monetary and exchange rate stability. His vision was supported by the Financial Committee of the League of Nations, which sent missions to a range of central European states in the mid-1920s as part of creating a coordinated international monetary system. Sir Otto Niemeyer and others from the Bank of England toured emerging markets to advise on monetary policy, "sound money," and to promote the establishment or reform of central banks. His advice was sometimes controversial, as, for example, in Australia where his recommendations of austerity to restore exchange rate stability were greeted with indignation (Attard 1992, 82). Many Western Hemisphere states looked to the United States; Edwin Kemmerer of the Federal Reserve Bank toured a number of countries from 1917 to 1931 advising on the organization of central banks, including Colombia, Chile, Ecuador, Bolivia, and Peru (Singleton 2011, 60). With the increased prominence of central banks and the establishment of the Bank for

International Settlements, the interwar gold standard (while itself a failure of cooperation and coordination) set the foundations for central bank cooperation for the next century.

The gold exchange standard collapsed amid the shocks of the Great Depression. Many argue that adherence to the gold standard caused the Great Depression because of "golden fetters"—due to the gold constraint, countries could not follow lender of last resort policies (Temin 1989; Eichengreen 1992), and because of the collapse of the global money supply gold multiplier (Bernanke 1995). Others argue that the Depression was caused by inappropriate Federal Reserve monetary policy (Friedman and Schwartz 1963; Meltzer 2003). The collapse in the US money supply was then transmitted to the rest of the world by the fixed exchange rate gold standard.

Two major attempts at monetary policy coordination were undertaken in the 1930s as the gold exchange standard collapsed, one a disaster and one quite successful. The League of Nations sponsored the London Monetary and Economic Conference in June 1933 to try to stabilize exchange rates and achieve concessions on trade restrictions. The planning for the summit was already in place when the United States abandoned its gold peg in April 1933, and the timing meant that there was little prospect for a successful outcome. The French were adamant about a return to gold but would not agree to reflate their economy to support the targets in Britain and the United States for recovery of prices, or to relax French trade restrictions (Eichengreen 1992). In the wake of this now traditional French unwillingness to cooperate, the British and American administrations opted firmly to prioritize their domestic goals for price stability. The United Kingdom turned to monetary and trade cooperation with the sterling bloc of countries pegged to the pound, the gold bloc centered on France bolstered its defenses, and the United States embarked on its own independent path.

Three years later, the timing was more propitious for successful cooperation under the Tripartite Agreement of 1936 between the United States, the United Kingdom, and France as the French position had become untenable when the dollar and sterling depreciated against gold. France needed a coordinated devaluation to prevent a free fall in the franc, and the United States and United Kingdom also had an interest in an orderly depreciation of the franc. With this coincidence of interest, it was possible to agree to a common strategy not to manipulate exchange rates for national advantage. Each country's Exchange Stabilization Fund (ESF) engaged in daily coordinated exchange market intervention to produce an orderly devaluation of the French franc. It ended at the outbreak of World War II (Bordo, Humpage, and Schwartz 2015, ch. 3).

Monetary policy cooperation and coordination certainly contributed to the interwar gold exchange standard's problems by propping up a flawed system and possibly even helping fuel the 1920s asset price boom. Central bankers were later blamed for the Great Depression and had their powers and independence stripped, with important consequences for the postwar period. Unlike the prewar gold standard, although the gold exchange standard was rules based, the circumstances and implementation of the rules were flawed from the beginning. Central bank monetary policy cooperation and coordination did not function well in this environment.

4. The Bretton Woods international monetary system, 1944 to 1973

During the World War II, the Great Depression was characterized as a failure of coordination in international trade (protectionism) and also international monetary policy; US monetary policy mistakes spilled over to European economies, increasing the fragility of the global financial system. Thus, many have argued that destabilizing international short-term capital flows fueled competitive devaluations and "currency wars" in the 1930s that led to further disintegration of the global economy via protectionist trade barriers and capital controls (Nurkse 1944; Kindleberger 1986). A key goal of the postwar period was therefore to create a framework for cooperation and coordination underpinned by credible rules to ensure a lasting and prosperous peace (Giovannini 1993). For monetary policy, the rules were to maintain pegged exchange rates within narrow bands (plus or minus 1%) supported by controls on short-term capital flows and access to short-term credit (from the International Monetary Fund) to cover temporary balance of payments imbalances. Unlike the interwar system, member countries could adjust their parities in the event of a "fundamental disequilibrium" (which was never defined). The gold convertibility rule was preserved through fixing the gold price of the US dollar at $35 per ounce. Gold parities for other currencies were identified through the dollar. The cornerstone of the classical gold standard—convertibility— was restricted to current account transactions to promote multilateral trade and payments. Short-term capital flows were considered disruptive to cooperation and coordination and were sacrificed to enhance domestic monetary policy sovereignty in this solution to the Mundell-Fleming trilemma.

The history of the design of the Bretton Woods system is remarkable for the strong consensus that a return to a pegged exchange rate rule (and freer trade) was the best way to recapture the benefits of the nineteenth-century era of globalization under the gold standard. The general agreement on the appropriateness and effectiveness of the rule should have boded well for the success and credibility of the system, if every participant shared roughly the same tolerance for unemployment and inflation. But almost as soon as it started to operate as designed, it began to founder, requiring a series of repairs to keep it afloat.

In the immediate aftermath of the war, other systems of coordination were formed to allow multilateral trade without full convertibility: the European Payments Union (EPU) and the Sterling Area were the two most prominent examples. The EPU provided monthly clearing for European trade payments from 1950 to 1958, with settlement increasingly in dollars and gold. The Sterling Area (the United Kingdom, the British Commonwealth—except Canada—all British colonies, and several Middle Eastern states) operated exchange controls in concert against the dollar, denominated most of their foreign exchange reserves in sterling, and enjoyed freer international capital flows from 1945 to 1958 (thereafter the coordination eroded) (Schenk 2010). These interim solutions allowed trade liberalization to fuel growth, and current account convertibility was finally introduced by most countries at the end of 1958.

But the convertibility rule proved inconsistent with domestic priorities of full employment and growth once international capital markets could no longer be contained. Offshore markets in London and current account convertibility in the 1960s tested the credibility of adherence to the exchange rate rule, and there were repeated parity adjustments that undermined the system as a whole. The pegged rate rule was operated too inflexibly, so, instead of small and frequent adjustments, there were repeated speculative rushes on the deutsche mark, franc, and pound sterling, in particular, through the 1960s. By the end of the 1960s, these attacks had spread to the dollar at the heart of the system, and the gold convertibility rule was effectively abandoned in March 1968.

The Bretton Woods system is an example of an elaborate effort at institutionalized coordination that failed because of fundamental flaws in the rules underpinning the system (Schenk 2016). Instead, a set of cooperative initiatives were deployed to prop the system up on an ad hoc basis until the convertibility and exchange rate rules finally gave way in 1973. This cooperation among leading industrial economies (promoted in part by Cold War ideology) allowed the global economy to reap the benefits of freer trade and technological innovation during the first 30 years after the end of World War II so that the Bretton Woods era was characterized by low inflation and rapid growth (Bordo 1993).

The most serious vulnerability in the Bretton Woods rules arose from the use of the dollar as an international reserve currency, and therefore reliance on US monetary policy. The role of the dollar gradually polarized the main actors in the system and crystalized their distinctive competing interests, undermining efforts at coordination and eroding credibility in the system's rules. After European states declared current account convertibility at the end of 1958, Robert Triffin (1960) warned that, once outstanding dollar reserves held by the rest of the world surpassed the US monetary gold stock, this would increase the possibility of a run on the dollar and a collapse of the system. Thinking in terms of the interwar experience, Triffin worried that US monetary authorities would tighten policy, leading to a world depression. For him, the solution was the creation of an alternative reserve asset subject to coordinated management, like Keynes's (1943) proposed bancor. Closely related to the Triffin paradox was the critique that the United States gained an exorbitant privilege from the dollar's position in the system. Since the dollar was an international reserve currency, the United States did not have to adjust to balance of payments deficits and could promote outward direct investment (acquiring foreign assets), and the US government could borrow at lower rates than otherwise because of the global appetite for dollar-denominated assets. The French in particular resented this and periodically pressed for the world to return to the classical gold standard (with disruptive effects [Rueff 1961]). Recent efforts to measure the "privilege" accorded to the United States find it to be very small (McCauley 2015). Meanwhile, West Germans viewed the US deficits as inflationary, which ran counter to Germany's strong preference for stable prices and inhibited the Bundesbank from adjusting the deutsche mark or reducing persistent German balance of payments surpluses (Emminger 1967). Nevertheless, the dollar persisted at the core of the system because of its desirable properties as a vehicle currency and the unrivalled breadth and depth of US financial markets. At the time, Despres, Kindleberger and Salant (1966) argued that the United States acted as a financial intermediary borrowing short-term deposits and lending long-term foreign investment. In this view, as long as the Fed followed credible monetary policy, the dollar standard could persist.

As the Bretton Woods system crumbled through the second half of the 1960s, enormous energy was put into efforts to renew the framework for international policy coordination, with little tangible outcome. An army of international civil servants toured the world on behalf of the G10 industrialized countries, the OECD, the IMF, the Committee of 20 and the Group of 24 developing countries seeking to reform the system through schemes such as replacing the US dollar as primary reserve asset or broadening exchange rate bands (Solomon 1982; Williamson 1977). These efforts were plagued by a lack of consensus about the problem to be solved (too little international liquidity or too much) and the proliferation of interests that made a coherent focus more difficult to achieve as problems of unequal growth and development became more prominent during the 1960s. US Treasury Secretary Henry Fowler's call for a new World Monetary Conference in July 1965 fell on deaf ears as the prospects for a successful public meeting were too slim to risk the subsequent shock to confidence from a failure (Schenk 2010, 259). Even where a reform was achieved, in the case of the SDR (Special Drawing Rights) in 1967–68, there was no fundamental consensus about its purpose or operation, and it has remained for most of its life mainly a unit of account rather than an effective international monetary instrument (Schenk 2010). Prolonged discussions to make it more useful through a substitution account to supplement the US dollar during the 1970s failed (McCauley and Schenk 2015). Meanwhile, the credibility of the exchange rate rules evaporated with multiple adjustments, currency crises, and the end of consensus either on the diagnosis of the problems in the international monetary system or the solution.

The General Arrangements to Borrow (GAB) in 1961 created a line of credit at the IMF sufficient to satisfy a speculative attack on a large country like the United States. Its lasting importance is perhaps less through its direct effect and more from the creation of a new tier of leadership in the global system. The Group of 10 countries involved in the GAB became an alternative to the IMF Executive Board as leaders of reform and as a forum for cooperation, challenging the broader constituency of the IMF and the interests of emerging market economies.[2] The G10 as a coordinating forum was further reinforced, since the G10 central bank governors formed the governing board of the Bank for International Settlements.

In addition to these ambitious efforts at renewed coordination through the IMF, there was the increased intensity of central bank cooperation through the auspices of the Bank for International Settlements. The monthly meetings of G10 central bank governors, supported by a technocratic secretariat and a set of topic-based expert standing committees (Goodhart 2011; Toniolo and Clement 2005) provided an opportunity for "soft" cooperation through a sharing of ideas, policies, and instruments as well as flexible, simple, and effective responses such as coordinated lines of credit and swaps.

The meetings were private and secret, with no formal minutes, and this promoted a frank exchange of views. The monthly meetings of G10 central bank governors and their staffs in Basel did not attract political attention or require parliamentary oversight

2. The Group of 10 were Canada, the United Kingdom, the United States, Italy, France, Belgium, Netherlands, Japan, Sweden, and West Germany. Switzerland also participated in multilateral activities through the BIS. Luxembourg also joined for the Basel Committee.

in the way that IMF meetings and edicts did. The BIS, therefore, became a preferred venue for cooperation for countries such as the United Kingdom, which struggled to maintain the sterling exchange rate through the 1960s until it floated in June 1972 (Schenk 2010; Schenk 2016).

There were three main cooperative efforts among central banks to support the gold and exchange rate rules of the Bretton Woods system: the Gold Pool, multilateral Group Arrangements, and bilateral Fed swaps.

The Gold Pool began as an intergovernmental initiative from the US Treasury secretary in September 1961 to keep the market gold price at the official price. It was thrust upon the G10 central bank governors in November 1961; only the Bundesbank was an enthusiastic supporter from the outset (Toniolo and Clement 2005, 376–77). Each central bank pledged a set amount for gold sales to the pool, and the US Fed matched the amounts of the other members to a total of $270 million. On the other side, the Bank of England intervened to buy gold when this would not raise the gold price. Part of the proceeds from these operations ($30 million) was kept to fund sales, thus saving the formal Gold Pool for times when there was a sustained upward pressure on the gold price, which started from 1965.[3] The Gold Pool operated reasonably well until sterling was devalued by 14.3% in November 1967. This prompted a fatal loss of confidence in the gold value of the dollar and the market rate of gold was finally allowed to rise after a run in March 1968, although central banks and the IMF agreed to continue to trade at the official rate of $35 per ounce. At this point, it became clear that the resources of central banks could not "buck" the market for any length of time. From this date, the gold convertibility rule of the Bretton Woods system was essentially over and the entire system's days were numbered.

3. Canada, Japan, and Sweden joined in 1964, creating the G10 Gold and Foreign Exchange Committee, the precursor to the current Markets Committee.

A second (and less well-known) support was the arrangement of coordinated lines of credit among the G10 central bank governors at the BIS starting in 1960 (Schenk 2010; Toniolo and Clement 2005). A spike in the London gold price to $40.00 in October 1960 on fears that John F. Kennedy would follow an inflationary policy if elected led to a flurry of attempts at cooperation (including gold swaps) between the ESF and a range of European central banks, a $1 billion credit line of gold from the BIS, and finally revaluation of the deutsche mark and Dutch guilder in March 1961.

In this context of dollar fragility, the British convinced the G10 that supporting sterling was a vital bulwark for the continuation of the Bretton Woods system and thereby garnered multilateral support. The Italian lira received significant support but sterling was the main beneficiary, repeatedly arranging emergency short-term lines of credit: $904 million in 1961, $250 million in March 1963, $1 billion in September 1964, $3 billion in November 1964. To put this in perspective, $3 billion in 1964 is equivalent to $37.7 billion in 1997, which is close to the value of the $40 billion rescue package arranged for Mexico in 1997 by the IMF, the World Bank, BIS, and bilateral swaps combined—and much more than the $10 billion pledged to Mexico by the G10 central banks through the BIS. Even for the 1997 Korean Crisis, the 13 contributors to the coordinated rescue package only pledged $20 billion.

From 1965 the Bank of England began to negotiate a longer-term solution to the retirement of sterling as a reserve asset, culminating in the First Group Arrangement in 1966, for up to $1 billion in support to be activated by a specific fall in global sterling reserves (Schenk 2010). As with the other lines of credit, the First Group Arrangement was not fully drawn, partly because its very presence improved confidence. Only $75 million of the BIS's own pledge was used, and the facility was renewed without much discussion in March 1967. However, the credit was completely exhausted by the time of the sterling devaluation of November 1967, as well as a further line of credit of $250 million organized by the BIS. But this was not the end of the G10 central bankers' cooperation to support the decline of sterling.

In the midst of a run on the dollar and the collapse of the Gold Pool in March 1968, the Bank of England tried unsuccessfully to get a new package of $5 billion in credit. Instead, central banks pledged $1.175 billion, almost half from extending the Fed's UK swap facility from $1.5 billion to $2 billion. Soon after, the BIS began to plan a Second Group Arrangement to retire sterling, supported by a $2 billion line of credit (equivalent to $38 billion today). This time, the United Kingdom was forced to negotiate bilateral agreements with each individual country that held substantial sterling reserves (34 in all) to limit the diversification of their reserves.[4] This Second Group Arrangement was finally concluded in September 1968, popularly known as the Basel Agreement. It was renewed several times (despite the depreciation of the dollar in 1971 and the float of sterling in 1972).

A third defense for the dollar was the Federal Reserve's series of bilateral swap lines between the US and major currencies begun in 1962. The swaps were covered short-term loan facilities between the Fed and other central banks, usually for three months, and served two purposes. Countries outside the United States drew dollars to intervene in foreign exchange markets to support their currencies (the Bank of England drew $8.65 billion from 1962 to 1971. On the other side, the Fed drew on the swaps to support the dollar price of gold. These swaps provided a short-term exchange value guarantee and thereby discouraged central banks from converting their unwanted or "excess" dollars to gold. The Fed drew $11.6 billion in foreign currencies from 1962 to 1971 (Bordo, Humpage, Schwartz 2014). These swap lines were sometimes retired with foreign exchange or Roosa bonds (US Treasury

4. In 1968, 23 countries held over half of their reserves in sterling.

securities denominated in foreign currencies) (Bordo, Humpage, and Schwartz 2015, ch. 4). The swap network expanded from less than a billion dollars in 1962, when the first swap was made with France, to close to $12 billion by August 1971 and $20 billion by in mid-1974, by which time the network included 14 central banks (including the BIS).

These tools and rescue packages all worked in the short run to head off the "crise du jour," but the system was no longer consistent with US domestic policy goals. By the spring of 1971 the French and British threatened to convert their outstanding dollar holdings into gold (Garber 1993; Bordo 1993), and in August 1971 President Nixon closed the US gold window on the advice of Treasury Secretary Connolly. The Bretton Woods system did not collapse into deflation as Triffin prophesized; rather the problem was inflation. The United States followed the key gold standard rule of keeping inflation low until 1965, but from then on the Fed followed expansionary monetary policy to help finance the Vietnam War and Lyndon B. Johnson's Great Society. It thus broke the basic rule of the Bretton Woods system, and the Europeans became increasingly critical of US inflation (Bordo 1993).

Like the interwar system, Bretton Woods was a rules-based system, but the rules were both analytically flawed and incompatible with the political economy environment of the time. In each case the exchange rate rule was formally set (and in Bretton Woods there was an elaborate institutional framework to promote coordination), but there was no underpinning domestic policy rule to support the system. Policymakers at the time had an incomplete understanding of the role and effect of monetary policy, and they prioritized the pursuit of full employment over price stability (to varying degrees). To top this off, the United States as center country broke the key rule of the system by running an inflationary policy. That the Bretton Woods system lasted as long as it did was due in a significant way to effective central bank cooperation encouraged by a deep fear of floating exchange rates and of the impact on the global economy of a collapse of the exchange rate rules. This cooperation transcended the collapse of the system that it was supposed to defend.

5. The transition to floating, 1968 to 1973

Although most currencies abandoned their dollar pegs in the early 1970s (starting with sterling in June 1972, followed by the deutsche mark and yen in a rush in February–March 1973), there was still a reluctance to abandon the pegged exchange rate rule (Schenk and Singleton 2011). Most developing and emerging markets retained some form of peg either to the dollar, sterling, SDR, or a trade-weighted basket. Most Western European countries took deliberate steps toward narrower exchange rate margins through the "snake" and plans for economic and monetary union (Mourlon-Druol 2012). During the 1960s, the trade integration of the European economies during the creation of the common market increased the cost of exchange rate fluctuations and led them down an exceptional path to monetary union, which we leave to others to discuss. Meanwhile, the US economy had more to gain from floating (or sinking) the dollar exchange rate while Europe and Japan had more to lose through uncontrolled appreciation of their currencies. The extraordinary tenacity of the appeal of a system based on a pegged exchange rate rule was clearly demonstrated in the ill-fated Smithsonian Agreement of 1971.

In August 1971 President Nixon finally ended the charade of the gold convertibility rule by closing the gold window, abruptly calling time on the efforts to resolve persistent imbalances by threatening a trade war and shifting the responsibility for adjustment to surplus countries. Within the US Treasury and Fed, there was increasing support for jettisoning the exchange rate peg as well, but the interim goal was for greater flexibility at an adjusted rate. The Nixon

Shock also belatedly woke the G10 and the rest of the world to the importance of Japan as a crucial player in coordination. Where the focus during the 1960s had been mainly on German surpluses, Japan was the main target of US pressure for adjustment in the negotiations in 1971. The Smithsonian Agreement rebuilt the pegged exchange rate system at new parities with wider bands, but the credibility of the system quickly evaporated in repeated runs on the dollar, until most countries had abandoned their dollar pegs by the spring of 1973.

As in the 1930s, the system was pulled apart by persistent imbalances, partly caused by two oil price shocks in 1973–74 and 1979. The end of the era of rapid growth with relatively low inflation prompted a loss of confidence among policymakers, and they mostly abandoned efforts at cooperation and coordination in an attempt to shore up their domestic economies. The seemingly endless circus of panels and meetings to reform the international monetary system continued throughout the 1970s in Paris, London, Washington, and Bonn, but there was little consensus on how to achieve stable monetary policy and no rules to underpin efforts at monetary cooperation and coordination.

Instead, the focus turned to how to correct persistent global imbalances through rules to force countries in surplus to adjust their exchange rates (a direct reversal of the burden of adjustment under the Bretton Woods system). Investigations had begun during the Bretton Woods era in the US Treasury as a way to redress the US deficit as well as to introduce greater exchange rate flexibility into the system, drawing on ideas from Richard Cooper (1970) and others (Schenk 2016). The so-called Plan X emerged from a special policy group led by Paul Volcker from 1969. By 1972 (before sterling floated), the proposal was for a set of indicators including the size of reserves to prompt multilateral pressure on a country to adjust its exchange rate. Although not initially gathering support from European states such as France, which were averse to floating exchange rates, the concept retained its attractions and versions re-emerged in the mid-1980s and again in the 2000s as a way to discourage the accumulation of global imbalances. The key lesson from this period was the difficulty of reviving an international rules-based system when domestic policy priorities diverged.

6. Managed floating, 1973 to the present

6.1. 1973 to 1980

The international monetary system switched to a managed floating regime in 1973. Milton Friedman (1953) argued that floating rates had the advantages of insulating the domestic economy from external monetary shocks and giving monetary authorities the independence of conducting monetary policy to satisfy domestic goals without imposing capital controls. According to Friedman, independence from the constraint of pegged exchange rates required monetary authorities to follow stable rules-based monetary policies. His preferred rule was for the Fed to follow a constant money growth rate equal to the growth rate of real GDP adjusted for the trend growth rate of velocity. Otherwise, monetary instability, in addition to producing instability in prices and real income, would also lead to instability in the nominal exchange rate.

It took close to two decades for the Federal Reserve and other central banks (with the principal exceptions of the Bundesbank and the Swiss National Bank) to learn this lesson. The 1970s was a decade of monetary instability manifest in high and variable inflation. This was reflected in exchange rate volatility. There is an extensive literature on the Great Inflation (Bordo and Orphanides 2013). Many attribute it to flawed monetary policy by central banks trying to manipulate the Phillips Curve trade-off to achieve full employment. Others attribute it to the accommodation of supply shocks (Blinder and Rudd 2013). Inflation began to rise in the mid-

1960s and, as mentioned above, contributed greatly to the collapse of the Bretton Woods system.

Monetary authorities engaged in extensive intervention to stem the perceived volatility of exchange rates. The Fed and other central banks believed that foreign exchange markets were inherently unstable and that exchange market intervention was required to keep exchange rates close to their fundamentals and to reduce unexplained volatility (Bordo, Humpage, and Schwartz 2015, ch. 5). It was not until the next decade that the Fed and other central banks learned that stable domestic monetary policy geared to low inflation would reduce instability in nominal exchange rates.

Two of the props designed for the Bretton Woods system were retained through the 1970s. Even though sterling was meant to be floating, the G10 central banks were reluctantly convinced to launch a Third Group Arrangement in February 1977 of $3 billion (equivalent to $28.7 billion today) to finally kill off sterling's residual reserve role (Schenk 2010). This time the coordinated support was contingent on the IMF conditionality from the 1976 stand-by; the G10 had shifted their monitoring responsibilities to the IMF. The prolonged support for the orderly retirement of sterling from 1960 to 1978 was an important example of coordination among central banks to try to avoid a crisis in the global monetary system and manage an orderly transition.

The Fed's central bank swap system also continued, although the exchange rate cover offered to foreign central banks was removed, and as a consequence no G10 foreign central bank drew on the swaps from 1973 to 1980. The Fed, however, increasingly drew on the swap system to support their intervention to stabilize the dollar. By 1978, total facilities totaled $29.4 billion, although, at its highest point (in 1978), outstanding Fed swap obligations amounted to only $5.5 billion. The publicized ceilings had a largely representational purpose to demonstrate the commitment of the partners (Bordo, Humpage, and Schwartz 2014).

Against the background of rising inflation and with the dollar depreciating against the deutsche mark and yen and other currencies, the Federal Reserve engaged in frequent and massive sterilized exchange market intervention. Many of the sales of deutsche marks and yen were financed by borrowing via swap lines with the Bundesbank and other central banks until 1980. Some of the Fed interventions were coordinated with similar operations by the Bank of Japan, Bundesbank, and other central banks. After December 1975, the Fed cooperated closely with other central banks, keeping them informed daily of their actions, although all of the operations in this period were covert. Empirical evidence suggests that much of the intervention had very small and possibly very temporary effects in reversing exchange rate movements. Bordo, Humpage, and Schwartz (2015, 236) concluded that for the 1974 to 1977 period "only 49 per cent of the active interventions to support the dollar and only 64 per cent of the passive interventions to acquire German marks appear successful."

The situation worsened in the next three years. In 1978 the dollar went into a free fall reflecting the Fed's lack of success in arresting inflation. On November 1, 1978, the Carter administration (along with the Fed) announced a massive dollar defense package consisting of a one percentage point increase in the discount rate to 9½%, a $30 billion increase in foreign resources, and closer cooperation with Germany, Japan, and Switzerland. The foreign currency package included a $47.6 billion increase in the Fed's swap lines with these countries. The Treasury also would issue up to $10 billion in German mark and Swiss franc denominated securities, called Carter bonds (Bordo, Humpage, and Schwartz 2015, 243). Massive coordinated exchange market interventions with the Bundesbank and other central banks followed in the next two months. In reaction to these actions, the dollar began appreciating against the mark.

But the evidence for the period September 1977 to October 5 1979 suggests that "despite the changes in amounts, frequency, objectives, and openness, US operations were no more effective than the earlier operations. As in the pre-1977 period, they demonstrated some tendency to moderate exchange rate movements" (Bordo, Humpage, and Schwartz 2015, 247).

In reaction to the volatility in the dollar and the public's reaction to rising inflation and inflation expectations, President Carter appointed Paul Volcker as chairman of the Federal Reserve Board in October 1979 with the mandate to end the inflation. The Volcker shock of October 5, 1979, when the Fed shifted to a tight monetarist-type monetary (nonborrowed reserves) targeting strategy, raised the discount rate, imposed reserve requirements, and allowed interest rates to rise dramatically, eventually broke the back of inflation and inflationary expectations and reversed the decline of the dollar. Similar policies were followed in other countries.

The 1970s was a low point for the IMF as the official hub of international monetary coordination. It was only in 1976 that the IMF finally recognized the legitimacy of flexible or floating exchange rates, and from this time the IMF, seeking a role to replace the one it had lost, turned more resolutely to focus on the interests of developing economies rather than governance of the international monetary system. This effort also brought mixed success as the gap between rich and poor countries widened and many economies accumulated unsustainable amounts of debt, which erupted in the 1982 sovereign debt crisis.

Instead, the mid-1970s gave rise to the G- summits, starting with the G6 at Rambouillet in 1975 and adding Canada in 1976 and then Russia in 1998 to form the G8. These were annual meetings of political leaders supported by finance ministers' meetings and meetings of central bankers. For central banks, of course, the summits supplemented the regular monthly meetings among G10 central bank governors at Basel. The summits generally resulted in rather mundane and repetitive public statements committing the participants to ensuring stable markets, but they also provided an opportunity for sharing of ideas and approaches to global economic challenges informally. The 1975 G7 Summit pledged members to "closer international cooperation and constructive dialogue among all countries" to combat inflation and unemployment, and members resolved that "our monetary authorities will act to counter disorderly market conditions, or erratic fluctuations, in exchange rates." Very similar language is used in the joint declarations ever since, usually with reference to working in conjunction with the IMF. A more ambitious initiative at the Bonn Summit of 1978 saw each government explicitly committed to specific goals of growth, low inflation, and/or fiscal policy "to bring about a better pattern of world payments balances and lead to greater stability in international exchange markets"; it was dubbed "the locomotive." But these efforts were derailed by the second oil crisis so that the next summit at Tokyo in 1979 focused instead on targets to cut oil imports and consumption.

Monetary cooperation via coordinated exchange market intervention (EMI) and other strategies did not work in this period. This was because most central banks did not follow a rules-based policy of keeping domestic inflation low, consistent with being on a floating exchange rate.

6.2. The 1980s

The 1980s saw a return to a consensus in monetary theory and policy. Paul Volcker's success in stemming inflation in the United States was applauded by central bankers and governments across the developed world. An examination of the minutes of the monthly meetings of the G10 central bank governors shows that in the 1970s they shared their common frustrations with their governments' inability to be consistent in their policy guidance and with the ensuing lack of credibility of monetary policy. They wriggled under their lack of independence when orders came from ministries to reverse tight money to promote growth targets at the expense of higher inflation. Through these regular meetings at the BIS, the G10 central bank governors created an epistemic community with shared goals for inflation but also a general commitment to avoiding destabilizing short-term exchange rate changes. As the operational arm for coordination, this forum was important for sharing information, debate, and forming opinion even though they lacked policy independence. This observation goes beyond Eichengreen's (2013a) identification of the Basel Committee on Banking Supervision as an epistemic community to include the formative development of common approaches to monetary policy.

Volcker's policy shift was apparently taken with almost no external consultation (there was advance notice for the Bundesbank) so it cannot be classified as an example of cooperation or coordination. Instead, it set the stage for a new domestic based rule for monetary policy. During the 1970s central bankers had complained to each other at their monthly meetings in Basel about inconsistent ministers and treasury officials, the conflict between inflation and employment targets, and the lack of credibility of their monetary policy in this political environment. Volcker's "unconventional" monetary policy in 1979 was therefore applauded at the subsequent BIS governors' meeting, and Volcker's colleagues asked what they could do to help make the policy effective. Their enthusiasm was tempered by interest rate instability and perceived spillover effects through 1980 and 1981, but they continued to accommodate US monetary policy, and the communication at the monthly Basel meetings no doubt enhanced that process of cooperation through the sharing of information. At the same time, the system of swaps and coordinated short-term intervention to smooth foreign exchange market volatility that had been developed in the 1960s was continued.

The ability to follow a monetary rule was dramatically reinforced by innovations in smaller countries. New Zealand's experiment with central bank independence and transparent inflation targeting set the model for the transformation of the credibility of monetary rules, just as economic theory and understanding of monetary policy was enhanced by the identification of the Taylor rule. By the end of the 1980s, therefore, we had returned to a rules-based system founded on domestic monetary policy actions by independent central banks acting in their own countries' interests, which seemed to generate a lasting period of moderate inflation. But the lingering ambitions for more elaborate coordination had much less success.

While central bankers moved closer to a common understanding on monetary policy, governments and Treasury bureaucrats continued to seek exchange rate stability or at least the "orderly exchange markets" described as the agreed goal in the revised IMF statutes. Exchange rate volatility continued as central banks learned to adopt and operate the new set of domestic monetary rules, and the 1980s witnessed a series of grand-gesture summitry to coordinate exchange rate and fiscal policy that produced mixed results.

The Volcker shock and three years of tight monetary policy led to a decline in inflation from a peak of 15% in 1979 to 3% by the mid-1980s. This led to a marked appreciation in the dollar to advanced countries—by 55% on a trade weighted basis. By 1985 Germany and other countries were complaining about the imbalances, and the Bundesbank had been intervening to offset the depreciating mark. More important, the strong dollar was harming the exports of US manufactured goods and this led to threats in the Congress to raise tariffs. The incoming secretary of the Treasury, James Baker, was a much bigger fan of macroeconomic policy coordination and of EMI than his predecessor, Donald Regan (under whose watch there was only limited EMI). So at the G7 Finance Ministers Summit meeting at the Plaza Hotel in New York City on September 22, 1985, ministers agreed that coordinated EMI would be used to depreciate the dollar. They also agreed that the United States would follow expansionary monetary policy and Japan would do the opposite. Immediately upon the announcement, the dollar declined. However, it had been falling since February 1985, and the increase before the meeting was only a temporary blip. Massive coordinated intervention by the Fed, Bundesbank, and Bank of Japan lasted two weeks, but the evidence that it was successful is limited (Feldstein 1986). On the one hand, Humpage (1988) argued that monetary policy had turned looser well before the Plaza meeting and that this more likely explained the turnaround in the dollar. Bordo, Humpage, and Schwartz (2015, 304) found that the EMI did not have much effect on the exchange rate. On the other hand, Dominguez and Frankel (1993) found that coordinated EMI did have significant effects, and Frankel (2016) argued that the Plaza Accord was a success. However, the part of the agreement that urged Japan to follow tighter monetary policy than would be consistent with macro fundamentals led the Bank of Japan to keep rates higher than would be the case had it followed a Taylor rule in 1986 (IMF 2011; Taylor 2016).

The dollar declined through 1986, leading to concerns that it had fallen too far. Members at the G7 meeting at the Louvre on February 22, 1987, agreed to coordinate policies to stabilize the dollar. This meant coordinated EMI in the opposite direction than at the Plaza, and it meant that Japan would follow more expansionary monetary and fiscal policy while the United States and Germany and the others would keep their macro policies constant. As with the Plaza Accord, there is strong evidence that the EMI had little effect (Bordo, Humpage, and Schwartz 2015), but there were longer lasting effects on the Japanese economy that were devastating. After the Louvre Accord, policy rates deviated in a negative way from a rules-based policy, and many argue that this expansionary monetary policy triggered Japan's asset price boom and bust leading to a serious banking crisis, and to over a decade of stagnation.

6.3. The Great Moderation, 1985 to 2006

By the late 1980s, most advanced countries had low inflation, had adopted central bank independence, and were following rules-based monetary policy. This led to a 20-year period of stable and low inflation, and stable and rapid real growth. Most of the disturbances in the global economy arose in emerging economies rather than industrialized countries at the core of the global trade and financial system.

Beginning in the late 1980s, the Federal Reserve began to turn away from the use of exchange market intervention as a significant policy tool. An extensive debate at the FOMC and in the academy argued that sterilized EMI and credible monetary policy were conflicting goals. By 1995, Chairman Greenspan agreed, and the United States has only undertaken such actions on three occasions since. Also in this period, economists argued, based on game theory and multicountry econometric models, that central banks that pursued credible rules-based monetary policy minimized the spillovers that were believed to have necessitated coordinated policies (Taylor 1985). As it turned out, in this period there were fewer occasions when there was a call for monetary policy coordination other than the mundane statements at G7 summits. Instead, the main focus of cooperation and coordination returned to the lender of last resort role of the 1960s and 1970s.

6.4. Return to lender of last resort

While industrial countries mainly adopted floating or managed floating exchange rates, many emerging market economies with underdeveloped financial systems, and thin and shallow domestic foreign exchange markets, opted for adjustable pegged exchange rates. Through the mid-1980s, many of these economies grew quickly through export oriented industrialization, particularly in East Asia. They were encouraged by the IMF and World Bank to liberalize their capital markets, but their institutions were not strong and this contributed to a rash of financial and currency crises in the 1990s as the dollar appreciated.[5] These episodes were viewed as posing systemic threats via contagion to the advanced countries and prompted calls for international cooperation, with central banks serving as lenders of last resort to supplement the resources of the IMF. The pattern of support packages echoed several aspects of the Basel agreements of the 1960s and 1970s: the reluctance of debtors in crisis to submit to the IMF as a first line of defense, the insistence of creditors on an IMF seal of approval before offering coordinated bilateral support, the preference of central banks and governments to provide only contingent lines of credit that they hoped would not be drawn. But they differed significantly because the operations were bailouts rather than rescues (in the lender of last resort sense) (Bordo and Schwartz 1999, 2000), and this heightened the moral hazard.

In each case (Mexico, Thailand, Indonesia, South Korea, Brazil, Argentina, Russia), the crisis arose from overvalued currencies pegged to the US dollar, which were toppled by a sudden reversal of capital flows that prompted uncontrolled devaluation and a financial crisis. Weak financial sectors, heavy foreign-currency-denominated borrowing, government guarantees, and exuberant investors contributed to the fragility of the system (Bordo and Meissner 2016). In each case the debtor country initially sought to bypass the conditionality of the IMF and activate swaps or bilateral support (Boughton 2012). But, in line with the final coordinated support offered by the G10 to the United Kingdom in the 1970s, creditor countries insisted on an IMF "seal of approval" through a contingent (smaller) standby agreement with a letter of intent. The IMF insisted on devaluation, restructuring financial markets, and fiscal

5. In the 1990s many emerging market countries were advised to adopt firm pegs or currency boards to import credible noninflationary monetary policies.

retrenchment, with mixed success. International policy coordination was thus operated through the IMF Executive Board and then central banks and finance ministers supplemented this credit, often in larger amounts. The difference from the 1960s and 1970s was that the funds were used to bail out creditors rather than as a resource for central banks to gain a breathing space. The coordinated operations therefore created moral hazard that was only partially offset by the IMF-induced restructuring programs (more successful in some countries than others).

We judge that the coordinated response to the emerging market financial crises was not a full success. Although the crises were eventually stemmed and growth returned under more flexible exchange rates, they left a legacy of institutional problems that exposed the weaknesses of these regimes a decade later. The bailouts did not remove the incentive of countries to accumulate substantial precautionary reserve. The fragility of the global system was increased by many countries aiming to run persistent balance of payments surpluses during the 2000s as insurance against a future sudden stop and to avoid the necessity of submitting again to the disciplines of a future rescue package.

While the currency crises of the 1990s pushed most emerging market economies to greater flexibility by 2000, the People's Republic of China became an increasingly important nonconformist. The renminbi exchange rate was not devalued in the wake of depreciations elsewhere in Asia, and this helped to support export recovery in the region as Chinese economic growth accelerated in the run-up to World Trade Organization accession in 2001. From claims that the renminbi was overvalued in the early 1990s, critics soon pointed to China's huge surpluses as proof that the renminbi was undervalued. Capital controls and consistently high growth allowed China to resist calls to appreciate its currency, but the increasingly large and persistent current account surpluses, most of which were unsterilized, came at some cost to price stability, particularly in volatile real estate and other asset markets. At the same time, China's role in the governance of the global monetary system became more and more distant from China's importance in the global economy. In 2005, the renminbi was appreciated slightly and a more flexible regime was adopted to allow an orderly appreciation, although the results were at first somewhat disappointing. China has had a challenging history with the IMF, mainly focused around their historically small quota (and therefore small voting rights), their iconoclastic international monetary policy, and continued exchange controls (Schenk 2015).

After the global financial crisis focused even more attention on the systemic risks of persistent imbalances, China and other large emerging economies were brought more closely into networks of cooperation and coordination through the G20 from 2009, including the renminbi in the SDR in 2016 and the eventual ratification of the 2010 IMF quota enlargement at the end of 2015. But challenges persist because of the nature of the Chinese political regime and slowing growth. Without a shift to open capital markets and liberalization of the financial system (which seems a long way off), China remains a threat to global stability.

Thus the coordinated rescues during the emerging market crises of the 1990s were quite far removed from rules-based policy. First, the rescues were bailouts to countries facing insolvency and not to countries facing a temporary liquidity shortfall, hence violating a key Bagehotian principle and engendering moral hazard for future crises. Second, these countries did not follow rule-like domestic monetary policies because they had not developed sufficiently in the sense of having weak institutional structures and governance and not having deep and liquid financial markets, and in other ways. Some of these countries in recent years have adopted rule-like policies, for example, Mexico and South Korea, but not all, for example, China.

6.5. 2007 to the present

The Great Moderation ended with the subprime crisis of 2007–2008. There is a voluminous literature on the causes of the crisis. The main ones are: departures from rules-based policy fueled the housing boom bust; global imbalances; and lax supervision and regulation of the financial sector that led to the development of mortgage-backed securities and other derivatives combined with excessive leverage (Bailey and Taylor 2014).

The response to the crisis in 2007 was for the central banks individually to follow very expansionary monetary policies. By early 2008, they were worried about a commodity induced inflation and so they stopped expansionary policy. The events of the summer of 2008, leading to the collapse of Lehman Brothers, created a full-scale global financial panic reminiscent of the summer of 1931. This led to massive unprecedented lender of last resort actions (although many did not follow classical Bagehot's rules [Bordo 2014]) by the Fed, the Bank of England, and other central banks. It also led to a reactivation of the swap lines by the Federal Reserve in September 2008 to provide dollar liquidity to the ECB and other foreign central banks who faced dealing with the liquidation of the dollar denominated mortgage-backed securities and other toxic derivatives held by their banks. This cooperative policy may have averted a global panic. Indeed, something similar might have averted the international aspect of the meltdown of 1931.

In addition to the swaps, at the G20 Summit in Washington, DC in November 2008, leaders of the G20 committed themselves "to stabiliz[ing] financial markets and support[ing] economic growth," with particular emphasis on "the importance of monetary support" as well as fiscal expansion. They also committed themselves anew to reforming the architecture of the international financial system, and the governing board of the BIS was extended to allow nine other central banks to be members.

By the end of 2008, the financial crisis had ended, but the real economy was still contracting and the federal funds rate and other central bank's policy rates had hit, or were close to, the zero lower bound. The Fed announced its policy of quantitative easing (QE1) in December 2008—the unconventional policy of large-scale open market purchases of long-term Treasury securities and agency mortgage-backed securities. In addition to the purchases, the Fed began forward guidance to manage financial markets expectations. The Bank of England similarly engaged in quantitative easing from March 2009 and forward guidance from August 2013, related to a target unemployment rate of 7%. The ECB followed in May 2009. Japan had a longer history of QE from March 2001 to 2006 and renewed its policy in October 2010. These initiatives were successful in arresting the Great Recession by June 2009 in the US, but the recovery that followed has been anemic. Further, the spillover effects have been controversial.

QE policies deployed by advanced economies were particularly criticized for adverse effects on emerging market countries, primarily through capital flows and exchange rates. Investors surged into emerging markets, increasing asset prices and appreciating currencies. These spillover effects undermined export competitiveness, increased exchange risk on debt, and threatened asset price bubbles. In May 2013, when Federal Reserve Chairman Ben Bernanke suggested that QE would be "tapered," volatility in emerging market asset prices led to renewed calls for greater coordination. The specter of the interwar crisis returned, and (as in the interwar period) there were calls for greater monetary cooperation to avert a "currency war" (described in Eichengreen 2013b).

The extent and cause of spillover effects is disputed. Certainly, US monetary policy has global implications because of the importance of US capital markets and the role of the dollar. Spillover effects appear greatest when Fed announcements surprise the markets, and there is evidence that these effects were greater after the global financial crisis than before it (Chen et al. 2014). However, there are structural factors in emerging market economies which can make them more resilient to spillovers—such as higher growth, stronger balance of payments, lower share of local debt held by foreigners ex-ante, and liquidity of financial markets. The evidence seems to suggest that advanced economies should avoid surprises and carefully signal their policy to the market while emerging market economies should reinforce their economic fundamentals and market liquidity to increase their resilience.

Moreover, allowing a free float of the exchange rate ensures that emerging markets can target independent monetary policy on domestic price stability (and in the short-run output stability also known as flexible inflation targeting) even in the presence of spillovers. If monetary policy is instead aimed at exchange rate stability or promoting exports, then there may well be challenges for emerging market economies to absorb spillovers (Ammer et al. 2016). Taylor (2016) argued that it is deviations from rules-based policies since 2002 that have led to the spillovers and that the solution is to return to the policies followed in the Great Moderation. The case that greater monetary cooperation is a necessary solution to spillover effects is not proven.

But there is also evidence of externalities that promote procyclicality and systemic risk in financial markets, which has prompted calls for macroprudential policymaking to increase financial stability (Claessens 2015). These policies may complicate the effective use of monetary policy dedicated to low inflation.

At the November 2008 G20 meeting (as the world clamored for a solution and villains were identified), new institutions were created to provide fora for cooperation. The IMF was tasked with monitoring spillover effects, publishing an annual report. The Financial Stability Board (2009) brings together central banks, finance ministries, and supervisory agencies to encourage "coherent implementation" of good practice and implement agreed-upon standards and codes, undertaking peer reviews of macroprudential policy frameworks. While easily dismissed as "talking shops," the exchange of information, ideas, and communication may bear some fruit in the long term in creating consensus around a common or agreed-upon framework of rules.

7. Conclusions

A number of conclusions follow from our survey;

1. Monetary policy cooperation generally is successful when done in a rules-based environment. This was the case under the gold standard and in the Great Moderation. Cooperation in these regimes was done for technical or lender of last resort reasons and supported the communication needed to develop a shared consensus about what rule was best.
2. Monetary policy cooperation does not work when domestic and international policy priorities are inconsistent, that is, when an international policy rule (for example, exchange rate stability) conflicts with domestic goals of price stability or full employment. Thus, the agreed-upon international rules conflicted with domestic priorities during the interwar gold exchange standard, the Bretton Woods system, and the early 1980s. Under the classical gold standard and during the Great Moderation, by contrast, the nominal anchor rules were consistent with price stability.
3. It follows that short-term efforts at international monetary policy coordination do not work when they involve a departure from domestic policy fundamentals, for example, Long Island 1927 and the Plaza and Louvre accords.
4. The coordinated rescues of the emerging countries in the financial crises of the 1990s were mainly bailouts and were not based on Bagehot's principles. This promoted future risky behavior. Moreover, in a number of cases, the recipients did not graduate to the

monetary policy strategies of the advanced countries, leading to later instability. Recent cooperation, largely through the BIS, has helped to create an epistemic community of central banks that has learned to follow rules-based policy. This has been beneficial but will be challenged by the addition of new members to the BIS governing board and by the proliferation of multiagency groups.

5. A return to a rules-based system under floating exchange rates now that the Great Financial Crisis is long past would provide an environment conducive to stable economic growth and low inflation for the world, as was the case during the Great Moderation.

The evolution of central bank cooperation and coordination since the classical gold standard has closely followed the evolution of central bank credibility (Bordo and Siklos 2014, 2016). Under the classical gold standard, central banks had high credibility because the gold standard rule was primarily a domestic rule and the international gold standard rule followed from that (Bordo and Kydland 1995). Central bank cooperation was perfectly consistent with that arrangement. In the Great Moderation, central banks enjoyed high credibility because under floating exchange rates they learned to follow domestic rules-based policy focused on price stability and had the independence to pursue their targets consistently.

But in the intervening seven decades, central bank credibility declined because the underlying theoretical and political economy framework dramatically changed towards maintaining domestic aggregate demand and full employment along with fixed exchange rates and the gold convertibility rule—an impossible task, which became evident in the interwar and, later, the Bretton Woods era, even with capital controls. Central bank cooperation and coordination was effectively used to prop up the Bretton Woods system through short-term fixes, but ultimately these regimes were doomed by the growing inconsistency of policy goals. It took the strains of the Great Inflation to create the learning environment to restore central bank credibility and identify a sustainable rule based on domestic monetary policy.

References

Ahamed, L. 2009. *Lords of finance: The bankers who broke the world.* New York: Penguin.

Ahrend, R. 2010. Monetary ease: A factor behind financial crises? Some evidence from OECD countries. *Economics: The Open Access, Open Assessment E Journal* 4: 1–30.

Ammer, J., M. de Pooter, C. Erceg, and S. Kamin. 2016. International spillovers of monetary policy. IFDP Notes.

Attard, B. 1992. The Bank of England and the origins of the Niemeyer Mission, 1921–1930. *Australian Economic History Review* 32 (1): 66–83.

Bailey, M., and J. Taylor. 2014. *Across the great divide: New perspectives on the financial crisis.* Washington, DC: Brookings Press.

Bazot G., M. D. Bordo, and E. Monnet. 2016. International shocks and the balance sheet policy of the Banque de France under the classical gold standard. *Explorations in Economic History* Volume 62 (October 2016): 87–107.

Bernanke, B. 1995. The macroeconomics of the Great Depression: A comparative approach. *Journal of Money Credit and Banking* 27 (1): 1–28.

Blinder, A., and J. Rudd. 2013. The supply shock explanation of the Great Stagflation revisited. In *The Great Inflation: The rebirth of modern central banking,* ed. M. Bordo and A. Orphanides, 119–180. Chicago: University of Chicago Press.

Bloomfield, A. I. 1959. *Monetary policy under the international gold standard, 1880–1914.* New York, Federal Reserve Bank of New York.

Bordo, M. 1981. The classical gold standard, 1880–1914: Some lessons for today. *Federal Reserve Bank of St. Louis Review* (April).

Bordo, M. 1984. The gold standard: The traditional approach. In *A retrospective on the classical gold standard, 1821–1931,* ed. M. D. Bordo and A. J. Schwartz. Chicago: University of Chicago Press.

Bordo, M. 1993. The Bretton Woods international monetary system: A historical overview. In *A retrospective on the Bretton Woods system: Lessons for international monetary reform,* ed. M. D. Bordo and B. Eichengreen, 3–108. Chicago: University of Chicago Press.

Bordo, M. 2014. Rules for a lender of last resort: An historical perspective. In *Frameworks for central banking in the next century: A special issue on the occasion of the Founding of the Federal Reserve*, ed. M. D. Bordo, W. Dupor, and J. B. Taylor. *Journal of Economic Dynamics and Control* (December).

Bordo, M., O. Humpage, and A. J. Schwartz. 2014. The evolution of the Federal Reserve swap lines since 1962. *IMF Economic Review* 63 (May): 353–72.

Bordo, M., O. Humpage, and A. Schwartz. 2015. *Strained relations: US foreign exchange operations and monetary policy in the twentieth century*. Chicago: University of Chicago Press.

Bordo, M., and F. Kydland. 1995. The gold standard as a rule: an essay in exploration. *Explorations in Economic History* 32: 423–64.

Bordo, M., and J. Landon-Lane. 2012. Does expansionary monetary policy cause asset price booms: Some historical and empirical evidence. Sixteenth Annual Conference of the Central Bank of Chile, Santiago.

Bordo, M., and R. MacDonald. 2005. Interest rate interactions in the classical gold standard, 1880–1914: Was there monetary independence? *Journal of Monetary Economics* 52: 307–327.

Bordo, M., and C. Meissner. 2016. Fiscal and financial crises. *North Holland Handbook of Macroeconomics*, (eds.) John B. Taylor and Harald Uhlig. New York: North Holland Publishers.

Bordo, M., and A. Orphanides. 2013. *The Great Inflation: The rebirth of modern central banking*. Chicago: University of Chicago Press.

Bordo, M., and A. J. Schwartz. 1999. Under what circumstances past and present have international rescues of countries in financial distress been successful? *Journal of International Money and Finance* 18 (4): 683–708.

Bordo, M., and A. J. Schwartz. 2000. Measuring real economic effects of bailouts: Historical perspectives on how countries in distress have fared with and without bailouts. *Carnegie Rochester Conference Series on Public Policy* 53 (December): 81–167.

Bordo, M., and P. Siklos. 2014. Central bank credibility, reputation, and inflation targeting in historical perspective. NBER Working Paper 20693.

Bordo, M., and P. Siklos. 2016. Central bank credibility: An historical and quantitative exploration. In *Central banks at a crossroad: What can be learned from history*, ed. M. Bordo, O. Eitrheim, M. Flandreau, and J. Qvigstad. New York: Cambridge University Press. 62–144.

Borio, C., and G. Toniolo. 2005. One hundred and thirty years of central bank cooperation: A BIS perspective. BIS Working Paper 197.

Boughton, J. 2012. *Tearing down walls: The International Monetary Fund 1990–1999*. Washington, DC, IMF.

Chen, K., T. Mancini-Griffoli, and R. Sahay. 2014. Spillovers from US monetary policy on emerging markets: Different this time? IMF Working Paper 240.

Claessens, S. 2015. An overview of macroprudential policy tools. *Annual Review of Financial Economics* 7: 397–422.

Clarke, S. V. O. 1967. *Central bank cooperation 1924–31*. New York: Federal Reserve Bank of New York.

Cooper, R. 1970. Flexing the international monetary system: The case for gliding parities. In *The international adjustment mechanism*, Federal Reserve Bank of Boston, reprinted in *The international monetary system: Essays in world economics*, by R. N. Cooper, 87–102. MIT, 1987.

Despres, E., C. Kindleberger, and W. Salant. 1966. The dollar and world liquidity: A minority view. *Economist* 5 (February): 526–29.

Dominguez, K., and J. Frankel. 1993. *Does foreign exchange intervention work?* Washington, DC: Institute for International Economics.

Eichengreen, B. 1992. *Golden fetters*. New York. Oxford University Press.

Eichengreen, B. 2010. *Exorbitant privilege: The rise and fall of the dollar and the future of the international monetary system*. New York: Oxford University Press.

Eichengreen, B. 2013a. International policy coordination: The long view. In *Globalization in an age of crisis: Multilateral economic cooperation in the twenty-first century*, ed. R. Feenstra and A. M. Taylor, 43–82. Chicago: University of Chicago Press.

Eichengreen, B. 2013b. Currency war or international policy coordination? *Journal of Policy Modeling* 35: 423–33.

Eichengreen, B., M. Flandreau, A. Mehl, and L. Chitu. 2017. *International currencies past, present and future: Two views from economic history*. New York: Oxford University Press (forthcoming).

Emminger, O. 1967. Practical aspects of the problem of balance of payments adjustment. *Journal of Political Economy* 75 (9): 512–22.

Feldstein, M. 1986. New evidence on the effects of exchange rate interventions. NBER Working Paper 2052.

Ferguson, N., and M. Schularick. 2012. The "Thin Film of Gold": Monetary rules and policy credibility. *European Review of Economic History.*

Flandreau, M. 1997. Central bank cooperation in historical perspective: A skeptical view. *Economic History Review* 50 (4): 735–63.

Frankel, J. 2015. International coordination. NBER Working Paper 21878 (January).

Frankel J. 2016. The Plaza Accord 30 years later. In *International monetary cooperation: Lessons from the Plaza Accord after thirty years,* ed. C. F. Bergsten and R. A. Green, 53–72. Washington, DC: Peterson Institute for International Economics.

Friedman, M. 1953. The case for floating exchange rates. In *Essays in Positive Economics,* ed. M. Friedman, 157–203. Chicago: University of Chicago Press.

Friedman, M., and A. J. Schwartz. 1963. *A monetary history of the United States 1867 to 1960*. Princeton: Princeton University Press.

Garber, P. 1993. The collapse of the Bretton Woods fixed exchange rate system. In *A retrospective on the Bretton Woods system: Lessons for international monetary reform*, ed. M. Bordo and B. Eichengreen, 461–94. Chicago: University of Chicago Press.

Giovannini, A. 1993. Bretton Woods and its precursors: Rules versus discretion in the history of international monetary regimes. In *A retrospective on the Bretton Woods system: Lessons for international monetary reform*, 109–47, ed. M. Bordo and B. Eichengreen. Chicago: University of Chicago Press.

Goodhart, C. 2011. *The Basel Committee on Banking Supervision: A history of the early years*. Cambridge: Cambridge University Press.

Humpage, O. 1988. Intervention and the dollar's decline. *Federal Reserve Bank of Cleveland Economic Review* 2492: 2–16.

International Monetary Fund. 2011. Did the Plaza Accord cause Japan's lost decades? *World Economic Outlook* box 1.4 (April).

Irwin, D. 2013. The French gold sink and the Great Deflation *Cato Papers on Public Policy* 2: 3–45.

James, H. 2016. International cooperation and central banks. In *Oxford Handbook of Banking and Financial History,* ed. Y. Cassis, R. Grossman, and C. R. Schenk, 364–394. Oxford: Oxford University Press.

Keynes, J. M. 1925. *The economic consequences of Mr. Churchill.* Reprinted in *Keynes collected writings*, vol 9. London: MacMillan.

Keynes, J. M. 1943. Proposals for an International Clearing Union. In *The International Monetary Fund, 1945–1965: Twenty years of international monetary cooperation*, by J. K. Horsefield, 1969, vol. 3, *Documents,* 19–36. Washington DC: International Monetary Fund.

Kindleberger, C. 1986. *The world in depression 1929–1939.* Rev. ed. New York: Penguin.

Kydland, F., and E. Prescott. 1977. Rules rather than discretion: The inconsistency of optimal plans. *Journal of Political Economy* 85: 473–91.

McCauley, R. N. Does the US dollar confer an exorbitant privilege? *Journal of International Money and Finance* 57: 1–14.

McCauley, R. N., and C. R. Schenk. 2015. Reforming the international monetary system in the 1970s and 2000s: Would an SDR substitution account have worked? *International Finance* 18 (2): 187–206.

Meltzer, A. 2003. *A history of the Federal Reserve vol 1: 1913–1951*. Chicago: University of Chicago Press.

Mourlon-Druol, E. 2012. *A Europe made of money: The emergence of the European monetary system*. Ithaca: Cornell University Press.

Nurkse, R. 1944. *International currency experience*. Geneva: League of Nations.

Polanyi, K. 1944. *The Great Transformation*. London: Farrar and Rinehart.

Rueff, J. 1961. The West is risking a credit collapse. *Fortune,* July.

Schenk, C. R. 2010. *The decline of sterling: Managing the retreat of an international currency 1945–92*. Cambridge: Cambridge University Press.

Schenk, C. R. 2015. China and the International Monetary Fund 1945–1985. In *History of the IMF: Organization, Policy and Market*, ed. K. Yago, Y. Asai, and M. Itoh, 275–309. Tokyo: Springer.

Schenk, C. R. 2017. Coordination failures during and after Bretton Woods. In *From Great Depression to Great Recession: The elusive quest for international policy cooperation*, ed. M. Qureshi and A. Ghosh. Washington, DC: International Monetary Fund (forthcoming).

Schenk, C. R., and J. Singleton. 2011. Basket pegs and exchange rate regime change: Australia and New Zealand in the mid–1970s. *Australian Economic History Review* 51 (2): 120–49.

Schenk, C. R., and T. Straumann. 2016. International monetary policy regimes: Historical perspectives. In *Central banks at a crossroad: What can be learned from history,* ed. M. Bordo, O. Eitrheim, M. Flandreau, and J. Qvigstad, 319–55. New York: Cambridge University Press.

Singleton, J. 2011. *Central banking in the twentieth-century*. Cambridge: Cambridge University Press.

Solomon, R. 1982. *The international monetary system*. New York: Harper and Row.

Taylor, J. 1985. International coordination in the design of macroeconomic policy rules. *European Economic Review* 28: 53–81.

Taylor, J. 2013. International monetary coordination and the Great Deviation. *Journal of Policy Modelling* 35: 463–72.

Taylor, J. 2016. A rules-based cooperatively managed international monetary system for the future. In *International monetary cooperation: Lessons from the*

Plaza Accord after thirty years, ed. C. F. Bergsten and R. A. Green, 217–36. Washington, DC: Peterson Institute for International Economics.

Temin, P. 1989. *Lessons from the Great Depression.* Cambridge: Harvard University Press.

Toniolo, G., with P. Clement. 2005. *Central bank cooperation at the Bank for International Settlements, 1930–1973.* Cambridge: Cambridge University Press.

Triffin, R. 1960. *Gold and the dollar crisis.* New Haven: Yale University Press.

Tullio, G., and J. Walters. 1996. Was London the conductor of the international orchestra, the second violinist, or the triangle player? *Scottish Journal of Political Economy* 43: 419–43.

Williamson, J. 1977. *The failure of world monetary reform, 1971–1974.* Sunbury on Thames: Thomas Nelson.

DISCUSSION BY ALLAN MELTZER

Today's paper is another in the long list of excellent historical surveys by Michael Bordo and his many coauthors. This time the topic is the changing role of cooperation and coordination in international monetary arrangements as the international system evolved from the classical gold system through the gold exchange system of the 1920s to Bretton Woods and finally to floating exchange rates with areas of regionally fixed exchange rates and considerable intervention.

Although some countries suspended the standard on occasion, the classical gold standard is an example of successful rule-based market coordination of policy action. A member was obligated to increase or reduce reserves and interest rates in response to gold flows. Full-time adherents like Britain generally avoided disruptive discretionary actions. The future gold exchange rate was as certain as it could be. Once that rule-based arrangement for policy coordination ended in 1914, it was never fully restored. Subsequent arrangements never achieved the degree of cooperation that existed under the pre–World War I gold standard because they did not prevent discretionary policy action as the classical gold standard had. Bretton Woods came closest but only in the early years when the United States followed the rules. By the mid-1960s, the United States and the Europeans could not agree to cooperate by adopting a rule for adjusting the misaligned dollar exchange rate.

I liked the section on the working of the gold exchange standard because it is not often examined so thoroughly. Despite efforts by Benjamin Strong and Montagu Norman to restore much of the automaticity of gold standard rules for coordination, British responses to economic problems, French lack of cooperation, and capital flows to the New York equity market were not subject to rules for cooperation and coordination. In fact, as Bordo and Schenk report, efforts to cooperate by assisting Britain in 1927 aroused members of Congress. Some later accused Strong of causing the Great Depression by cooperating with British efforts to maintain the gold exchange rate. This suggests the widespread ignorance about or opposition to gold standard rules.

My succinct summary of the main lesson learned from the exchange rate policies that followed the gold exchange standard is that no system of fixed or floating rates can achieve exchange rate stability as long as major countries do not adopt and follow rules for monetary policy. The most frequent violation of a monetary rule arises when governments finance expansive or contractive fiscal policies by issuing or reducing debt and expanding or contracting money growth by buying or selling government bonds or other assets. Countries' commitments to rules for cooperation and coordination are not often strong enough to counter domestic pressures to spend to reduce unemployment rates or respond to other major changes such as an oil shock.

Two very different ways of maintaining exchange rate stability have been tried since World War II.

Keynes tried to manage international coordination by getting countries to agree to a rule for fixed but adjustable exchange rates. Under the Bretton Woods system, governments could use fiscal and monetary actions for domestic economic stabilization, but their actions were limited by the fixed exchange rate. Keynes innovation was an IMF rule that allowed countries to adjust exchange rates rather than deflate, but the rule required IMF approval of the change. Early on, France violated the rule by devaluing without IMF approval. The rule was not enforced.

As Bordo and Schenk note, the United States was the more important cause of Bretton Woods's failure. The Johnson administration ran large budget deficits. By the 1960s, Chairman Martin accepted that the Federal Reserve had to keep interest rates from rising by financing administration budget deficits. By doing so, he abandoned the principle on which the Fed was founded that barred the Fed from financing government spending and deficits.

The Martin Federal Reserve concerned itself with domestic policy, leaving the exchange rate and trade deficit to the Treasury. During the Johnson administration, each new exchange rate crisis brought new regulations and restrictions, but the actions were temporary palliatives that neither permanently changed the real exchange or enforced monetary rules. International cooperation at the time was limited.

The Nixon administration appointed Paul Volcker as Undersecretary for Monetary Affairs. Within a few weeks of taking office, Volcker wrote about the need to devalue the dollar. He proposed taking two years to reach agreement with the other members on an adjustment of the dollar exchange rate. After two years, he said, the United States would have to act unilaterally. Little more than two years later, President Nixon suspended gold payments.

Bordo and Schenk discuss the short life of the Smithsonian Agreement that devalued the dollar. The United States did not change policy to support a cooperative agreement, and other countries did not support the dollar. After the new international agreement failed, Treasury Secretary Shultz floated the dollar. The new arrangement did not restrict government monetary and fiscal policies or outlaw exchange rate intervention. Soon after, the Arab oil countries raised the oil price in an effort to recoup losses caused by dollar devaluation. The first oil shock imposed real as well as monetary changes in all countries. Countries pursued their separate interests with no coordination attempted.

The Federal Reserve and some other central banks misinterpreted the change in the relative price of oil as evidence of inflation. Contractionary policy actions introduced additional exchange rate adjustment. At the end of the 1970s, the Federal Reserve repeated the misjudgment or error by treating a second oil price increase as evidence of increased inflation. Markets efforts to find equilibrium exchange rates failed. No one could correctly anticipate future policy. Exchange rates reflected the prevailing uncertainty about current and future policy.

Talk of unstable floating rates, as is often done, seems misplaced. The problem is best described as absence of a policy rule guiding major countries, especially the United States, because the dollar continues to serve as the principal international currency.

Those who claim that greater exchange rate stability without a monetary rule would improve economic outcomes should look at the ECB. It has a fixed nominal exchange rate but lacks an agreed-upon rule for adjusting real exchange rates. There is no agreement among the members on a monetary rule. Principal members France and Germany follow very different, incompatible policies.

The European Central Bank has a negative interest rate to encourage expansion. President Draghi should look across the border to Switzerland, where the Swiss National Bank has a negative interest rate to discourage capital inflow. The negative rate has slowed the Swiss economy from an average of above 2% to less than 1%. The ECB and the SNB cannot both be right. I believe the data support the Swiss.

During the period from 1986 to 2002, Alan Greenspan more or less followed a Taylor rule at the Fed. This produced the best long period outcome in Federal Reserve history. Uncertainty declined, and exchange rates were relatively stable. Economists call it the Great Moderation. Stable monetary policy also reduced exchange rate variability.

Current Federal Reserve policy responds to current or recent announcements of economic data. Policy actions are ad hoc and unpredictable. The Fed gives out no information that could be used to predict its medium term actions. It probably does not have a medium-term strategy. Any cooperation with other central banks is entirely ad hoc.

To sum up, what do we learn from more than 100 years of exchange rate policy? I draw three major lessons from the more than one hundred years of history that Bordo and Schenk summarize for us. First, the way to increase exchange rate stability, whether of fixed or floating rates, is to reduce policy uncertainty. If the exchange rate floats, the central bank should adopt and follow a monetary rule. The rule should include an enforcement mechanism and restrictions on fiscal actions. Second, rules enforced by market responses, like the classical gold standard, are likely to work better than rules that leave enforcement to central banks. Domestic pressures in most countries are usually much stronger than commitments to international cooperation. Third, the Federal Reserve has not developed either a domestic strategy or decided on its responsibilities as the world's major currency.

Finally, a few words about actual current and recent exchange rate policy. After the bad prewar experience with competitive devaluation in the late 1930s, major countries agreed at Bretton Woods that they would avoid competitive devaluation, called at the time "beggar thy neighbor policy." The Bernanke Fed broke that promise and hid their action by calling it QE. The correct name was competitive currency depreciation. Japan and the ECB followed. Both called their actions QE presumptively to hide what they were doing.

As in the 1930s, competitive devaluations have not brought export growth. They have two main effects on third countries. If they expand output in the devaluing country, some third countries might experience an increase in their exports. But this effect currently seems small. All third countries experience a rise in their exchange rate when the dollar, euro, or yen depreciate. The current problems of the third world suggest they have been hurt on balance. There is no cooperation, no coordination because there is no policy rule. Restoring the agreement to rule out competitive devaluation should be high on the monetary reform agenda.

GENERAL DISCUSSION

ANDREW LEVIN: I want to follow up on something that Secretary Shultz said. He referred to this era of social media and instant communications around the world. I'm wondering, the tradition of central banks meeting in relative confidentiality or secrecy, depending on how you want to characterize it, at the Bank for International Settlements and other forums, obviously has benefits. But there are also costs. And I'm just wondering how the two of you view that. Is it time for a change? The same kind of discussions have happened about trade agreements. In the old days, those were made behind closed doors and not released until the very end. To the extent to which central banks do cooperate or coordinate, how transparent should it be?

CATHERINE SCHENK: There is obviously a tradeoff between transparency and effectiveness sometimes, and maybe it depends on what it is that you're trying to achieve. I think that the difficulties and challenges of going through the International Monetary Fund diverted a lot of energy back through the BIS, and that has its advantages and disadvantages. In the longer term, it made countries very averse to going to the IMF for support. It led to the precautionary accumulation of insurance reserves, for example after the 1990s. So there are dangers to that kind of publicity as well. I think, talking about the BIS group, looking at the minutes—and I know there are no official minutes, but the Reserve Bank of New York representatives took verbatim minutes, and they can be found in their files—there is argument, quite frank argument, amongst the central bankers. And that's partly because they're not being observed, and they don't feel they're being recorded. And there is a move towards an understanding of sharing of best practice, of operational skills, and tools and instruments, that is possible in that kind of environment, that wouldn't be if it were more public.

ALLAN MELTZER: Andy, I think the strength of congressional pressures, market pressures, the pressures of the unemployed or those who are suffering from inflation, are just too strong in democratic countries these days to be able to have coordinated policies of that kinds. So the best that we can hope for, I would think, would be that each country would follow a rule, and then you could at least, to a much greater extent than you can at present, figure out for yourself what the likely effect of that will be over the near term and over the medium term. We don't have the gold standard, not because people don't know about the gold standard, but because they do. It's a standard that maintains exchange rate cooperation. What the public wants is macroeconomic coordination.

CHRISTOPHER ERCEG: The ability of central banks to achieve their monetary policy objectives clearly depends on financial stability, and financial stability in turn depends on effective cross-border macroprudential regulation, given the potential for large financial spillovers across national borders. In this vein, I am interested in knowing if you are any more sanguine or optimistic about the possibilities for effective macroprudential policy coordination across countries, particularly in economies in Europe that would seem to face significant challenges.

MICHAEL BORDO: I'm somewhat pessimistic about that. Because of the European Union and Economic and Monetary Union, the Europeans need to do more coordination. Indeed, for Europe to succeed, it must have a banking union like we have. But for other countries, I'm not so sure. These issues are being discussed at the BIS today, and that is a good thing. Information sharing, especially, via the BIS is very helpful. But trying to constrain sovereign countries to do things that they wouldn't have done otherwise will always backfire.

CATHERINE SCHENK: And can I just add, in terms of the Basel Committee and the Basel process, Basel I, Basel II, Basel III—they were always responding to the last crisis, so it is quite a backward looking and prolonged process that incorporates the banks in developing the regulations for themselves. It's the Basel process that brought in the rating agencies; it's sort of fundamental to the credit risk weighting and that sort of thing. So I'm also quite critical, I think, of that aspect.

ALLAN MELTZER: The great problem in trying to get financial stability is to try to get market solutions to these things. I testified four times in the Dodd-Frank hearings. Eventually, I helped to write a bill with Senator David Vitter, and he was wise enough to make it a bipartisan bill by getting a Democratic liberal senator to sign on to it. But the banks, especially the New York banks, opposed it. So it never got into committee. The pressure is from the big banks to regulate to their benefit, and so, What has been the result of that? We had, not very long ago, 1,400 banks in the United States. We're now down to around 550. The middle-sized banks are going out of business. They're the people who used to do the lending to small and medium-sized startups. They didn't do it on the basis of income sheets and balance statements. They did it on the basis of being local and knowing the character of the borrowers. That part of America is rapidly disappearing because of the heavy cost of regulation under Dodd-Frank and the low interest rates, so they can't find loans to make to these people at interest rates where they want to take on the risk. So we're losing an important part of the mechanisms that created growth and new enterprises in this country.

HARALD UHLIG: I always learn important insights when I hear Mike Bordo and coauthor Catherine Schenk talk about economic history. So one thing that struck me in particular was the story that essentially the 1927 clandestine meeting on Long Island, where the New York Fed decided to help out the pound sterling, subsequently triggered the expansion in the stock market, the subsequent stock market crash, and the subsequent depression. That's almost what it sounded like. I mean, that statement strikes me as wild, but if you say to us that it's true, I would imagine just highlighting that more and bringing it out more would be interesting. If it's really true, it sounds like you should never, ever allow central bankers across the world to meet. Right? That's such a disastrous outcome, and I'm probably happy about the forces that Allan described about domestic considerations nowadays being much more important in preventing that sort of really disastrous type of coordination. Is that the sort of conclusion you'd like to draw from the analysis? I'm just wondering, because that's how it sounded to me.

The second thing is you also emphasized that, going forward, it would be nice to go back to a rule-based regime. And that sounds all good and nice, and then I thought, What rules? Right? I think what the financial crisis has shown to us, all those Eurobank considerations and so forth, is that all the nice rules that we used to preach and teach our students, they're kind of all out of the window. I mean, what do we do now? I can't follow the Taylor rule if there is a zero lower bound. Is the Friedman rule a good one? What rule? Where's the solution to that one coming from? I guess you're saying, we should get back to the drawing board and find some good rules that will be useful in the future.

MICHAEL BORDO: The jury is out on the 1927 meeting as a catalyst to the disasters that followed but other factors like major Fed monetary policy mistakes are more important. Liaquat Ahamed's *Lords of Finance*, nicely dramatizes this story. That said, it is not clear that Benjamin Strong's actions in 1927 were the bellows that fueled the fire, that led to the assets price boom, that led to the crash. There is some evidence, however, and Friedman and Schwartz and others discuss it, that the policy was not necessarily dictated by fundamentals and that the Fed was following too expansionary a policy. How much? We don't know. What happened was that several years later in 1931, after Benjamin Strong's death, Carter Glass and one of the governors of the Federal Reserve, Adolph Miller, picked up on this, and, and they blamed him for all that had happened. Then Herbert Hoover in his memoirs in 1951 said that, if it hadn't been for Benjamin Strong and Montagu Norman (governor of the Bank of England), he would have stayed in office for another term. And so this is where the story comes from. But the evidence is not overwhelming that 1927 was the key cause of the Great Contraction.

With respect to the second issue, I'm thinking in terms of something like a Taylor rule, in an environment where we have already moved beyond quantitative easing and are getting back towards conditions that prevailed during the Great Moderation. What our survey tells us is that if you have a rules-based system, you tend to do better. And then going forward, the question of what rule to be picked is another question.

CHRISTOPHER MEISSNER: I thought Chris Erceg's point was really interesting, and I was going to bring up something similar, maybe something to follow up with. Two other examples of coordination or lack thereof, domestic monetary policy in the United States in the 1920s and 1930s—Gary Richardson and Billy Troost showed major disagreements about the correct response to banking panics. Does that fit your model? I don't know. And then what about European monetary system crises of the early 1990s. I didn't notice it in the paper. I only skimmed through it, but where is that situated in this idea?

CATHERINE SCHENK: I'll take the 1990s maybe. We have pushed Europe to one side. It is an exceptional story towards economic and monetary union. We've heard a little bit about it here today. I don't think it's a successful example of international monetary coordination, as we're seeing, and we'll see how long it lasts. So the European Exchange Rate Mechanism (ERM) in the 1990s—again it follows a period where there's a decline in average deflation rates, and there seems to be some kind of convergence during the ERM period but also a lot of disruptive departures, of course in 1992 and elsewhere.

ROBERT KAPLAN: Given that, over the last number of decades, manufacturing as a percentage of GDP by country has changed dramatically, and the nature of global trade has changed dramatically; I would think those shifts would have an impact on the issue of exchange rate policy coordination. How do you think about that? How might these shifts impact the way we think about attempts to coordinate policy?

MICHAEL BORDO: I'm not quite sure I understand why that would matter. But here's what I think, if what you're saying is that, because there's been much more of a move toward services and financial services, that creates a potential for instability, which we didn't have before. Perhaps the difference in structure matters, but I am not sure about it. I still think if you just look at the record and follow the message that comes out of our paper, which is that, if rules-based policies are followed, these problems could be dealt with regardless of the composition of output and trade. I'm just not quite sure why it would matter.

ALLAN MELTZER: I would think that the main way in which it would show up would be in the current account deficits, that is, if the short-term—certainly maybe longer-term—has effects on the current account deficit. If you're following a monetary rule and allowing exchange rates to float, then you get at least a response. It may not be a perfect response, but you get a response to the shifts in the current account deficits.

BILL ENGLISH: I have a question for Michael. I think you use the term "rules-based policy," but it isn't clear to me what you mean by "rules-based policy." Alan Greenspan in 1990 or so probably didn't know he was following something along the lines of a

Taylor rule. He thought he was making policy from meeting to meeting. But nonetheless, I guess you view him as having been rules-based. What about Paul Volcker? I'm not sure Volcker should be seen as a rules-based policymaker. He certainly generated a lot of policy surprises. If he was rules-based, I'd be interested to know what the rule was.

ALLAN MELTZER: I don't know what Alan Greenspan had in his mind, but if you look at what he did, and compare it to what you would do if you were more or less following a Taylor rule, they look pretty similar. Now I say that because Alan Greenspan was much too wise to say publicly that he was going to commit himself to any rule. That would be a signal to all the people who didn't like what he was doing to complain about what he was doing and blame the rule. So I don't know about that. Volcker was not following a rule. Volcker was following something that the Fed, to its unbelievable mistake, paid attention to. He looked at what was happening to money and credit, and the current Fed, as I understand it pays interest on reserves so it can keep the money growth from rising.

CHAPTER SIX

Rules-Based International Monetary Reform

John B. Taylor, Richard Clarida, and George P. Shultz

PART 1

An International Monetary System Built on Policy Rules and Strategies

John B. Taylor

For nearly two decades in the 1980s and 1990s, economic performance and stability improved in major parts of the world as monetary policy tended to be more focused and rules based. During much of the past decade, monetary policy has deviated from a rules-based approach in much of the world, and economic performance and stability has deteriorated, remaining poor today. As Paul Volcker (2014) has put it, "the absence of an official, rules-based, cooperatively managed monetary system has not been a great success."

In these remarks I discuss a new approach to international monetary policy. The proposed reform is based on years of experience and economic research which suggest that a rules-based reform in each country will deliver a rules-based international monetary system that "can better reconcile reasonably free and open markets

---

These remarks were presented at the conference on International Monetary Stability: Past, Present, and Future, Hoover Institution, Stanford University, and are based on Taylor 2016a. More details and related issues are discussed in Taylor 2016b and 2016c.

with independent national policies [and] stability," the sensible goal called for by Volcker (2014).

I start with a review of the economic principles that indicate that such a rules-based policy will lead to good global economic performance. I then provide evidence—consistent with those principles—that shows that adhering to more rules-based policy has been associated with good performance while deviating from rules-based policy has been associated with poor economic performance. Building on this experience and the principles, I then describe the reform proposal and its implementation.

The international monetary system: A rules-space or strategy-space approach

Economic research going back to the 1980s showed that simple rules-based monetary policy would result in good global economic performance (Carlozzi and Taylor 1985; Taylor 1985). In this research, the monetary policy of each central bank was viewed as a rule or strategy for the instruments of policy, and questions of international coordination or cooperation were addressed in "rules-space" or "strategy-space" rather than in terms of the setting for the policy instruments. If each central bank adopted a rules-based monetary policy that was optimal for its own country's price and output stability, it would contribute to global stability. Moreover, there would be little additional gain from the central banks also jointly optimizing their policy rules or strategies. In other words, the research showed that the Nash equilibrium—where each country chose its monetary strategy taking as given other countries' strategies—is nearly optimal, or nearly an internationally cooperative equilibrium.

In the models used in this research, capital is mobile, which is largely appropriate for the modern global economy, and rigidities exist, including the fact that prices and wages are sticky. There are cross-country linkages: the price of foreign imports affects domestic prices, and the real exchange rate affects output. Shocks from abroad can hit anywhere. Monetary policymakers face a macroeconomic tradeoff between price stability and output stability, and they have the task of finding a policy strategy in which they adjust their monetary policy instrument to reach an optimal point on that tradeoff. The strategy must respond to shocks while not creating its own shocks either domestically or internationally.

The tradeoff is like a frontier. Monetary policy cannot take the economy to infeasible positions off the frontier. But suboptimal monetary policy—due to policy deviations, reacting to the wrong variables, and other factors—can take the economy to inferior points off the tradeoff. Along the frontier, lower price variability can only be achieved with greater output variability corresponding to different values of the reaction coefficients. The existence of such a tradeoff is quite general, and the modeling framework has been used in many different monetary policy studies going back to the 1970s and continuing today.

The important result for international policy is that such models imply that the central bank's choice of a policy *strategy* has little impact on output and price stability tradeoff in the other countries. The tradeoffs for other countries are virtually the same regardless of which optimal policy strategy is chosen by each country. This is the sense in which there is little to be gained by countries coordinating their choice of policy rules with other countries if all are following policy rules that are optimal domestically.

The converse situation where monetary policy in one or more countries does not follow an optimal rule is less clear-cut theoretically because it requires defining the nature of the deviation. Nevertheless, the tradeoff concept can be used to illustrate how such deviations from an optimal policy rule can lead to a breakdown in the international system.

Suppose a country deviates from its policy rule and moves in the direction of an inefficient policy. There are two types of impacts on other countries. First, the tradeoff in other countries shifts in an unfavorable direction, perhaps due to more volatile capital flows, exchange rates, commodity prices, and export demand. Second, less efficient monetary policy in one country brings about a less efficient monetary policy in other countries. For example, if the policy change in one country brings about an excessively easy policy with very low interest rates, then the policymakers in other countries—concerned about exchange rate appreciation—may deviate from their policy rule by setting interest rates that are too low.

History has validated many of these theoretical predictions. As the United States and European central banks moved toward rules-based monetary policies, economic performance improved in the 1980s and 1990s, especially when compared with the instability of the 1970s. Evidence for this shift in policy was provided early on by Clarida, Gali, and Gertler (2000). When central banks in many emerging market countries started moving toward more rulelike policies with their inflation targeting approach, economic performance also improved, as shown by De Gregorio (2014).

During the past decade, however, policy has changed. I refer here to the departures from rules-based policy before and after the panic in the autumn of 2008, not to the lender of last resort actions taken by the Fed and other central banks during the panic. Empirical research by Ahrend (2010), Kahn (2010), and Taylor (2007) shows that a deviation from rules-based policy in the United States and other countries started more than a decade ago—well before the financial crisis. Hofmann and Bogdanova (2012) and Shin (2015) show that there has been a "Global Great Deviation," which is continuing, as can be seen especially when unconventional central bank interventions and large-scale balance sheet operations are included. Nikolsko-Rzhevskyy, Papell, and Prodan (2014) uncover these changes in policy using modern time-series techniques. Associated with the change has been deterioration in economic performance, including the Great Recession, the slow recovery, large negative international spillovers, and an increase in the volatility of capital flows and exchange rates. Policymakers in emerging market countries, including Agustin Carstens (2015) and Raghuram Rajan (2016), have noted the adverse spillovers, and many have had to resort to unusual policy actions. Policymakers in developed countries, including Japan and Europe, have reacted to the adverse exchange rate effects of monetary policies. International economists have raised concerns about currency wars.[1]

While there is general agreement about the first shift in policy in the early 1980s, there is still disagreement about the second shift and its timing. An alternative view is that the monetary policies have been appropriate during the past dozen years, even if they are not rulelike, and the recent deterioration in economic performance was not due to monetary policy deviating from a rules-based approach. Mervyn King (2012) argues that the policy tradeoff in many countries shifted in an unfavorable direction because financial stability eventually bred instability as investors got complacent. "Relative to a Taylor frontier that reflects only aggregate demand and cost shocks," he writes, "the addition of financial instability shocks generates what I call the Minsky-Taylor frontier."

And there is also disagreement about the international spillovers and the related problems with the international monetary system. Bernanke (2013) argues that it was appropriate for coun-

1. See Bergsten (2013).

tries around the world to deviate during the years from 2009 to 2013 from the policies that worked during the 1980s and 1990s.

Empirical evidence on global effects

Because of these disagreements about the more recent shift in policy and especially the international impacts, it is important to look for and examine evidence that bears on this shift and its effects.

According to the IMF's main multicountry monetary model, GPM6 described in Carabenciov et al. (2013), the impact of a deviation from a monetary policy rule in the United States has impacts on real output around the world. A deviation which initially causes the US interest rate to decline results in a negative effect on output in Latin American emerging economies (including Brazil, Chile, Colombia, Mexico, and Peru) and Asian emerging economies (China, India, South Korea, Indonesia, Taiwan, Thailand, Malaysia, Hong Kong, Philippines, and Singapore). For each percentage point monetary-policy-induced increase in output in the United States, output falls by .25 percentage points in the Latin American countries and by .13 percentage points in the emerging Asian countries. As described by the builders of the IMF's GPM6 model, this occurs because "the exchange rate channel is stronger than the direct output gap effect." The impact on other developed economies' output is not negative, but it is quite small. For example, Japan's output increases by only about 1/20th of the US output increase in the model.

Note that these simulations contradict the view that deviations from the rules-based policy are beneficial abroad. Bernanke (2013) argued that "The benefits of monetary accommodation in the advanced economies are not created in any significant way by changes in exchange rates; they come instead from the support for domestic aggregate demand in each country or region. Moreover, because stronger growth in each economy confers beneficial spillovers to trading partners, these policies are not 'beggar-thy-neighbor' but rather are positive-sum, 'enrich-thy-neighbor' actions." The policy simulations do not support an enrich-thy-neighbor view.

Given these simulations it is not surprising that policy deviations at one central bank put pressures on other central banks to deviate also. A reduction in policy interest rates abroad causes their exchange rate to appreciate, and even with offsetting effects due to economic expansion abroad, the overall spillover effect may well be negative. For the emerging market countries in Latin America and Asia, the exchange rate effect dominates. Central banks will tend to resist large appreciations of their currency, and one way to do so is to reduce their own policy rate relative to what it would be otherwise. This will reduce the difference between the foreign interest rate and the domestic interest rate and will thus mitigate the appreciation of their exchange rate.

There is considerable empirical evidence of the impact of foreign interest rates on central bank decisions.[2] The best evidence comes from central bankers themselves, many who readily admit to these reactions in conversations. The Norges Bank provides a great deal of detail about its decisions and the rationale for them. In 2010, for example, the Norges Bank explicitly reported that it lowered its policy interest rate because interest rates were lower abroad. It also reported that a policy rules with external interest rates included came much closer to describing the actual decisions than the policy rules without external interest rates.

Regressions or estimates of policy rules provide considerable evidence of the international spread of central bank policies. The recent work of Edwards (2015), Carstens (2015), and Gray (2013) is quite definitive. The usual approach is to estimate policy rate reaction functions in which the US federal funds rate or other measures of foreign interest rates are entered on the right-hand side as

---

2. See Taylor (2013) for more details.

deviations from their respective policy rules. The usual finding is that the reaction coefficient on the foreign rate is positive, large, and significant.

In addition, this type of deviation from interest rate policy rules can create large international multiplier effects. In a two-country model in which one central bank's policy rate has a response coefficient of .5 on the second central bank's policy interest rate and the second central bank has a response coefficient of 1 on the first central bank's interest rate, an initial cut in interest rate results in a reduction in global interest rates of twice as much.

Just as interest rate policy deviations can be transmitted globally, so can quantitative easing. Following the financial crisis and the start of the US recovery from 2008 to 2012, the yen significantly appreciated against the dollar while the Fed repeatedly extended its large-scale asset purchases along with its zero interest rate policy with little or no response from the Bank of Japan. However, the adverse economic effects of the currency appreciation in Japan became a key issue in the 2012 election, and, when the Abe government came into power, it urged the Bank of Japan to implement its own massive quantitative easing, and this is exactly what happened. As a result of this change in policy, the yen reversed its course and depreciated to the same levels as those before the panic of 2008. In this way the quantitative easing policy of one central bank appeared to cause quantitative easing at another central bank.

The moves of the ECB toward quantitative easing in the past year seem to have similar motivations. An appreciating euro was, in the view of the ECB, a cause of the weak European economy, and the response was to initiate another large round of quantitative easing. At the Jackson Hole conference in August 2014, Mario Draghi spoke about his concerns about the strong Euro and hinted at quantitative easing. This shift in policy was followed by a weaker euro and a stronger dollar.

These actions were accompanied by widespread depreciations of currencies in emerging market countries as capital flows reversed. The dollar index rose sharply against a large group of countries: Mexico, China, Taiwan, Korea, Singapore, Hong Kong, Malaysia, Brazil, Thailand, Philippines, Indonesia, India, Israel, Saudi Arabia, Russia, Argentina, Venezuela, Chile, and Colombia. The Taper Tantrum of May–June 2013, in which the Fed first indicated it was going to wind down QE, was a big turning point for currency markets and capital flows.

With these currency developments in the background, the actions of China to start to let the yuan move with other currencies and away from the dollar in August 2015 are understandable. There is also econometric evidence that quantitative easing has an impact on monetary policy decisions abroad. Chen et al. (2012) find that "the announcement of QE measures in one economy contributed to easier global liquidity conditions."

Concerned about the ramification of deviating from their normal monetary policy, many central banks have looked for other ways to deal with the impacts of policy deviations abroad. These include imposing capital controls, the proliferation of macroprudential tools, and currency intervention.

Controls on capital flows, or what the IMF staff calls "capital flow management," are usually aimed at containing the demand for local currency and its appreciation, but they also mitigate risky borrowing and volatile capital flows. However, capital controls create market distortions and may lead to instability as borrowers and lenders try to circumvent them and policymakers seek even more controls to prevent the circumventions. Capital controls are one reason why the output and price stability frontier will shift adversely. Capital controls also conflict with the goal of a more integrated global economy and higher long-term economic growth.

Currency intervention is another way countries try to prevent unwanted changes of a currency, either as an alternative, or as a supplement, to deviations of interest rates from normal policy. Currency intervention has been used widely in recent years by many emerging market countries. However, currency interventions can have adverse side effects even if they temporarily prevent appreciation. If they are not accompanied by capital controls, they require a change in monetary policy (nonsterilization) to be effective.

The spread of macroprudential policies is another impact of monetary policy deviations from abroad. This is most obvious in small open economies closely tied to the dollar. With low interest rates, those central banks have had no choice but to resort to discretionary interventions in housing or durable goods markets. These policies are also becoming more popular in inflation targeting countries with flexible exchange rates. But so-called macroprudential actions are inherently discretionary, and they expand the mission of central banks and bring them closer to politically sensitive areas. They also run the risk of becoming permanent even after unconventional policies abroad are removed. A regulatory regime aimed at containing risk-taking is entirely appropriate, but that entails getting the levels right, not manipulating them as a substitute for overall monetary policy.

The flows of capital in and out of emerging markets as well as the recent swings in exchange rates seem quite related in time to changes in monetary policy. Regarding the volatility of capital flows, Rey (2014) writes that "our VAR analysis suggests that one important determinant of the global financial cycle is monetary policy in the center country, which affects leverage of global banks, credit flows and credit growth in the international financial system." Carstens (2015) showed that there has been a marked increase in volatility of capital flows to emerging markets since the recent deviation from rules-based policy began. Regarding exchange rate movements, there has also been an increase in volatility. The 12-month percent change in the US dollar index against "major" currencies as defined by the Federal Reserve (Euro Area, Canada,

Japan, United Kingdom, Switzerland, Australia, and Sweden) has showed an increase in volatility.

A proposal for implementing a rules-based international monetary system

The evidence indicates that the key foundation of a rules-based international monetary system is simply a rules-based monetary policy in each central bank. There is already an established body of research showing that the move toward rules-based monetary policy in the 1980s led to improved national and international performance in the 1980s and 1990s. And, although more research is needed, economic evidence indicates that the recent spread and amplification of deviations from rules-based monetary policy in the global economy are drivers of current instabilities in the international monetary system. Finally, research shows that each country following a rules-based monetary policy consistent with achieving national economic stability—and expecting other countries to do same—would take the world toward an international cooperative equilibrium.

The process of each country reporting on its monetary policy strategy and agreeing to commit to that strategy can be an important means of building this foundation. It is essential that the process not impinge on other countries' domestically optimal monetary strategies. Emerging market countries should be part of the process. A clear commitment by the Federal Reserve—still the world's most significant central bank, with responsibility for the world's most significant currency—to move in this rules-based direction would help start the process.

The barriers to implementing an international agreement along these lines may be surprisingly low. Of course some form of renormalization of monetary policy, or at least intent to renormalize, is needed. After that come goals and strategies for the instruments of policy to achieve the goals. The major central banks now have explicit inflation goals, and many policymakers use policy rules that describe strategies for the policy instruments. Thus, explicit statements about policy goals and strategies to achieve these goals are feasible. That there is wide agreement that some form of international reform is needed would help move the implementation along.

Such a process poses no threat to either the national or international independence of central banks. It would be the job of each central bank to formulate and describe its strategy. Participants in the process or parties to the agreement would not have a say in the strategies of central banks in other countries or currency unions other than that they be reported. And the strategies could be changed or deviated from if the world changed or if there was an emergency. A procedure for describing the change in strategy and the reasons for it would presumably be part of the agreement.

Many policymakers and economists have called for reforms of the international monetary system, reflecting concerns about instabilities, international policy spillovers, volatile capital flows, risks of crises, or simply less than stellar economic performance. I already cited Paul Volcker (2014). In addition, Jaime Caruana (2012) at the Bank for International Settlements has been researching the issues and also making proposals. Raghuram Rajan (2016) argues that "what we need are monetary rules that prevent a central bank's domestic mandate from trumping a country's international responsibility." Hélène Rey (2014) argues that we need macroprudential policies or even capital controls to slow down the flow of capital that she connects to independent monetary policy actions.

The approach suggested here is supported by historical experience and extensive research over the years. It is attractive because each country can choose its own independent strategy, avoid interfering with the principles of free and open markets, and contribute to the common good of global stability and growth.

References

Ahrend, R. 2010. Monetary ease: A factor behind financial crises? Some evidence from OECD countries. *Economics: The Open Access, Open Assessment E-Journal* 4.

Bergsten, C. F. 2013. Currency wars, the economy of the United States and reform of the international monetary system. Stavros Niarchos Foundation Lecture. Peterson Institute for International Economics, Washington, May 16.

Bernanke, B. 2013. Monetary policy and the global economy. Speech at the Department of Economics and Suntory and Toyota International Centres for Economics and Related Disciplines (STICERD), London School of Economics, London, March 25.

Carabenciov, I., C. Freedman, R. Garcia-Saltos, D. Laxton, O. Kamenik, and P. Manchev. 2013. *GPM6: The global projection model with 6 regions*. IMF Working Paper WP/13/87. Washington, DC: International Monetary Fund.

Carlozzi, N., and J. B. Taylor. 1985. International capital mobility and the coordination of monetary rules. In *Exchange rate management under uncertainty*, ed. J. Bhandhari. Cambridge: MIT Press.

Carstens, A. 2015. Challenges for emerging economies in the face of unconventional monetary policies in advanced economies. Stavros Niarchos Foundation Lecture, Peterson Institute for International Economics, Washington, DC, April 20.

Caruana, J. 2012. Policymaking in an interconnected world. Paper presented at the Federal Reserve Bank of Kansas City Policy Symposium on The Changing Policy Landscape, Jackson Hole, August 31.

Chen, Q., A. Filardo, D. He, and F. Zhu. 2012. *International spillovers of central bank balance sheet policies*. BIS Paper 66p. Basel, Switzerland: Bank for International Settlements.

Clarida, Richard, Jordi Gali, and Mark Gertler. 2000. "Monetary Policy Rules and Macroeconomic Stability: Evidence and Some Theory," *Quarterly Journal of Economics* 115, 1 (February): 147–180.

De Gregorio, J. 2014. *How Latin America weathered the global financial crisis*. Washington, DC: Peterson Institute for International Economics.

Edwards, S. 2015. Monetary policy independence under flexible exchange rates: An illusion? NBER Working Paper 20893. Cambridge, MA: National Bureau of Economic Research.

Gray, C. 2013. Responding to a monetary superpower: Investigating the behavioral spillovers of US monetary policy. *Atlantic Economic Journal* 21 (2): 173–184.

Hofmann, B., and B. Bogdanova. 2012. Taylor rules and monetary policy: A global Great Deviation? *BIS Quarterly Review*, September.

Kahn, G. A. 2010. Taylor rule deviations and financial imbalances. *Federal Reserve Bank of Kansas City Economic Review* 2nd quarter: 63–99.

King, M. 2012. Twenty years of inflation targeting. Stamp Memorial Lecture, London School of Economics, London, October 9.

Nikolsko-Rzhevskyy, A., D. H. Papell, and R. Prodan. 2014. Deviations from rules-based policy and their effects. In *Frameworks for central banking in the next century*, ed. Michael Bordo and John B. Taylor. Special issue, *Journal of Economic Dynamics and Control* 49 (December): 4–18.

Rajan, R. 2016. New rules for the monetary game. *Project Syndicate*, March 21.

Rey, H. 2014. Dilemma not trilemma: The global financial cycle and monetary policy independence. In *Global dimensions of unconventional monetary policy*, symposium sponsored by the Federal Reserve Bank of Kansas City, Jackson Hole, WY, August 22–24, 2013.

Shin, H. S. 2015. Macroprudential tools, their limits and their connection with monetary policy. Presented at IMF conference entitled Rethinking macro policy III: Progress or confusion?

Taylor, J. B. 1985. International coordination in the design of macroeconomic policy rules. *European Economic Review* 28: 53–81.

Taylor, J. B. 2007. Housing and monetary policy. In *Housing, housing finance, and monetary policy*. Federal Reserve Bank of Kansas City, September: 463–76.

Taylor, J. B. 2013. International monetary coordination and the Great Deviation. *Journal of Policy Modeling* 35 (3): 463–72.

Taylor, J. B. 2016a. A rules-based cooperatively managed international monetary system for the future. In *International monetary cooperation: Lessons from the Plaza Accord after thirty years*, ed. C. F. Bergsten and R. Green, 217–36. Washington, DC: Peterson Institute for International Economics.

Taylor, J. B. 2016b. The Federal Reserve in a globalized world economy. In *The Federal Reserve's role in the global economy*, ed. M. Bordo and M. Wynne, 195–217. Cambridge: Cambridge University Press.

Taylor, J. B. 2016c. Rethinking the international monetary system. *Cato Journal* 36.2 (Spring/Summer): 239–50.

Volcker, P. A. 2014. Remarks. Bretton Woods Committee Annual Meeting, Washington, DC, June 17.

PART 2

National Monetary Policies often Correlate, May Sometimes Coordinate, but Rarely Cooperate (And That's Probably a Good Thing!)

Richard Clarida

The topic of this panel is "rules-based international monetary reform," and my goal is not only to offer a perspective informed by macroeconomic models that give a prominent role to policy rules but also, by my ongoing effort as a student of global monetary policy—and of the two panelists I am sharing the stage with—to square those models with what we (think we) see in the world. The title of this note reveals the punch line: we *observe* that national monetary policies are often correlated (eras of global monetary easing; global rate hike cycles), and they also *appear* sometimes to be coordinated (after all, what else are central bankers doing at all those G7, G20, IMF, and Basel meetings?), but rarely (if ever) do major central banks respect a binding commitment to pursue cooperative policies, policies that would differ from non-cooperative policies aimed solely at satisfying their objectives for domestic inflation and employment. It has long been well appreciated (Taylor 1985) that, in small- or large-scale open economy macro models, the calibrated gains to international monetary policy cooperation (see, for example, Obstfeld and Rogoff 2002) are found to be modest relative to the welfare achieved under a Nash equilibrium in which each country runs a sensible policy, taking as given the (sensible) policy of the other countries. Today, I will make a somewhat different and less often discussed case against global monetary policy cooperation, namely, that, in practice, adopting it—or succumbing to it!—could plausibly erode central bank credibility and public support for sound, rules-based policies. If I'm right, the all-in cost to a regime of policy cooperation could swamp the theoretical benefits, and, if so, we should not bemoan the absence of formal monetary policy cooperation—we should celebrate it!

In a world in which policy rules provide (or should provide) an important reference point and anchor for monetary policy, international monetary policy *coordination*—which I define as including the sharing of information and analysis regarding estimates of the unobservable inputs to policy rules such as the equilibrium real rate of interest and potential output as well as the considerations that would govern the timing and trajectory of a baseline policy (rule) path as well as triggering deviations from such a path—can enhance the design and effectiveness of baseline policy rules. I will give examples below. But while international monetary policy *coordination* may enhance the efficiency of a policy rule framework if it is in place, I am skeptical that in practice there are additional material, reliable, and robust gains that would flow from a formal regime of binding monetary policy *cooperation*, at least among major G7 economies and even a number of emerging economies with flexible exchange rates and relatively open capital accounts. In such a regime, national monetary policies in *each* country are constrained to be set so as to jointly maximize *world* welfare. In these models, as in the earlier literature they build on, there are externalities to monetary policy that create such theoretical gains to cooperation. However, as Clarida, Gali, and Gertler (2002) and Engel (2009) illustrate in "new Keynesian" models, to achieve the theoretical gains to international monetary policy cooperation, policy rates in *each* country must be set with reference to an index of inflation deviations from target in both *the home and the foreign countries.* In other words, whereas optimal policy in the absence of cooperation can be implemented with a policy rule that reacts to domestic inflation, output gaps, and the appropriately defined equilibrium—or neutral—real interest rate, a policy increasing global welfare must bind central banks to policy rules that react to *foreign* as well as domestic inflation, policy rules that they would not chose were they not bound.

I believe that, in practice, beyond the time consistency problem, there could well be another problem with policy cooperation that is absent from most theoretical discussions. Simply stated, the problems as I see them are the threat to the credibility of the central bank, the challenges to central bank communication, and the resulting potential loss of support for its policy actions from the public when the policy choices required by cooperation react not only to home inflation but also to deviations of foreign inflation from target. For example, if home inflation is above target but foreign inflation is below target, the optimal policy rule under cooperation calls for the home (real) policy rate to be lower—more accommodative—than it would be in the absence of cooperation (Clarida, Gali, and Gertler 2002). In theoretical models, the commitment to the inflation target is just assumed to be perfect and credible, but in practice credibility appears to be a function of central bank communication and of the policies actually implemented pushing inflation toward—and, in the absence of shocks, keeping inflation at—target. I suspect that, in practice, central banks would have a hard time maintaining credibility as well as communicating a policy that kept home real interest rates low—or in extreme cases negative—not because home inflation is too low but because foreign inflation is too low! Or, imagine the opposite case, with home inflation below target when foreign inflation is above target. In this case, the optimal policy rule under cooperation calls for the home (real) policy rate to be higher—less accommodative—than it would be in the absence of cooperation, not because home inflation is too high but because foreign inflation is!

While, perhaps for these reasons, we do not have many confirmed sightings of genuine monetary policy *cooperation,* we do perhaps observe rather more examples of what I think of as policy *coordination.* The Clarida, Gali, and Gertler (2002) model provides an illustration of the value of policy coordination in the noncooperative Nash equilibrium of that two-country model. In the "home" country, the optimal Nash monetary policy rule can be written as a forward-looking Taylor rule:

$$R_t = \overline{rr}_t + \left(1 + \frac{\lambda(1-\rho)}{\alpha\rho}\sigma_0 + \frac{\lambda}{\rho}\right)E_t\pi_{t+1} + \alpha\tilde{y}_t$$

where $\overline{rr}_t$ is the equilibrium real interest rate consistent with the flexible price equilibrium given by

$$\overline{rr}_t = \sigma_0 E_t\{\Delta\overline{y}_{t+1}\} + k_0 E_t\{\Delta y^*_{t+1}\}.$$

Here $\sigma_0 = \sigma - \gamma(\sigma - 1) > 0$, $\kappa_0 = \gamma(\sigma - 1)$, and Δy^*_{t+1} is growth in foreign output with $1 / \sigma < 1$ the intertemporal elasticity of substitution, $\gamma < 1$ the share of imports in the consumption basket, λ the slope of the open economy Phillips curve, ρ the persistence of "cost push" shocks, and α the relative weight the policymaker places on stabilizing output. Thus, the best Nash policy in this two-country model is a Taylor type rule for setting the policy rate as a function of expected home inflation, the home output gap y_t, and time varying equilibrium home real interest rate, *which is a function of expected foreign output growth!* In the baseline specification $\kappa_0 > 0$, the equilibrium real interest rate that is relevant for setting home monetary policy depends on expected foreign, as well as home, output growth. Thus, to the extent the foreign central bank has some comparative advantage in tracking or forecasting foreign output growth and the foreign equilibrium real interest rate, sharing this information with the home central bank can improve its estimate of the home equilibrium real interest rate and thus the effectiveness of its policy rule in meeting its domestic objectives.

As discussed above, to achieve the theoretical gains from monetary policy cooperation in these models, it no longer suffices for the policymaker to follow an instrument rule based solely on domestic variables. Instead, under cooperation the home central bank must set the policy rate as a function of home and foreign variables. In its simplest form, this rule can be written as

$$R_t = \overline{rr}_t + \left(1 + \frac{\lambda(1-\rho)}{\alpha\rho}\sigma_0\right) E_t\pi_{t+1} + \frac{\kappa_0}{\kappa}\left(\frac{\lambda(1-\rho)}{\alpha\rho}\sigma_0\right) E_t\pi^*_{t+1}$$

with the parameter $\kappa > 0$. In sum, not only do the quantitative gains from time inconsistent cooperative monetary policy rules appear to be modest, but also the policy rules required to implement the cooperative outcome could well be difficult to communicate and to adhere to without sacrificing the credibility of the inflation target and the policy regime itself.

To conclude, we have reviewed some simple examples based on rigorous models which can (1) generate monetary policy correlation via the global factor present in each country's equilibrium real interest rate; (2) rationalize the alleged benefits to monetary policy coordination; but (3) provide some intuition for why binding monetary policy cooperation is rare in practice if not in academic papers.

References

Clarida, R., J. Gali, and M. Gertler. 2002. A simple framework for international monetary policy analysis. *Journal of Monetary Economics* 49: 879–904.

Engel, C. 2009. Currency misalignments and optimal monetary policy: A reexamination. Mimeo. University of Wisconsin, January.

Obstfeld, M., and K. Rogoff. 2002. Global implications of self-oriented national monetary rules. *Quarterly Journal of Economics* 117 (May): 503–536.

Taylor, J. 1985. International coordination and the design of macroeconomic policy rules. *European Economic Review* 28: 53–81.

PART 3

Reforming the International Monetary System in Practice

George P. Shultz

I'm going to tell three stories—first, about international monetary reform; second, about saving the monetary system while not bailing out firms; and, third, about the dangers of monetary policy drifting away from market principles. Then I'll make two observations about the Federal Reserve that are relevant for reform.

International monetary reform through diplomacy, negotiation, and prayer

The first story involves the international exchange rate system. The story begins when I was director of the Office of Management and Budget. It was obvious that the United States couldn't keep the gold window open. There was too much demand; it would end Fort Knox. So the gold window was closed in August 1971, and that meant the exchange rate system was totally shifted around, and it was sort of sloppily floating. John Connally, who was secretary of the Treasury—it was the Treasury's responsibility—developed something called the Smithsonian Agreement in December 1971, which really didn't work. I kept asking the Treasury people what their plan was, and they said it was a secret. So then I become secretary of the Treasury in June 1972, and I say, "Okay, what's the plan?" They say, "We don't have one," and I say, "Okay, that's what I thought."

I had a terrific consultant. His name was Milton Friedman. And Paul Volcker was my undersecretary. Milton thought—and I agreed with him—that we should have a much more flexible exchange rate system, and Paul kept pointing out that that wouldn't sell internationally. The Europeans, the Japanese, all wanted something more formal, a par value system. And so through discussion, we designed a floating exchange rate system in the clothing of a par value system. It was very clever. Milton was a big contributor. He was a good consultant, and the price was right: it didn't cost anything. The idea was that we'd have a par value system, but the par values would change automatically when the reserve balances changed. So we proposed this system. We had it all written out, and I orchestrated it within the US government. Arthur Burns even signed on, which was hard. We had the big World Bank/IMF meeting coming up in September 1972, and the president was to speak, and I was to speak. I took a draft over to the president and said, "Mr. President, here's your speech." He looked it over and said, "That's not my speech, that's your speech." And so he goes before this big gathering and says, "Tomorrow my secretary of Treasury will unveil the United States' plan." The pressure was on.

So I did something that seemed natural to me, but I learned later it had never been done before. I invited the finance ministers of the key countries—France, Germany, Japan, Britain—to come in and look at my speech and give me their observations, so they all did. And they were good people, such as Helmut Schmidt and Valéry Giscard d'Estaing. Later, Takeo Fukuda was added to this group. They looked at it, and nobody touched the structure of the speech, but they all had little changes and words they thought would go down a little easier. I took practically all of their suggestions, so the speech I read had a usual kind of support. And I think in the spirit of those days, people didn't do what the United States wanted, necessarily. But when the United States comes to the party with ideas, and substance, and readiness to discuss, constructive outcomes take place. That's leadership in these areas, and in that way we reached an international agreement.

These discussions led to the formation of a little group that came to be called the Library Group. As a means to facilitate a meeting between all these countries, I mentioned to the president that I wanted to have a meeting before the IMF/World Bank meetings. He said, "Well, I'm not going to be in the White House that weekend. Why don't you use the White House? It'll give your meeting a little class." So we met in the library on the ground floor of the White House. It's a beautiful room with a fireplace.

At the time, a larger group of 20 countries was supposed to be working on reform, but it was too unwieldy to get anything done. Everyone knew the key countries had to come together and figure out what they thought, but nobody wanted the whole world to know that. You wanted a meeting to happen, but you didn't want everyone to know. So we met, and we said, "Well, we've got to have a name for our group that doesn't disclose what it's about," so we decided to call ourselves the Library Group. And we became very good friends in the sense that members of the group were always candid about their views and what they intended to do, so that developed trust.

I learned a lot from this process, which served me well when I was secretary of state. One of my observations in these international meetings and other kinds of dealings is that trust is the coin of the realm. You've got to be able to develop that kind of relationship with people.

Then there was the Arab oil boycott and the huge increase in the price of oil that had enormous international financial implications. So in the winter of 1974, there was a meeting in Rome of the finance ministers of the world, and two things happened there that impressed me. First, Takeo Fukuda, who was there as the finance minister of Japan, took me aside and said, "George, you're going to be visited by a stream of businesspeople and bankers and other officials from Japan complaining about me. So I want to explain to you what I'm doing." He said, "Inflation in Japan right now is out of control. I, Fukuda, am going to wring inflation out of the Japanese system, and I know how to do it, namely, restrict the money supply." Then he said, "And I am going to run the policy; I have a deal with the LDP, my party, that I, Fukuda, alone am in charge of economic policy."

So when people did come and complain, I supported my friend Fukuda and he brought about the softest landing from an inflation problem I think anyone has ever done. It was a beautiful piece of work.

The other thing that I remember about that time in Rome involved my late wife, O'Bie, who was a devout Irish-Catholic girl. Somehow, I managed through the White House to arrange a private audience with the Pope, knowing that it would be a high point of her life. So we go to the Vatican, and we are put in a little holding room. A rather severe monsignor comes out and looks at me and says, "When the Holy Father is ready, you will come in for ten minutes." And he looks at my wife and says, "And then you will come in for two minutes, during which time there will be pictures." And he leaves.

We look at each other: well, if that's the deal, that's the deal. A little while later, out comes an American cardinal, who says, "The Holy Father's ready! Come on in!" So I start to go in, and my wife hangs back. "Come on in, come on in!" he says. So we both go in. And we start talking with the Pope about oil prices and the financial repercussions and the impact on the poor countries. I'm astonished at how much the Pope knows about the subject. He was well versed and a lot of his instincts were very much compatible with what we in the US delegation were saying in these meetings. Fifteen minutes go by, half an hour goes by, three-quarters of an hour go by, and we're still talking. And I say to myself, maybe it's up to me to bring this to an end, and I ought to do it on a humorous note. So I say, "Your Holiness, the finance ministers of the whole world have been meeting for two full days and nothing we've been able to think of has done as much good in dealing with this problem as the mild weather we're having this winter. We thank you for your intervention." He did not laugh. He said, "Mr. Secretary, you can be sure it will continue." And I noticed we had another mild winter the following year, so it's not all economics.

Saving the monetary system without bailouts

My second story also begins when I was at the Office of Management and Budget. In 1970, I have just become the director, so I'm finding out what's happening on a broader scale than I did as secretary of labor. I find out there's a company named the Penn Central (a big financial organization) that has mismanaged its affairs and is about to go bankrupt. I also find out that Arthur Burns, the chairman of the Fed, thinks that this would put big stress on, maybe destroy, the financial system. And he has arranged through a reluctant David Packard, who was deputy secretary of defense, for what amounted to a bailout.

I think it's a lousy idea, for obvious reasons, so I'm arguing with Arthur and half of me is saying, "What am I doing arguing with Arthur Burns about financial markets? I'm a lousy labor economist. What do I know?" But I had some views. At a critical moment, in walks the savviest political counselor the world has ever seen, a guy named Bryce Harlow. He says, "Mr. President, the Penn Central, in its infinite wisdom, has just hired your old law firm to represent them in this matter. Under the circumstances, you can't touch this with a ten-foot pole." So there was no bailout.

What happened? The financial system was strengthened. It was not ruined. And everybody had to look around and say, "Hey, they let them go. We have to look at our hole card." Arthur did not have the pleasure of intervening and being the guy who saved the system, but he was not idle. He flooded the system with liquidity. So it allowed the market to sort things out. It seemed to me that's the right role for the Fed: to protect the system and not the company.

Dangers of monetary policy drifting away from market principles

The third story goes back further. To my way of thinking, it explains something about the problems in the 1970s. In the 1960s, there was a lot of talk from the Council of Economic Advisors about guidelines for wage and price changes. I'm at the University of Chicago listening to this, and I'm saying to myself, this is the underlying conceptual structure for wage and price controls, so it's not a good idea. And with a colleague named Bob Aliber, I organized a big conference. Milton talked. Bob Solow had a wonderful talk called "The Case against the Case against the Guideposts." Bob Aliber and I published a book on the conference in 1966.

The subject is on my mind by the time I become OMB director. I can just feel that the wage and price control issue is going to be a big problem. So I give a speech called "Steady as You Go" arguing that we have the budget under control and a good monetary policy and that "if you have the guts to stay with it," the policy will work.

But inflation was increasing, and closing the gold window gave John Connally an additional argument that we needed to deal with this inflationary pressure. So we had the big Nixon decision to close the gold window and we also put on wage and price controls. It was a battle I lost, but it happened, and it was very destructive.

For a while, it seemed to work very well and was almost intoxicating. It scared the hell out of everybody. It started with a wage-price freeze, and we could see the economy beginning to get badly distorted. At any rate, after I become secretary of the Treasury, the office in charge of wage and price controls now reports to me. And guess who is running it: Don Rumsfeld and Dick Cheney. Later on, I said to them, "I don't see on your resume that you ran the wage and price controls." We were trying to diminish them, very quietly getting rid of this and getting rid of that. We had a good program going.

Then, over my objections, the president reinstituted wage and price controls in a big way. And I had to say to him, "Mr. President, it's your call. I think it's a mistake, so you have to get yourself a new secretary of the Treasury. I resign." And my opinion is, as these controls stayed on, they were a huge regulatory impediment to the economy. I remember the Jimmy Carter gas lines. And they were responsible for the stagflation that we had. I was glad to see that in the first three days of his presidency, Ronald Reagan abolished them all. He also eliminated the group of people who were administering them, so there was nobody left to administer anything. That gave us a chance to get loose from this.

I mention this story at this conference on the Fed because the Fed chair Arthur Burns kind of liked the guidelines. Arthur was chairman of the Council of Economic Advisors in the Eisenhower administration, where I was an economist for a while, and we became good friends. Back then he had the idea that it's not enough to look at the statistics, though he was good at that; he wanted to get out and talk to businesspeople and get a feel for their attitudes. He wanted to talk to labor leaders, but he didn't have a way of doing it, so I figured out a way for him to meet quietly with Walter Reuther and George Meany and a few other people.

Though Arthur and I were friends, we battled about wage and price controls. Arthur liked the idea that somebody other than the Fed was going to do something about inflation. And I think part of that was a reason why the Fed had a looser policy during this period than they should have.

Diversity of views and a limited purpose as preconditions for reform

Those are my three stories, but I now want to make a couple of observations. The first is that, as I look at it, the Fed was originally organized in a very interesting way, though with Allan Meltzer here, I hesitate to say anything about the history of the Fed. If you're managing over diversity, how do you do that? You have to set yourself up so you understand that diversity. And the way the Fed is organized, it isn't just the guys in Washington. There are regional banks, and they come to the meetings and are heard. They rotate in being able to vote, so there's genuine representation of the huge diversity of our country. And I think as time goes on and as people think about how the Fed should be organized, one essential feature should be to keep the strength of our regional entities and their ability to talk. So this isn't a beltway organization. It's an organization that has to listen to the great diversity of our country.

The other thing that worries me a lot is the drift in the Fed to become an all-purpose organization. I have read some testimony where somebody says to the chairman of the Fed, "Look, Congress can't do anything. Nobody can do anything. You're the only people who can do anything, so you've got to do everything." It's a mistake. There is no such thing as an all-purpose organization. You have things you can do, and, when you go too much beyond that, you do things that you don't want to do.

Right now, the Fed is kind of driving the exchange rate system along with the actions of other banks. That's not their role. That is one of the reasons people are calling again for some kind of international monetary reform.

The huge liquidity plows into the stock market and other assets. That exacerbates the inequality of wealth. It's almost as if there's a deal with Bernie Sanders to give him something to complain about. But it's an unintended consequence of trying to do too much. I think there should be a sense of, "Look, our job is to do this. It would be nice if other problems got solved, but we can't do anything about that." We have to have some ability to say no, and that comes through the stories I've been telling.

I'll wind up by describing a cartoon I've always liked that goes back to the Eisenhower administration. The first secretary of state who traveled a lot was John Foster Dulles. And Ike—who knew something about the world, too—was a little annoyed by all the time he spent flying here and there. In the *Washington Post* cartoon, Ike's got his hands on his hips and he's looking at Foster Dulles. He says, "Dammit, Foster, don't just do something! Stand there!" Sometimes you have to stand there and not be the guy who reaches out and tries to solve all the world's problems.

GENERAL DISCUSSION

STEVE CHAPMAN: I just had a question for John Taylor, which is: Given that so many countries were following the Taylor rule in the 1990s and the early part of this century, and the results were very good, why do you think so many of them deviated from that afterward?

JOHN TAYLOR: Well, I've thought about that question a lot. My answers are mostly speculative. I've talked to many people at the Fed who were there at the time of the deviation, and their explanations vary. Alan Greenspan's explanation differs from that of Ben Bernanke, who was on the board at the time. To paraphrase Greenspan, he would say, "Well, if we raised the interest rate, it would not do much to long rates or to mortgage rates. The long rate is determined by other forces—global forces." That's the so-called Greenspan conundrum. Ben Bernanke argues that there was a global savings glut creating a capital inflow into the United States holding interest rates down. I've studied both of those explanations and discussed them in my 2009 book, *Getting Off Track,* where I argued that they do not add up to a satisfactory explanation. But it is interesting that different people who were a part of the decision have different explanations. So I've come to the conclusion that it's more of the "perfect becomes the enemy of the good" story. Greenspan's term as chair was, until that time, extraordinary. It was the Great Moderation continuing what Volcker had begun. And in that situation, you might think, "Well, I can do even better." For example, there was the idea of "risk management," which meant holding the rate a little bit lower could reduce downside risks. That was kind of the argument that was made. So I think it was more or less like that. Things were going well, but they tried to do even better, and that way of thinking frequently gets you off course. That's my explanation for the Fed.

And then there is the question of other central banks. To some extent there was contagion. I gave a paper about this in 2007; it was called "Globalization and Monetary Policy: Missions Impossible." In it I reviewed two successful missions of monetary and financial policy: the end of the 1970s stagflation with much improved performance in the 1980s and 1990s and the taming of emerging market crises in the early 2000s: two good missions that had been accomplished. I then asked, "What's the third mission?" And I argued that it was dealing with contagion of policy between countries. I looked at the ECB decisions around the same time as the Fed's low interest rate decisions and found that there was some evidence of extra low interest rates at the ECB. I think that was the beginning of the policy contagion that we're now talking a lot about today.

DAVID PAPELL: What John Taylor and Rich Clarida are saying is that if each country picks its own policy rule and says what it's doing, then you're going to get a good outcome. I would add to that what George Shultz said that the Fed should not try to do too much and what John said in his answer to Steve Chapman about not trying to be too ambitious. The policy rule legislation that has passed the House of Representatives does all of this. It just asks the Fed to pick its own rule and be transparent—say what the rule is, how it would adhere to it, or, if it's not adhering to it, explain why. But the reaction within the Fed has not been tremendously positive, to say the least. And so my question is for John. You seem optimistic that the barrier to reform is low while, as far as I can see, the barrier has, at least so far in the United States, not been particularly low. So do you have any ideas for how to get there from here?

JOHN TAYLOR: Well, first of all, it's not unusual for the Fed to resist suggestions like this. I give the example of when the money growth requirements came in the 1970s. Arthur Burns was the chair, and he objected strenuously to any notion that they would have to report on money growth. But as soon as it became apparent that some legislation was going to pass, he and his staff started working with the Hill, and they came up with something that the Fed could live with. It didn't specify what aggregates to report. And it was a little vaguer than maybe what was aimed for, but they decided to go along. It took time. It didn't happen overnight. So that's the way I think about it now. It's something on the shelf ready to be implemented. Implementing it, to me, is fascinating. I think George's stories, especially the one about implementing the flexible exchange rate system, are very important to understand. Ultimately, he and Milton Friedman wanted a flexible exchange rate system. So what do they do? They come up with this little adjustment mechanism with exchange rate and reserves, and, without emphasizing that it was their idea, they got people to adopt it. And sometimes you have to be there to make it happen, and I'm not there. I'm outside of the system.

A more recent example, from last year, was the proposal to increase the voting rights of emerging market countries at the IMF; the proposal had been sitting around without Congressional approval since 2010, when the Obama administration negotiated it. I saw there was a simple deal to solve this: if the IMF would reinstate its exceptional access framework for making loans, the Congress would approve the negotiated agreement. I was not there to work the deal internally, but I could talk and write about it, and eventually it happened. It was such a simple deal. And it worked.

GEORGE SHULTZ: I wonder, John, if one of the reasons is that the Fed gets distracted with other things. You act as though monetary policy is the only thing it does. But it does a lot of other things. It's a major regulatory agency, and it will intervene. Whenever there's some kind of economic crisis, the Fed will think it has to do something about it. So it has a wide range of impacts.

JOHN COCHRANE: And it increasingly—sorry to put two cents in there—is mixing its regulatory and macroeconomic roles. This new call for macroprudential regulations says, well, if I don't like the way the economy's going, and I don't want to fiddle with interest rates, I'll just tell banks who they should lend to.

GEORGE SHULTZ: But I think, listening to all you people here today, it seems obvious that everybody agrees that having some sort of a rules-based policy that John has proposed is essential. That will work. And somehow, it's important to get the politics such that it can happen within the Fed and around the Congress and elsewhere where it's needed.

ANDREW LEVIN: One obstacle to adopting a systematic policy benchmark is that some people think it would be too mechanical, and Secretary Shultz's remarks today are really helpful for dispelling that notion. In fact, John Taylor's Carnegie-Rochester paper specifically says that a rules-based approach should not be purely mechanical. But it seems like a purely semantic obstacle is that the word "rule" sounds too rigid and mathematical, whereas just referring to a "strategy" may be a bit too vague. Perhaps the use of the phrase "systematic and transparent strategy" would help avoid that sort of confusion and move this debate forward.

I think it's been very unfortunate that Federal Reserve officials started promoting the idea of making "meeting-by-meeting" decisions, because that doesn't sound like a systematic strategy at all. And it's not sufficient to state that policy will be "data dependent." Any effective strategy has to be data dependent. But policymakers need to explain what that means in practice. Which types of data? Which specific indicators? What magnitude of responses? And again, the strategy doesn't necessarily just have to be a mathematical rule; it can also be very helpful for the central bank to emphasize alternative scenarios and contingency plans.

Moreover, as Secretary Shultz has noted, there are real benefits of transparency. When you become more transparent, you open yourself up to criticism and critique. And as John Taylor has suggested, it would be terrific to have an international forum at which every central bank would explain its own systematic and transparent strategy and other central bankers could provide comments and feedback. That would enable economists at the IMF and elsewhere to analyze and assess these strategies. We can even imagine that John would test those strategies in his multicountry model to determine whether or not there's a unique and stable global equilibrium. But that sort of analysis can only happen when there's a sufficient degree of transparency about each central bank's policy strategy.

Finally, it may be helpful to envision the development of an international standard for the essential elements of a systematic and transparent strategy. Perhaps it could be named the "Taylor Standard for Transparency" or TST. Such a TST framework would be similar in spirit to accounting standards like GAAP (Generally Accepted Accounting Principles). In fact, there could even be a verification process for assessing whether each central bank's strategy is consistent with the international standard. And if a central bank fell short, it would have an incentive to refine and clarify its strategy in order to achieve the certification.

CHRISTOPHER CROWE: I just wanted to ask a quick question, and it has a little bit of an element of devil's advocate to it, because I don't think I disagree with what's been said. But I just have a query and sort of a concern, that when we use economic models and say, "Well, the model suggests that rules-based policy is best." I just wonder whether there's an element of tautology to that, because a model is basically a set of rules itself. You say the economy follows a set of rules. And so, isn't it kind of inevitable that the best policy will also look like a rule?

RICHARD CLARIDA: Well, I think, yes. But I think the point is models often times have 80—the big ones have 87—equations, and what comes out through all the permutations and the literature is not that there's a rule. You're right. At some level, that will be a tautology of an optimal control system. It's that in comparison to the general solution of the optimal control problem, as we know from John Taylor's work 35 years ago, instead of getting 87 variables on the right-hand side to get the optimal path, you can oftentimes get it with 2. So the insight is not that there is a solution, but that a similar solution across countries and regimes and periods within a pretty narrow range of parameters does a good job. So that's the sweet spot.

JOHN COCHRANE: I'd like to abuse my privilege and ask one question of John Taylor. You put up a graph with a policy rule with 18 years of downside deviations bigger than we've seen since the 1970s, and yet there's no inflation. You must have a story for that.

JOHN TAYLOR: The graph is based on research by Hyun Shin at the BIS, which I refer to in my paper. It pertains to policy deviations in many countries. There are two periods in that graph. One was prior to the crisis in which inflation did pick up. I didn't look at every country in that chart, but the US inflation rate rose fairly substantially actually—1.7% to 3.4% in terms of the GDP deflator during that period. But you also had other inflationary forces. The housing price boom accelerated at that point. There's an inflexion point there. And so I think we want to take that into account. I also think that there's different ways to measure the effect of monetary policy. It can cause high inflation, but also it can cause other bad things, too. To the extent that it caused a search for yield, risk taking, it was a factor, not the only factor, in the financial crisis crash that came about.

Then during the panic, I think the Fed did a good job as lender of last resort, and that was kind of rules-based policy. Maybe you can quibble with some of it, and I have, but it basically was on the right track during the panic of 2008. Then you move to the QE and the changes in forward guidance, and there's a question about whether that even had a contractive effect. Evaluating monetary policy during that period is still very hard.

CHAPTER SEVEN

International Monetary Stability and Policy

James Bullard, Robert Kaplan, Dennis Lockhart, and John C. Williams

PART 1

International Monetary Stability: A Multiple Equilibria Problem?

James Bullard

Introduction

Should monetary policy be better coordinated across countries? This has been a classic question in international macroeconomics. In recent years, this question has again moved to center stage. The use of unconventional monetary policy in the United States, in particular, has been met with criticism from emerging markets. The so-called "Taper Tantrum" of the summer of 2013 reenergized the debate. The surprise renminbi devaluation in the summer of 2015 seemed to cause substantial volatility in global financial markets. One characterization of both of these events, along with others during this period, appears to be that a seemingly small adjustment to the policy stance in one country may have an outsized impact on global financial markets and, through that channel, an important

This draft reflects comments made at the workshop on "International Monetary Stability" at the Hoover Institution, Stanford University, on May 5, 2016. Any views expressed are those of the author and do not necessarily reflect those of the Federal Open Market Committee.

impact on real activity in other nations. Expectations alone seemed to drive these macroeconomic events. How can such phenomena be reconciled with standard theories that are used to guide thinking at many of the world's central banks?

In these remarks, I will lay out some well-established conventional wisdom concerning international monetary stability based on a standard, multicountry New Keynesian model. I will then present an alternative interpretation based on a very similar multi-country New Keynesian model, but with some policymakers in some countries pursuing "bad" monetary policy. The notion of what constitutes "bad" monetary policy will have a precise definition in this story.

The bottom line of these remarks can be described in two parts as follows.

The conventional wisdom as I describe it suggests that under "good" monetary policy in each country, worldwide equilibrium is unique and international monetary policy coordination is unnecessary. The key condition that defines "good" policy in each country is that policymakers follow a rule that adheres to the Taylor principle, that is, that nominal interest rates are adjusted more than one-for-one with deviations of inflation from target. If this is the way the world economy operates—and much of modern central banking is indeed intellectually based on New Keynesian theory with flexible exchange rates—then there would be little need to discuss international monetary policy coordination further.

In the alternative interpretation, the Taylor principle is not adhered to by every central bank worldwide, and this defines "bad" monetary policy for the multicountry model. Research shows that the worldwide equilibrium is not unique in this case. In fact, there are a lot of equilibria and shocks to expectations alone could drive macroeconomic volatility. This may be one way to interpret events like the 2013 Taper Tantrum or the 2015 renminbi devaluation without departing from an otherwise standard New Keynesian model. In addition, there is a very good reason to think that the world's central banks have had a harder time adhering to the Taylor principle in recent years: they have encountered the zero lower bound, which makes it difficult to lower nominal interest rates more than one-for-one with declines in inflation. If this is the way the world economy operates, then there may be more scope for international monetary policy coordination.

Conventional wisdom

In my characterization of the precrisis, traditional view of the international economy, there are many interacting "New Keynesian" economies.[1] Capital is mobile internationally. All exchange rates are perfectly flexible. Shocks occur at the country level. Each country has an independent monetary policy characterized by a Taylor-type monetary policy rule. This policy rule has a "good" property in that it adheres to the Taylor principle—nominal interest rates are adjusted more than one-for-one with deviations of inflation from an inflation target.

Should the world's central banks coordinate monetary policy in this environment? The short answer is no. In this baseline situation, research shows that the worldwide equilibrium is unique and that the payoffs from international monetary policy coordination are small. In principle, to be sure, there are gains to be had, and they would accrue in the worldwide equilibrium if all central banks augmented their policy rules to include a response to foreign inflation as well as to domestic inflation. But policymakers do almost as well with respect to their goals by simply ignoring this effect. Hence, the gains are small.

Many have concluded from this precrisis line of thinking that it does not pay to worry too much about international monetary

1. See, for some examples in the literature, Obstfeld and Rogoff (2002) and Clarida, Gali, and Gertler (2002).

policy coordination. The possible gains seem to be small, and, practically speaking, it would be difficult to get the world's policymakers to play the cooperative equilibrium.

Some of the recent empirical evidence in international macroeconomics raises questions about the traditional view. Edwards (2015), for instance, conducts an analysis of the 2000–2008 data for Chile, Colombia, and Mexico, countries with relatively free capital flows and flexible exchange rate regimes. He concludes that monetary policy across these countries is nevertheless closely related to US monetary policy. Rey (2015) also documents spillovers from US monetary policy to the United Kingdom, Sweden, Canada, and New Zealand using data stretching from the mid-1980s or mid-1990s (depending on the country) until 2012. These results are viewed by the authors as potentially invalidating traditional New Keynesian conceptions of the international monetary economy. But the alternative view, detailed below, suggests that it is not clear what to expect in these VAR-based analyses if at least one country is not adhering to the Taylor principle.

An alternative view

In the alternative view, all the features of the multicountry New Keynesian economy are the same as in the traditional view.[2] The only difference is that monetary policymakers in one or more countries are not following "good" monetary policy. This means that at least one national policymaker does not adjust the degree of policy accommodation more than one-for-one in response to deviations of inflation from target. In short, monetary policy does not adhere to the Taylor principle in at least one country. Precrisis, this situation might have been thought to characterize Japan as op-

2. For more detail on the alternative view, see Bullard and Singh (2008). See also Bullard and Schaling (2009).

posed to the United States or the euro area.[3] Postcrisis, deviations from the Taylor principle are arguably widespread.

Why is it reasonable to assume that some countries are following the "bad" monetary policy—that is, not adhering to the Taylor principle? These are not normal times for monetary policy in the United States or across the world economy. In particular, in many countries, it is difficult for monetary policy to respond to declines in inflation when the policy rate is subject to the zero lower bound. Many central banks, including the Fed, have tried to substitute for lower policy rates through unconventional policies, including forward guidance and quantitative easing. These types of approaches may or may not provide a good substitute policy, an issue that continues to be debated.[4]

If we suppose that one or more national policymakers are deviating from "good" policy in the sense defined here, then we have a clear result: worldwide equilibrium is no longer unique. This means that many volatile equilibria exist, and they are all consistent with market clearing and rational expectations. Observed volatility could be—but would not have to be—much larger than what would be observed if national central banks were adhering to the Taylor principle in their Taylor-type policy rules away from the zero lower bound. Shocks to expectations around the world could be important drivers of global macroeconomic volatility.[5]

In summary, under the alternative view the problem is that monetary policymakers in some countries are not adhering to the Taylor principle, possibly because they cannot do so due to the zero lower bound. The result is multiple equilibria and, potentially, a

3. This was the motivation for Bullard and Singh (2008).

4. Another way to think about deviations from the Taylor principle could be that central banks have been too slow to raise their policy rates even when standard Taylor-type rules advised otherwise. See Nikolsko-Rzhevskyy, Papell, and Prodan (2014) for estimates of whether the Fed adhered to the Taylor principle postcrisis. Their estimates suggest the Fed did not respond to inflation at all during this period.

5. Size matters in this argument, so it is really a question of whether the central banks affiliated with the largest economies are adhering to the Taylor principle.

lot of excess volatility in the worldwide equilibrium. Whether the United States or other countries are following the Taylor principle today hinges on what one thinks about unconventional monetary policy. If unconventional monetary policy is largely an ineffective substitute for nominal interest rate reductions, then a stronger case can be made in favor of the alternative view and hence in favor of some form of international monetary policy coordination. The alternative view may be one way to represent recent events in global financial markets in response to monetary policy decisions, such as the 2013 Taper Tantrum or the 2015 renminbi devaluation.

Relation to Taylor

Taylor (2013) interprets recent monetary policy developments in the United States and other advanced economies, such as extended periods of near-zero nominal interest rates and quantitative easing programs, as deviations from rules-based policy. Deviations from rules-based monetary policy at some central banks may create incentives for other central banks to deviate from rules-based policy. This process can cause a breakdown in global monetary policy arrangements and lead to an inefficient global equilibrium.

This idea has a flavor similar to the one presented here. I interpret the Taylor concept of central banks "deviating from rules-based policy" as the Bullard-Singh concept of central banks "following a Taylor-type rule that does not adhere to the Taylor principle."

Conclusion

The conventional wisdom on international monetary policy coordination as I have described it provides a good baseline for thinking about the precrisis situation in international monetary policy. In that view, domestic policymakers should take care of their own affairs and, in doing so, would create a worldwide equilibrium which is nearly the best attainable. The alternative multiple equilibria view of worldwide equilibrium is more radical and less established. It has the virtue of adopting a nearly identical set of assumptions relative to the conventional wisdom, except that monetary policymakers in some countries no longer adhere to the Taylor principle. In this situation the worldwide equilibrium may be excessively volatile and subject to expectations shocks in a way that would not be possible in the conventional view. This may be one way to make sense of some postcrisis global macroeconomic developments. The difference between the conventional wisdom and the alternative view is essentially a judgement on whether global monetary policymakers have been able to effectively replicate "good" monetary policy rules in the aftermath of the global financial crisis through unconventional policy.

References

Bullard, J., and E. Schaling. 2009. Monetary policy, determinacy, and learnability in a two-block world economy. *Journal of Money, Credit, and Banking* 41 (8): 1585–1912.

Bullard, J., and A. Singh. 2008. Worldwide macroeconomic stability and monetary policy rules. *Journal of Monetary Economics*. Suppl. 55 (October): S34–S47.

Clarida, R., J. Gali, and M. Gertler. 2002. A simple framework for international monetary policy analysis. *Journal of Monetary Economics* 49 (5): 879–904.

Edwards, S. 2015. Monetary policy independence under flexible exchange rates: An illusion? NBER Working Paper 20893 (January).

Nikolsko-Rzhevskyy, A., D. Papell, and R. Prodan. 2014. The Taylor principles. Working paper, University of Houston (November).

Obstfeld, M., and K. Rogoff. 2002. Global implications of self-oriented national monetary rules. *Quarterly Journal of Economics* 117 (2): 503–535.

Rey, H. 2015. International channels of transmission of monetary policy and the Mundellian trilemma. Mundell-Fleming Lecture, *IMF Economic Review* (forthcoming).

Taylor, J. B. 2013. International monetary policy coordination: Past, present, and future. Bank for International Settlements Working Paper 437 (December).

PART 2

International Monetary Stability and Policy

Robert Kaplan

Discipline is an essential element of effective monetary policy. Part of being disciplined is clearly articulating the key drivers of monetary policy decisions as we try to achieve full employment and price stability.

One difficulty is that distinctions and complications that were once of second-order importance for the conduct of monetary policy loom much larger today as companies, economies, and financial markets become more globally integrated. Below, I discuss these distinctions and complications in the context of the original 1993 formulation of the Taylor rule, which suggests that the central bank adjust the stance of monetary policy in response to deviations of inflation from target and deviations of real activity from potential (Taylor 1993). However, these issues are relevant to broader discussions concerning the role and appropriate stance of monetary policy as well.

Implementation of the Taylor rule

To implement the Taylor rule (or simply track its prescriptions), one must answer several very practical questions, including: (1) Which price index should be used for measuring inflation? (2) Which index of real activity should be used for measuring slack? (3) How can we gauge whether monetary policy is accommodative or not? In particular, what is the neutral rate? These questions are central to properly using rules-based decision-making tools. I will offer thoughts on each of these questions, but I'll spend most of my time discussing the third issue—the challenge of assessing the level of monetary policy accommodation.

Which price index?

The original formulation of the Taylor rule suggests that the Federal Reserve respond to changes in the gross domestic product (GDP) deflator—a broad measure of the prices received by US producers. The FOMC, however, uses the personal consumption expenditures (PCE) deflator as its principal inflation gauge. The PCE index measures the prices paid by US households and is influenced by what's happening to import prices. As the US economy has become more open, the distinction between price indexes which exclude and which include, imported goods and services has become more important. The correlation between quarterly GDP and PCE inflation rates was 0.90 in the late 1950s through the early 1980s (see table 7.1). In the 2000s, the correlation has dropped to 0.58. Similarly, the correlation between inflation as measured by the GDP and gross-domestic-purchases deflators has dropped from 0.99 to 0.75. Fifty years ago—even 30 years ago—it didn't significantly matter which of the major inflation gauges the Fed used to guide policy. Now, the choice is of some importance.

Which measure of real activity?

The original formulation of the Taylor rule has the Fed respond to the gap between real GDP and an estimate of the US economy's

TABLE 7.1. In a globalized economy, how you measure inflation matters.

	Correlation between Inflation Measures	
Time Period	GDP and PCE	GDP and GD Purchases
1956–1970	0.90	0.99
1971–1985	0.90	0.96
1986–2000	0.83	0.87
2001–2015	0.58	0.75

productive potential. One could argue, though, that the Fed's job is to stabilize aggregate *demand,* as measured by gross domestic *purchases,* rather than aggregate *output,* as measured by real gross domestic *product.* As international trade and capital flows have grown, the distinction has become more important. Over the 20 years from 1956 through 1975, gross domestic purchases averaged 1.6 percentage points above GDP, and the gap between the two measures of real activity had a standard deviation of just 0.6 percentage points (see table 7.2). Over the 20-year period ending in 2015, both the average gap and the standard deviation of the gap more than doubled, to 3.6 percentage points and 1.3 percentage points, respectively. The Taylor rule calls for a half-percentage-point change in the funds rate for each one-percentage-point change in slack, so the almost five-percentage-point increase in the gap between purchases and product that we saw between 1996 and 2005 means that the funds rate would have increased by almost 2.5 percentage points more over this period had the Fed followed a Taylor rule based on gross domestic purchases rather than GDP. (The more rapid pace of tightening would almost certainly have altered the course of the economy, and so the actual cumulative funds-rate impact of the counterfactual policy probably would have been less than 2.5 percentage points.)

TABLE 7.2. In a globalized economy, whether you look at purchases or at product matters.

	Gross Domestic Purchases as a Percent of Gross Domestic Product		
Time Period	Mean	Standard Deviation	Range (highest–lowest)
1956–1975	101.6	0.60	3.0
1976–1995	101.2	1.08	4.7
1996–2015	103.6	1.30	4.8

How should one gauge the level of monetary policy accommodation?

In the original formulation of the Taylor rule, policy is judged accommodative when the real federal funds rate is less than 2%, and restrictive when it is above 2%: the long-run equilibrium or neutral real interest rate (r*) is implicitly assumed to equal 2%.

However, the neutral rate, the rate that signifies the dividing line between an accommodative and a restrictive monetary policy, is "unobserved"—that is, we must infer this rate from other financial and economic data. Additionally, the neutral rate is not static, and I am strongly persuaded by arguments that declining expectations of future GDP growth (heavily impacted by aging demographics) in advanced economies, a decline in productivity growth, and the continued emergence of the United States as a source of safe assets have all contributed to a decline in the neutral rate.

Determining the neutral rate

Since the neutral rate is unobserved, policymakers use various methods to make an estimate of the neutral real rate. While different approaches yield varying estimates, they each indicate that there has been a significant decline in the real neutral rate over the past several years.

In January 2012, Federal Reserve policymakers submitted their projections of the appropriate path of the federal funds rate over the medium term. Since that date, the median projection of these policymakers has declined from a 4.25% longer-run nominal funds rate to 3.0% in the June 2016 submission. Given the Federal Open Market Committee's commitment to a 2.0% longer-run inflation target, these projections imply a reduction in the longer-run neutral real interest rate from 2.25% at the beginning of 2012 to 1.0% today. Yields on Treasury Inflation-Protected Securities (TIPS) have signaled a substantially similar decline in the longer-run neutral real rate.

John Williams, president of the San Francisco Fed, working with Thomas Laubach, on the staff of the Board of Governors, has done pioneering research on the neutral rate that argues that the longer-run neutral real rate depends on the economy's potential growth rate, which varies over time, as well as other unobserved factors (2003). As of the first quarter of 2016, the Laubach-Williams model implied a 0.2% neutral real rate.

Evan Koenig and Alan Armen (2015) at the Dallas Fed use movements in slack to help identify the neutral real rate. They focus on shorter-run r*, and rather than make r* a direct function of growth in potential output, Koenig and Armen draw on signals from the financial markets and changes in household wealth. They argue that wealth growth and long-term yields do a good job of picking up changes in growth prospects and capture movements in other r* determinants.

The Koenig-Armen model says that the short-run neutral real rate was -1.3% in the first quarter of 2016, about 1.5 percentage points below the latest Laubach-Williams estimate of the longer-run rate and only 15 basis points above the actual real rate. Policy was only modestly accommodative in the first quarter of 2016, according to Koenig-Armen.

Potential reasons for decline in the neutral rate

As discussed earlier, a major driver of the decline in the neutral rate is a decrease in estimates of future growth. In the first quarter of 2003, the Congressional Budget Office (CBO) projected five-year potential growth would average 3.25% per year; in the first quarter of 2008, the prospective five-year growth estimate was 2.88% per year, and today, prospective five-year growth is estimated to be 2.28% per year.

This growth slowdown has been mostly due to demographics—baby boomers are moving into their retirement years—but weaker productivity growth also contributes significantly to the decline. Given the deterioration in US growth prospects, it makes sense that the longer-run neutral real interest rate has fallen. This deterioration appears to be occurring across all advanced economies, which helps explain the historically low level of interest rates we are seeing.

To illustrate this point further, I refer to work done by the CBO that details the negative impact on potential GDP growth of weaker trend growth in the potential labor force, primarily due to demographics, as well as slower productivity growth (table 7.3).

Another likely reason for the decline in the neutral rate is the emergence of the United States as chief supplier of safe assets to the world. In an increasingly globally connected world, the search for safety and return occurs globally—meaning that low rates in one country can quickly impact interest rates in other countries. Robert Hall of Stanford University and the Hoover Institution argues that the representation of risk-averse foreign investors in US financial markets has increased and that this trend has contributed to downward pressure on the neutral real rate (2016).

TABLE 7.3. Sluggish labor-force growth has contributed to a weakening in potential GDP growth.

	Annualized Growth Rates (percent/year), CBO Estimates		
Time Period	Potential GDP	Potential Labor Force	Productivity
1956–1975	3.83	1.88	1.92
1976–1995	3.13	1.78	1.33
1996–2015	2.39	0.88	1.50
2016–2025	1.94	0.49	1.44

Short-run volatility in the neutral rate

Another challenge for policymakers is short-term volatility in the neutral rate. Financial markets are today much more global and interconnected than they were 25 years ago. Investment portfolios are increasingly global, and asset allocators increasingly think globally in making investment decisions. Because financial markets trade in real time, market strains or other challenges in one market now have the potential to rapidly affect currency, debt, and equity markets globally. We saw this unfold in January and February when the devaluation of the Chinese currency was accompanied by a steep sell-off in Chinese markets, which then transmitted to a tightening in global financial conditions.

This tightening threatened to impact underlying economic activity. In response, central bankers were forced to adjust the path of monetary policy and alter their communication.

Concluding Observations

A disciplined approach to monetary policy requires a discussion of the key inputs into decision-making tools. Appropriate measures of the price level, output gap, and the neutral rate must be identified. Of particular concern today is an apparent decline in the neutral rate as a result of lower levels of expected GDP growth as well as the emergence of the United States as a source of safe assets. These issues must be carefully examined as policymakers attempt to use monetary policy tools to help inform decision making.

References

Hall, R. E. 2016. Understanding the decline in the safe real interest rate. NBER Working Paper no. 22196 (April).

Koenig, E. F., and A. Armen. 2015. Assessing monetary accommodation: A simple empirical model of monetary policy and its implications for unemployment and inflation. *Federal Reserve Bank of Dallas Staff Papers*, no. 23.

Laubach, T., and J. C. Williams. 2003. Measuring the natural rate of interest. *Review of Economics and Statistics* 85 (4): 1063–70.

Taylor, J. B. 1993. Discretion versus policy rules in practice. *Carnegie-Rochester Conference Series on Public Policy* 39 (1): 195–214.

PART 3

Post-2008 Central Bank Operating Frameworks: Differences, Commonalities, and Implications for Reform

Dennis Lockhart

I think my copanelists James Bullard, John Williams, and Robert Kaplan probably had a similar experience to mine in preparing for this meeting. Last week was the April Federal Open Market Committee meeting. And then I had my own financial markets conference Monday and Tuesday, and a speech Tuesday night, so I first got into the subject matter of today's conference yesterday. And my first reaction to the topic of the international monetary system and reform was sort of a classic expectation that we would be talking about—and I should be talking about—the reserve currency system, the role of the dollar, the exchange system, and any international agreements that relate to that. These are questions of coordination of national monetary policies that have been touched on today, along with fault lines in these arrangements, the transmission of stress, and how to address imbalances through collective action. I then read John Taylor's speech delivered at the October 2015 Baker Institute conference titled Currency Policy Then and Now: 30th Anniversary of the Plaza Accord, in which he first put out the proposal for domestic establishment and reporting of rules-based monetary policies as the foundation for rules-based reform at the international level. I realized that John was suggesting more of what I'm going to talk about: that the individual policy frameworks of central banks around the world, if somewhat more uniform, taken collectively, can amount to some sort of reform of the international system.

I would say the "system" is currently more described as the sum of national policies. I'd like to make some key points that are not prescriptive but really observations about the changes in central bank operating frameworks post-2008. There are some common aspects, and there are a number of differences in these operating frameworks. Let me define "operating framework" as how a central bank interacts with the banking system and financial markets to implement monetary policy. And there are four topics that I think are worth looking at. First is the size and composition of central bank balance sheets. The second deals with questions that central banks are grappling with regarding counterparties and acceptable collateral. Generally, what institutions should have access to central bank facilities? A third topic is the shift, as opposed to traditional monetary policy, to floor systems, with administered rates and remuneration of reserves. And the fourth is the interaction of operating frameworks with regulation.

If you look at those four topics, I'd say some common themes emerge. We clearly are in the era of unconventional policy and the use of unconventional policy tools. That involves engagement in large-scale quantitative easing when needed and appropriate. Central banks are dealing with a broader range of asset classes, especially in crisis situations, and they are dealing with international counterparties as required. The differences between operating frameworks or operating approaches in the major central bank countries really are dictated by somewhat different circumstances, as well as institutional details in those countries, or, in the case of the European Currency Board, the currency area.

So let me take those four topics one by one and make a few observations, first about central bank balance sheets. There is a general recognition that quantitative easing and targeted lending or asset purchase programs are necessary in some circumstances.

But there is no consensus about what should be the nature of those programs. The Japan experience suggests to me that there are some limits to what quantitative easing programs can achieve, and I would make the observation that Japan has gone so far with their programs that they may run the risk of really distorting fairly materially sovereign debt markets in Japan. The ECB experience suggests complex programs may be less effective. One of my colleagues spent a full day studying the balance sheet of the ECB, trying to understand from the assets that had been acquired what they were doing. He found that to be a difficult process. They have a complex program. Since quantitative easing programs involve a fiscal aspect, there is nervousness about precommitting to programs, and there is some anticipation on the part of central banks of political controversy. And among central banks there is admiration for the 2008 Memorandum of Understanding (MOU) between the Bank of England and Her Majesty's Treasury, which created a new legal entity that bears all the profit and losses from unconventional monetary policy. But I would say at the same time, similar MOUs would be difficult, if not impossible, to achieve in most countries.

Turning to the subject of counterparties and collateral, before the crisis, central banks had rather strict requirements for collateral and counterparties. And during the crisis, those standards were liberalized. It raises the question, Are pre-2008 standards simply too tough for all circumstances, and how much of loosened or changed standards are likely to persist on a permanent basis? In the United States, the reverse repurchase agreement facility now has almost 140 counterparties, and the majority of those counterparties are money market mutual funds. In the United Kingdom, the Bank of England invited some nonbanks to apply for full access to Bank of England services, as if they were banks, if they were regulated, liquidity dependent, and Systemically Important Financial Institutions if you will. The ECB and the Bank of Japan are acquiring corporate securities as part of their QE programs. So in general, central banks are grappling with this question, and there is no clear consensus.

There has been a shift to floor systems with administered rates. The conditions are that reserves at almost all central banks are abundant, and so reserve requirements are a dead issue. Central banks are now willing to use floor systems with full reserve remuneration, because in a low rate environment, there's not a big expense involved. But there is a feeling that such big systems might become more difficult to manage when rates get back to more normal levels. Balance sheets are too large and the expense could lead to capital losses under certain scenarios, and that could give rise, of course, to what I euphemistically will call "political economy concerns." The current prevalence of floor systems has led to a new appreciation of their advantages: transparency and very simple administration.

So let me now turn to the final topic, and that is operating frameworks and their interaction with regulation. New regulatory frameworks have generally increased banks' demand for high-quality liquid assets. And in general, there is a recognition that there is tension between maintaining market liquidity and achieving the intent of macroprudential bank policy.

Let me close with these very simple observations. Major central banks have new operating frameworks with common themes at work but quite a number of differences based on their individual circumstances. All major central banks are grappling with the question, Where is this going? Where is this headed? And taken together, there is high uncertainty regarding the future of the sum of the parts of operating frameworks of major central banks.

PART 4

The Decline in the Natural Rate of Interest: An International Perspective

John C. Williams

First, I want to thank John and the other organizers for inviting me today. I try to attend this conference every year, and I've made it the past four. I come here for a number of reasons. One is that it brings together the best minds in monetary policy. Another is that it's always a wonderful experience to hear from Secretary Shultz, providing both his current views and a longer-term perspective. Some of the issues we're dealing with today aren't unique to our time, and we can learn from the experiences of the past.

Over the years, we've talked a lot about policy rules. We've discussed Fed governance, central bank strategies, and other related matters. As I listened to John Taylor's talk today, I agreed very much—as, I think, did most of us—with the notion that we should be systematic in our approach to making policy. We should be more transparent about what our policy strategy is and share that information with the public. To me it seems an admirable and excellent goal to work for a world in which central banks all not only follow their own domestic mandates but also pursue systematic, well-designed policies and share that information. And I hope that we can move towards that end.

But in my nine remaining minutes, I'm going to raise one challenge to that central-banking utopia, which I think is a serious concern. It picks up on what Rich Clarida said when he dangled the teaser of my topic today, which is r*, or the natural rate of interest. Rich actually asked Thomas Laubach and me to prepare a paper for a National Bureau of Economic Research conference this summer that looks more broadly at the question of r*. Instead of being entirely United States–focused, we take our methodology and apply it to other countries. The Laubach-Williams model is basically a vector autoregression (VAR) model overlaid with a Kalman filter, in which we try to infer the natural rate of interest based on the relationships between real output, real interest rate, and inflation.

For the United States, we found the striking result that in the past, the natural rate of interest—or the intercept in the Taylor rule, if you will—was running somewhere around two and a half percent, meaning that we would say r* was historically around two and a half. But our model indicates that it's come down dramatically over the past 25 years, reaching around zero in the United States. A lot of the decline in our estimate of the neutral rate transpired over the years since 2007; specifically, that drop was about two percentage points. A large share of the decline is explained in our model by the slowdown in estimated potential, or trend, output growth. But some of it is explained by other factors.

Because the model is based on a purely statistical method, the Kalman filter, I can't tell you exactly what these other factors are, though a number of people are doing research on the subject. But if you go back to John Cochrane's presentation, you get some idea. He showed an equation that relates the neutral real interest rate to the growth rate of consumption and some other factors, which I believe include changes in the risk spread, the discount factor, the distribution of income, and possibly much more.

The important point is that, based on a very simple VAR-type framework that we developed 15 years ago, these factors have also fallen quite a bit: our model estimate of the natural rate of interest in the United States has come down from around two and a half to close to zero.

Now let me share some other, more preliminary results. My coauthors probably won't appreciate me spilling the beans this afternoon, but here we go. We took the same basic methodology and applied it to the euro area, Canada, and the United Kingdom. What we find is much the same pattern that we see in the United States. For example, if you look at the euro area in 1990, our estimates come in at about two and a half. I think that's consistent with pretty much anybody's view of a normal natural rate of interest. Today, it's about minus one half percent. We also find a smaller, but still sizable, decline in the estimated natural rate of interest in both Canada and the United Kingdom. In all four of these major economies, r* has declined over the past 25 years. These estimates are generally stable over the 1960s, '70s, '80s, up until the '90s, when they are followed by a pronounced decline.

We see the same pattern in potential output growth. So to return to what Rob said earlier, the demographics we're seeing in the United States are happening across the globe. They're happening in the advanced economies. They're happening in Asia. Much more dramatically, in Japan, the labor force is already shrinking.

So what does this mean? There are two overarching takeaways. First, it is a lot harder to follow a Taylor rule with a two percent inflation target if the neutral real interest rate is as low as some of our estimates. Let's take one half percent as an example. You're hitting the zero lower bound much more frequently even if you're just following a standard Taylor rule. It's going to be very hard to achieve your inflation goal on a regular basis when you're constrained by the lower bound as often as that.

Second, there's a very strong correlation in these results across countries. This goes back to something Rich highlighted, which I think is very important: our estimates were done country by country. We were not imposing any linkages across geographies. However, economic theory tells us there should be global factors driving movements in r*. Again, we didn't incorporate global links in our estimates, but the movements in r* are clearly correlated across countries. We're undertaking formal econometric analysis to discover what the global r*, or should I say, the intergalactic r*, is [laughter].

Ultimately, there are a lot of similarities on the supply side of the economy, the trend in productivity growth, demographics, and other areas, which are affecting economies across the globe, not only the advanced ones but emerging markets as well. So this is not just a US issue. This isn't just a post-financial-crisis issue. This is more a concern about how monetary policy should operate in the future. And quite honestly, it raises the question of whether our inflation targeting framework, with a two percent inflation target, is really the right way to achieve our goals in a low r* global environment. I'm not going to try to answer that today. There's a lot of research being done on that question. But this is a topic that we should keep front of mind when we think about what kind of rules we should move towards, again, not just in the United States but in countries across the globe.

The last thing I would like to note—and I know John's going to say it, so I'm going to say it before he has a chance—is that these estimates are very uncertain. Our original paper, which we wrote 15 years ago, made two statements. First, "Here's our estimate," and second, "Don't trust our estimate." So I would again stress that there is a lot of uncertainty about r*. It's very difficult to extract from the data what the natural rate of interest is, and there are other models and estimates out there.

But when we're thinking about robust policy strategies, I would include the possibility that the natural rate of interest has fallen a good deal, that it is maybe even close to zero. Thank you.

GENERAL DISCUSSION

SEBASTIAN EDWARDS: We talk a lot about policy rules and coordination and Taylor rules and inflation targeting. What we haven't talked much about is what the target ought to be. And that probably it is more and more difficult, with an r* around zero, to follow these kinds of rules with two percent inflation targeting. So in order to make this an open-ended question, I would like to ask everyone in the panel what they think about the Olivier Blanchard 2010 proposal, which was a very simple one, which was, instead of a two percent target, let's go to a four percent target. And you may say you don't want to answer, but four percent as a target as we normalize the system—Is that something that you think is reasonable?

ROBERT KAPLAN: I'll help out by going first here. The Fed has a target of two percent, and my own view is that I shouldn't be speculating publicly about deviating from that. The most appropriate thing for me to do is to reaffirm that two percent is our target.

DENNIS LOCKHART: As a practical matter, I don't see any movement away from the target that was established in January 2012. And I personally think communicating that change would be extraordinarily difficult with the public. It could very well be disruptive. So in a very pragmatic sense, we have the two percent target, and I don't see there'll be a move away from that in the near term.

JOHN WILLIAMS: I'll delve a little bit further into this topic. We don't want to change horses midstream. We are close to our two percent inflation goal. The US economy is in a very good position. I'm optimistic in terms of how we're doing in achieving that goal. But, I am also watching what's happening in the euro area. I'm watching what's happening in Scandinavia, Japan, and other countries, where they are all struggling to get to their inflation goals. I think that we owe it to ourselves as researchers, academics around the world, and policymakers to be thinking really hard right now whether that's the right strategy for the future. Now, Evan Koenig is here, he's done some really good research on nominal GDP targeting, and there's been a lot of research on price-level targeting as well. I think there are other options in the literature besides raising the inflation target that I think will both provide a strong nominal anchor—because you don't want to lose that—and at the same time give us maybe more of a protection against these kinds of issues like the zero bound. But I do think this is the time to really think hard about this. I look around at what's happening, at what the ECB's doing, pushing every pedal to the metal, if you will, and how hard it is just to get to their inflation target. I mean, this is completely the opposite experience of what I was taught when I took economics. I thought that, you know, when you go into central banking, the thing was to make sure you didn't let inflation get too high. I didn't know that my career was going to be solving. . . . It was a Stiglitz transformation, right? The sign was the wrong one.

ROBERT KAPLAN: Evan Koenig is at the Dallas Fed, and, as you can imagine, we talk a lot about nominal GDP targeting. As a former businessperson, I'm very sensitive to the fact that global debt is high relative to GDP: if you look at advanced economies, it is extremely high. It takes nominal income to service nominal debt. Given that debt is a big challenge in the world, there's a lot to be said for thinking hard about nominal GDP targeting and doing more work on that approach.

BOB HALL: A complimentary question is, How negative are you willing to go? The Fed is the only major central bank that has absolutely refused to even think about a negative policy rate. At least, that's what it seems.

JOHN WILLIAMS: That's unfair, Bob! At our conference in March, Ben Bernanke was speaking, you asked him the question, and he answered.

BOB HALL: Well, he's not in charge anymore.

ROBERT KAPLAN: I'm happy to go first on this question also, because I've already addressed it publicly. I used to live in Japan. While their circumstances differ a little bit from the United States and Europe, the Japanese experience is indicative. Japan, as we know, is dealing with a number of issues, but most significantly Japan is aging so rapidly that its population is declining. They've tried to deal with their demographic problem by getting women into the workforce. And that has helped to some extent. Additionally, the Japanese have very high levels of debt to GDP.

In my view, what the Bank of Japan has done with interest rates might buy some time. It might. Alternatively, it might do more harm than good. But it will not address these fundamental issues of an aging population and high levels of debt to GDP. These issues will require structural reforms. That's the key point. Japan is a good example of the need for policies beyond monetary policy. Structural reforms and fiscal policy need to play a role.

Turning to the United States, you never want to dismiss a tool, but the issues we're facing are going to require structural reform and fiscal policy action. When I think about the effects that negative rates here would have on the money market industry and on commercial paper, which is a critical funding source for companies, and the impact on financial institutions more broadly, it makes me wonder whether negative rates wouldn't create more problems than solutions. I think we should be broadening the conversation to include tools beyond monetary policy.

ANDREW LEVIN: So just to follow up on the previous question for a second. When the FOMC adopted the statement on longer-run goals and strategy—let me just read you the final sentence of it.

It's really important: "The committee intends to reaffirm these principles and to make adjustments as appropriate at its annual organization meeting each January"—*make adjustments as appropriate.* Now I think what the Fed should do following the example of the Bank of Canada is to have a regular review. It could be a three-year review or a five-year—in Canada, it's a five-year process—where you systematically look at things like this and other elements of the longer-run goals and strategy, with input from academics and central banks around the world and discussions with government officials, just like they do at the Bank of Canada: could be enormously helpful. Now the Bank of Canada's done this five times. They've actually never changed the inflation target. But I think it's helpful to the public process to go through. As we've discussed, the Fed should adopt a systematic and transparent strategy. And the Fed should regularly revisit that strategy and change it periodically as appropriate.

So the other thing I wanted to ask about, my question was, about the longer term . . . about the r*. So I just checked, the Philadelphia Fed survey of financial forecasts is pretty much like any other. Their consensus for the ten-year average of the three-month Treasury bill rate is 2.5. And you subtract a two percent inflation, you're at 0.5. Very consistent with what President Williams said. I've actually been wondering for quite a long time, Why is the Federal Reserve's median assessment of r* systematically higher than professional forecasters? Now, I'm not saying it's wrong. And obviously, there is uncertainty. It seems to me the Federal Reserve needs to start engaging in a public process for key things like this, and potential output, and the nonacceleratng inflation rate of unemployment (NAIRU), and maximum employment, to have a public discussion and engage in views so people understand. Maybe they come along and decide the Fed's right and the professional forecasters' views are distorted. But it needs to be more transparent.

DENNIS LOCKHART: Well, some of John Williams's comments in meetings I've attended have been helpful in shaping my thinking. And I think what John was saying earlier is that r* may be zero now. But our projections of r* are time varying, and they rise with better economic conditions or with the achievement of our objectives. So the medium-term numbers are not necessarily consistent with what he said.

JOHN WILLIAMS: Can I respond quickly? As to Andy Levin's first point, I want to affirm I agree a hundred percent. The earlier point about longer-term strategies, whether it's price-level targeting, inflation targeting, and all that, that we should be having conferences, pulling together experts and policymakers, having really serious discussions exactly along the Bank of Canada model, I agree a hundred percent. That's why I'm raising this issue the way I'm doing it. Because we need to think about this in the same way that I think people thought about it very seriously when inflation targeting first was. . . . New Zealand introduced it on the fly, but other countries thought heavily about that. And my answer on the r* is that people's views are evolving, as Rob Kaplan said. As the data have confirmed that it's declined, estimates have been moving lower. And I'll admit my own estimates have been moving down over time.

ALLAN MELTZER: When you think about r*, and the possibility that it is substantially declined, do you relate that in your mind that this is the first recovery in the postwar period without any investment in the United States and in Europe? No investment at all. People are buying stock back at very high prices that you have created for them, and that's a sign of pessimism on the part of managers. Now in your mind is that pessimism in any way related to the fact that we have substantial new regulation of the economy that is putting fiscal burdens on companies that they don't like? That looking ahead, there is $20 trillion of government debt that somehow will have to be handled that nobody wants to talk about? That on top of that government debt, there's $90 trillion, estimated, of unfunded liabilities that nobody even mentions? And that that may have some substantial effect on resource allocation? And that, if you look at the European economies—France, Germany—and then go to Japan—declining populations, huge debt to GDP ratio. China, declining population: the estimate that I've seen is that the 1.4 billion Chinese by the end of this century will be 500 million. That's a decline of a little over one percent a year, which is not unimaginable. But these are real burdens. Does that have any effect on your thinking on low real rates of return?

JOHN WILLIAMS: Yes. And I believe there are potentially better solutions to the r* problem than to have a higher inflation target. The preferred solution would be to put into place fiscal, structural, and other policies that raise r*. By the way, Larry Summers says that, too.

ALLAN MELTZER: Amen!

JOHN WILLIAMS: So we finally have everybody in the whole range of economics agreeing. So I agree completely: r* is affected by all types of policies. After all, it's the intersection of aggregate demand and aggregate supply at a real interest rate. But until that happens, I think we need to be thinking about how to best conduct monetary policy.

DENNIS LOCKHART: The challenge of our times right now is becoming clear, and that is growth. And every major economic zone in the world is struggling with growth one way or another, even including China with a slowdown. And you cited a number of things that I think are much more structural in nature than simply headwinds, which we point to all the time as the reason why we haven't broken out from a two-percent world to a three-percent world. If someone presented me just a binary, pick-one-side-or-the-other question: Do you believe that in the foreseeable future, fairly long term, we're in a two-percent world, or is there a chance of a four-percent world? I'd have to side with two percent, and results may be below that. And there are a number of reasons. Allan, you've mentioned them: demographics; weak investment, sometimes influenced by fiscal issues; just a range of things that are not for the Fed to solve, that are in the way of breaking out of that kind of two-percent torpor, and I use that word generalizing for the term "low growth." The one that is I think underappreciated is demographics. Governor Shirakawa, the former governor of the Bank of Japan, made a tour of the United States and came through my bank a while back. And he basically has a slide show on Japanese demographics. And his message was twofold. One, 30 years ago he had no interest in the subject whatsoever, and it was not on his screen. And today, he thinks it is the number one problem of Japan. And two, his message was, you ought to pay attention to it as well. And so, I think the consequences of the demographic changes in the United States are not fully factored into the longer-term projections.

RICHARD CLARIDA: I guess it's sort of like Elvis is entering the building. So I guess I'll try to turn this into a question. But I think there are two things: one is a point that I think John would also agree with, which is, yeah, r* is unobservable, as is the natural rate of unemployment. But I think the analogy is a good one in that we're not entirely flying blind. I mean, if r* were really two or two and a half, we would see it in other parts of the economy, just like if the NAIRU were seven, or two even, you would see it. So I think that we don't want to be too pessimistic about it being a good input to policy with standard errors, just like the NAIRU's been an input to policy in the original Taylor rule.

And then the other point is, I think—and I applaud Andy Levin's point about thinking of a Fed discussion of a strategy at a periodic basis—I guess I would point out, as you think about alternatives to this strict two percent inflation target, I think there's a real difference in transitioning from where we are to some version of a price-level strategy versus the nominal GDP. Price level would be referring to some average rate of inflation over some interval that you can measure and define. The trouble with that nominal GDP target is you may lose the inflation angle. It depends on how you get to five-percent nominal GDP. If you get there with four percent inflation, one percent growth, that's not. . . . So, I don't view them as being equivalent as a practical matter, even though when I write down a model there might be more of a speech.

STEVE LIESMAN: John Williams, it's sort of consensus, I think, in this room that rules-based monetary policy is better and leads to better economic outcomes. So my question is, Do you agree with that conclusion, and do you agree that the outcomes have been better when you follow a more systematic rule? And I don't know if it's out of bounds for me to ask John Taylor to respond.

JOHN WILLIAMS: I think we agree actually. I think that where you can, you would want monetary policy to be as systematic and predictable, understandable, clear, transparent as possible. And that's why I've spent most of my career studying versions of the Taylor rule and other strategies related to that. I'm not picking which rule is the best rule here but really thinking seriously about that question. My own view is that, when we hit the zero lower bound, it made being predictable and transparent very difficult because we couldn't move the policy instrument in response to economic news the way we'd want, because we did not want to go to negative at the time but chose to use other policy instruments, like, QE and forward guidance. So during that whole seven years of essentially zero interest rates, we weren't able to demonstrate the systematic policy reaction to economic developments that we normally would and couldn't always clearly communicate and show how our thinking was evolving with the data. So I am looking forward to the time when interest rates are well away from zero, and you see our policy actions being data dependent in a predictable and consistent way, as in the past. The positive sign I would say that I'm already seeing—and I did an economic letter on this a few weeks ago—was that, during the zero lower bound period, clearly the markets were not paying attention to the macro news in terms of thinking what the Fed was going to do, because we were at zero, and we seemed to be locked down at zero, especially with our forward guidance. But now, as we've moved away from zero and as we've talked about being data dependent, market responses to macro news and other information seem to be moving closer to what we saw during the period that John Taylor highlights as a period of predictable monetary policy. So in our analysis we looked at how markets responded to news in the 1990s when policy was following something like the Taylor rule. Well, we're not quite there yet, but we're getting closer to seeing markets respond to the news just like they did back in the '90s. But I do want to see us get all the way there and have a policy that's as predictable and systematic as possible.

One thing I will push against a little bit is the notion that we, somehow, the nineteen of us, will agree to one policy rule. One of the strengths, and Secretary Shultz brought this up in his comments and I agree with him a hundred percent, one of the strengths of the Fed structure is that we have nineteen people of very different backgrounds, different perspectives, different experiences, and that's all sitting around the table, and we don't have to all agree that there's one rule to rule them all. We can actually have that debate, discussion, live every time. But I do agree that we should be agreeing on strategy, and I think that we do, and being as transparent as we can about how we are executing on that strategy.

DENNIS LOCKHART: My way of thinking about the rules-versus-discretion question and policy setting is, I'll pick up where John

Williams started, and that is predictable, systematic, disciplined, consistent over time, yes. I think we all agree with that.

In actually setting policy, I get a little uncomfortable with too much reliance on simply the calculation of an equation telling you what you should be doing. I think a certain amount of judgment is inevitably going to be in the process. I would not like to see the debate simply shift to the estimations within the equation, which can be all over the map depending on what a particular reserve bank president thinks, his or her r*, for example, or what the output gap might be, or whatever. So we could end up easily bogged down and not making a rule work. So I don't really gravitate to the extremes on this in terms of rules-based policy setting. At the same time, I understand discretion, if it is defined as "making it up as you go along, with much inconsistency over time," clearly a dangerous approach. So I see it as being guided by rules with inevitably some judgment involved.

JOHN TAYLOR: My concern here is that, even with the best of policymakers' intentions, policy rules can start to have other things come into play that look like discretion. I teach my students it's like the old story of the wolf in sheep's clothing, except it is discretion in rules clothing. For example, before Janet Yellen became chair, she wrote a piece about how the coefficient on output in the Taylor rule should be one rather than .5. And that's when the gap was big. As soon as the gap was zero, she started talking about another issue: r* as zero rather than two. It's an amazingly quick shift. Now that may be completely as policymakers see it. But you've got to worry about that. The reduction in estimated r* from four percent to three and a quarter percent occurred in only two years? Just to be candid, I worry about groupthink. The intentions I think are clear, but in practice?

GEORGE SHULTZ: Has the Fed made a careful study of the increase in the regulatory morass that's now gripping our country? You seem to be pessimistic about the future, and it seems to me that every way you turn, there's a regulatory arm telling you that you can't do it. Allan talked about the reduction in the number of banks. Here's a personal experience. I wanted to add a bedroom on the first floor of our house here on the Stanford campus. It took a year to get permission. And for a long while, they were saying I had to dig an eighty-foot-long, six-foot-deep trench around the house to find any evidence that an earthquake took place in California. Everywhere you turn, there's a regulator telling you that you can't do it. Suppose we just did away with all this regulation and let people struggle for themselves? Probably the economy would take off like a bird. Have you studied this question?

ROBERT KAPLAN: I will start with John Taylor's comment on the danger of groupthink. I would note that the four of us come from a variety of different backgrounds but, independently, are winding up with somewhat similar positions. That makes me think there's validity to these arguments. Turning back to regulatory burden: yes, I think there needs to be a broad cost-benefit analysis of regulation in the United States, not just financial regulation. Papers by Alan Krueger and others suggest that the problem is not confined to federal regulation. A lot of the burdensome regulation—and we see this in our Dallas Fed surveys—is state and local: fees, licenses. Cost-benefit analysis is not *the* answer, but it is a part—along with five or six other things—of the answer, and I would love to see a comprehensive review. It will not be done, as you know, by the Fed. But I think as Fed leaders, we can and do talk about this, because I think it is an issue that needs to be addressed.

JOHN COCHRANE: We were talking about low inflation, especially Europe's very low inflation, and what they should do about it. There was some discussion that maybe central bankers should just announce a higher inflation target. I was going to channel Jim Bullard and say, well, that probably isn't going to work, because if you can't get inflation up to two, and then you announce four, then the public finds out you're completely powerless to do anything you want. I was also going to see if Jim was still with me in considering the Fisherian heresy: if you look at the data, and if you look at every new Keynesian model, you see that inflation follows an interest rate peg. Maybe Europe is a giant case of pedal misapplication, and that by lowering rates, they are in fact stepping on the inflation brakes, and the answer is to raise rates? Jim, are you still on board with that? Or can I start a discussion on that issue?

JAMES BULLARD: When I talk about neo-Fisherian effects, I like to talk about them going down. You stay at a zero nominal interest rate for a long time: I can see that dragging inflation expectations down. This applies to a negative interest rate as well. I think it's a tougher story to tell going up, that you can set nominal interest rates higher and get inflation expectations to go higher. It seems plausible that you can set nominal interest rates low and stable, and that actually leads to lower inflation globally. So I think that's plausible given what's happened to inflation in the last seven to eight years globally. A pegged negative rate under that interpretation would lead to even lower inflation. So it depends on how much inflation you want, I guess.

V. V. CHARI: I couldn't resist a minor technical point for Jim Bullard. The issue of multiplicity or determinacy depends critically on the behavior of the policy rule off the equilibrium point. So that's something Andy and Pat and I have written about, so I just wanted to say that.

But I wanted to raise a broader question. I wanted to go back to John Taylor's proposal. Let me start with a terminological. . . . It's not really a quibble, but I think it goes to the heart of the issue. I think that the use of the term "rules" rather than "discretion" is not a helpful way of addressing this issue. Why? If I define a rule simply as something that is a relationship that describes how the history of past events leads to current policy, even when policy's conducted under discretion, that can be described as a rule. It goes back to something that Bill English said. So I think the right distinction is when the policies are chosen with or without commitment, not so much whether it's rules rather than discretion. I think that's the key difference.

Now if I think about policies being chosen under commitment, then they typically have the feature—in environments where commitment really matters—that they're going to be situations, states of the world in the future, where what you want to do, if you could do it and get away with it, is to deviate from whatever it is you chose earlier and committed to. So the key thing about all this is private agents have got to believe that you're going to follow that rule.

And so I want to put in a plug, a particular theoretical plug, for John Taylor's proposal. One of the insights from game theory is, it's a lot easier to get people to commit to a particular strategy for making policy if the consequences for deviating from that policy are more severe. They don't have to be catastrophic, but they're more severe. One of the advantages of John's rule is, to the extent that you have a traditional agreement on this and to the extent that you are warned that a significant deviation from whatever strategy you'd agreed upon earlier occurs, then that's more likely to lead to bigger problems internationally, which may help discipline individual policymakers. Anyway, taking all that as given, I think that at least two of the presidents here seem to be in favor of adopting a strategy and then trying to speak to it. I guess I'd like to hear from the other two whether they think it's a good idea, too.

TERRY JONES: I'll make this a more pragmatic question, since I write for an audience, and I regularly get letters and sometimes phone calls and whatever. People asking me, Well, what is the Fed going to do if something goes wrong? We see here in the first quarter we had a less than one percent GDP number. A lot of people brushed it off; they said we always have a bad number in the first quarter. Well, maybe so, but I've also seen a number of investment houses raising their estimates of the risk of a recession. What can the Fed do now should the economy reverse and go negative? Do you have tools other than negative interest rates? They don't seem to have worked in Japan very well or in Europe. Quantitative easing may have stabilized markets somewhat, but it sure didn't do much for economic growth. Do you have tools that can address a recession right now? Or is it basically going to come down to you arguing you've done all you can; it's now down to the fiscal policy types to takeover?

JOHN WILLIAMS: I'll answer that last one. First of all, I can't believe that you actually get letters and phone calls in this day and age. Second, I think we know what we would do. We'd do what we have done in the past. I disagree with your premise that it didn't work. In 2010, we had a very serious discussion about policy options. I wasn't on the committee at the time, but there was a discussion about what tools we should be deploying, and in the end they were asset purchases and eventually very strong forward guidance. My own view is the forward guidance clearly moved market expectations dramatically. QE moved asset prices pretty significantly as well. So if we get another significant negative shock, we have a list of things we can do. First, we won't raise rates. The markets expect us to raise rates over the next couple of years. If we get a negative shock, we'll change their expectation: we won't raise rates, which will add to policy accommodation. We can cut them closer to zero if necessary. We can go to QE4. This is an audience that doesn't want to hear this, but we could do QE4; we could do forward guidance again. So I think we've developed a playbook. I think it's worked. I think it was only appropriate given the extraordinary circumstances. But I think we know what we would do if that situation were to occur. Negative interest rates I still think is at the bottom of the list, because these other tools are the better tools. I don't think this is going to happen. I think this is a very unlikely scenario, because we're basically at full employment where core inflation is just a few tenths below our target. It's kind of a puzzling discussion. I keep hearing about negative interest rates in the United States, when really we're on the road to normalizing policy, at least from my perspective. Oh, was I supposed to put a disclaimer on that? I only speak for myself.

DENNIS LOCKHART: I think John Williams covered anything I would cover. Do we have a new rabbit to pull out of the hat? I am not aware of one. It's the tool bag we have used in the past, and we have some scope for applying that if the conditions require.

ROBERT KAPLAN: I don't have anything to add to that.

JAMES BULLARD: I think negative rates are very unlikely.

DAVID MALPASS: We've been talking today about r* being near zero and potential GDP estimates coming down quite a bit. How is that consistent with the forward communication that's trying to get people to raise the probability of rate hikes? How do you put together rate hikes with the tone of the discussion earlier?—maybe to John Williams or anyone.

JOHN WILLIAMS: The way I'm usually asked this is, "Don't you believe your own model?" The answer is that the nominal Fed funds rate is below 50 basis points. Let's assume a value of r* of zero; I agree with Dennis's point that this may be a reasonable short-term r* estimate at this point in time. Core inflation is running at about 1.6%, and we're at full employment. That tells you that we need to be moving toward that r*. Put another way, the real Fed funds rate is below minus one percent, well below the estimate of r*, indicating that policy is very supportive of growth. So there is no inconsistency.

It is, though, consistent with the notion that we should be moving gradually. We're talking about two or three rate increases this year and a gradual path over next year. I think that's consistent with the view that the longer-run value of r* may not be zero, but it's much lower than it was in the past.

ROBERT KAPLAN: I'll make one other comment. Another reason for this impetus is that there is a cost to this level of accommodation: a cost to savers, which we hear about all the time, distortions in the process of making asset allocation and investment decisions, and other imbalances that are created, which can be costly and which can in fact be very painful to unwind and which are much easier to see in hindsight than in real time. So this is another reason why we're very focused on this effort to normalize the stance of policy. But on the other hand, we can't force it beyond what conditions allow.

DENNIS LOCKHART: I think a gradual path to a lower destination is really the picture that we're presented with. And I am concerned that, if the r* discussion, the growth discussion, the atmosphere that would suggest not moving, overpowers our decision making, we will lose credibility in the process. So there's a balancing act here. I see it as consistent to pursue normalization but, in all likelihood, to a lower destination.

JAMES BULLARD: I think one of the legacies of the crisis is that the Fed started using the "dot plot" to give forward guidance. And now that we've lifted off, we're still using the dot plot to give forward guidance. I've started to wonder if we really want to be doing that. That embodies an assumption that there is going to be some kind of mean reversion in productivity and in a variable like r*. Do we need to, or do we want to, make that kind of assumption? In the past, the Fed would have said, "We've set interest rates where we want to set them for today, and if the data come in in a different way, then we'll change the interest rates in a way that's appropriate for that," but the Fed would have not given this sort of forward guidance. Now we put a lot of words around that that say that the dots, of course, are dependent on how the economy evolves, and we think this is the most reasonable scenario, and so on. But in previous years, we used the dot plot to try to convey forward guidance. So I refer to it as "quasi-forward guidance," and I've been a bit concerned about that recently.

CHRISTOPHER ERCEG: So I just had a quick question on the issue of fiscal consolidation, that, in order to achieve fiscal sustainability, so we have the latitude to deploy fiscal policy when needed, if we prospectively hit the zero lower bound again, presumably, fiscal consolidation has to start at some point. But in an environment where r* appears to be very low, it makes it more complicated to pursue fiscal consolidation. So I was wondering about any sort of guidance you might offer in terms of how far a country has to be along in terms of recovery before it will be appropriate to pursue a strategy of fiscal consolidation.

HARALD UHLIG: When you look at inflation, it's been sort of remarkably stable. And we talk a lot about the New Keynesian theories all giving us kind of opposite conclusions. I mean you talk about inflation: How do you look at this? Do you think the Fed can tap itself proudly on its shoulder about having achieved this remarkably stable inflation since 2009? Or do you have this eerie feeling that you guys don't have anything to do with inflation at this point?

JAMES BULLARD: Low inflation is the question of our time in central banking. Why we did not get a repeat of the 1970s with central banks doing all the things that they've done in the last six or seven years is a fantastic question. I think that should lead us to doing a thorough reexamination of most monetary economics and monetary theory. We know a lot from that literature that I think maybe it doesn't get enough play in policy circles. A lot of things depend upon expectations, for instance. So to get to the bottom of why we have low inflation we really need to reexamine monetary theory.

ROBERT KAPLAN: My own view is that the Fed has done everything it can over the last several years. However, as a person with a markets background, I am sensitive to the fact that there are big, powerful secular forces at play. It's like going into the ocean when there's a big wave coming—you think that you can work through it, and it just crushes you. As has been said, aging demographic trends are extremely powerful, and they're unfolding in every advanced economy. Not everyone agrees with the implications of the second secular force: high (and growing) levels of debt to GDP. Increasing global interconnectedness is another important secular trend that can create spillovers back to the United States. For example, high levels of overcapacity and increasing levels of debt to GDP in China have the potential to impact the world economy and financial markets (as we saw in January and February of this year). These secular trends are powerful. It may not be fully appreciated just how powerful they are in impacting economic conditions.

DENNIS LOCKHART: I side with Jim's view that we may not be too far away, and, if we are not able to get inflation up to target or moving decidedly toward target, a rethink may be required; that there's a theoretical basis for believing that if we have a policy that resembles what we've had for several years, that is, essentially throwing everything we have at it, and we still can't get to target, it's time for a reappraisal. And when I vote—I was a voter last year—so when I voted in December for liftoff, I was comfortable enough with the idea of "reasonable confidence." That was just based on no evidence, just confidence. But I also said at the same time in public remarks that I'd be looking for real evidence as 2016 unfolded. And maybe we're seeing some real evidence of some firming. But if that all reverses and in another year or more we're still where we are, and we can't get inflation up, I think that the notion of a rethink really does come into play.

About the Contributors

DAVID BECKWORTH is a research fellow at the Mercatus Center at George Mason University and a former international economist at the US Department of the Treasury. He has done research on the assessment of monetary policy, the transmission mechanisms through which that policy works, and its impact on the global, national, and regional economies. He is the editor of *Boom and Bust Banking: The Causes and Cures of the Great Recession* and has published in scholarly journals such as *Economic Inquiry, B.E. Journal of Macroeconomics,* and the *Journal of Macroeconomics.* Beckworth's blogging at *Macro and Other Market Musings* has been cited by the *Washington Post, New York Times, Financial Times, Economist,* CNN/*Fortune, Bloomberg/Businessweek,* and *Newsweek;* his popular articles have appeared in the *New York Times, Washington Post, New Republic, National Review, Investor's Business Daily,* and *Barron's.*

MICHAEL D. BORDO is a Board of Governors Professor of Economics and director of the Center for Monetary and Financial History at Rutgers University, New Brunswick, New Jersey. He has held previous academic positions at the University of South Carolina and Carleton University in Ottawa, Canada. Bordo has been a visiting professor at the University of California at Los Angeles, Carnegie Mellon University, Princeton University, Harvard University, and Cambridge University, where he was the Pitt Professor of American History and Institutions. He is currently a distinguished visiting fellow at the Hoover Institution, Stanford University. He has been a visiting scholar at the International Monetary Fund; the Federal Reserve banks of St. Louis, Cleveland, and Dallas; the Federal Reserve Board of Governors; the Bank of Canada; the Bank of England; and the Bank for International Settlements. He is a research associate of the

National Bureau of Economic Research, Cambridge, Massachusetts, and a member of the Shadow Open Market Committee. He has a BA degree from McGill University, an MSc in economics from the London School of Economics, and a PhD in 1972 from the University of Chicago. He has published many articles in leading journals and sixteen books on monetary economics and monetary history. He is editor of a series of books for Cambridge University Press: Studies in Macroeconomic History. He is currently President of the Economic History Association.

JAMES BULLARD, as president and CEO of the Federal Reserve Bank of St. Louis, participates in the Federal Open Market Committee (FOMC) and directs the activities of the bank's head office in St. Louis and its branches in Little Rock, Arkansas, Louisville, Kentucky, and Memphis, Tennessee. He is an economist who joined the bank in 1990. His research has appeared in numerous professional journals, including the *American Economic Review*, the *Journal of Monetary Economics*, *Macroeconomic Dynamics*, and the *Journal of Money, Credit and Banking*. A peer reviewer for many periodicals, he currently serves as coeditor of the *Journal of Economic Dynamics and Control*. Since becoming president in 2008, Bullard has called for the FOMC to adopt state-contingent policy and give greater consideration to headline inflation than core inflation when deciding monetary policy. In the wake of the financial crisis, he supported quantitative easing and warned about the possibility of the United States' falling into a Japanese-style deflationary trap. He has also argued that the US output gap may not be as large as many estimates suggest. Bullard is an honorary professor of economics at Washington University in St. Louis, where he also sits on the advisory council of the economics department and the advisory boards of the Center for Dynamic Economics and the Wells Fargo Advisors Center for Finance and Accounting Research. He is the chairman of the U.S.A. United Way Board of Trustees and a member of the Worldwide United Way Board of Trustees, the University of Missouri–St. Louis Chancellor's Council, and the Greater St. Louis Financial Forum. Bullard also serves on the board of the St. Louis Regional Chamber and on the senior committee of the Central Bank Research Association. Bullard earned his doctorate in economics from Indiana University in Bloomington. He holds bachelor of science degrees in economics and in quantitative methods and information systems from St. Cloud State University in St. Cloud, Minnesota.

VARADARAJAN V. CHARI is the founding director of the Heller-Hurwicz Economics Institute; the Paul Frenzel Land Grant Professor of Liberal Arts in the University of Minnesota, Department of Economics; and an adviser at the Federal Reserve Bank of Minneapolis. He received a bachelor's degree in technology and chemical engineering from the Indian Institute of Technology, Bombay, and his PhD from Carnegie Mellon University. He has served on the board of editors of many journals, including *Econometrica*, the *Journal of Economic Literature*, and the *Journal of Economic Perspectives*. In 1998 he was elected a fellow of the Econometric Society and named a scholar of the college by the College of Liberal Arts, University of Minnesota, in 2008. His research interests are in banking, fiscal and monetary policy, and issues of economic development.

RICHARD CLARIDA is the C. Lowell Harriss Professor of Economics and International Affairs at Columbia University, where he has taught since 1988. From February 2002 until May 2003, he served as the assistant secretary of the US Treasury for economic policy, in which position he was the chief economic adviser to the Treasury secretary, advising him on a wide range of economic policy issues, including US and global economic prospects, international capital flows, and corporate governance. In May 2003 Treasury secretary John Snow presented Clarida with the Treasury Medal in recognition of his outstanding service to the Treasury. Since 2006 Clarida has been an adviser on global strategy to the asset management firm Pimco. From 1997 until 2001 Clarida served as chairman of the Department of Economics at Columbia University. Earlier in his career Clarida taught at Yale University and served in the administration of President Ronald Reagan as senior staff economist with the president's Council of Economic Advisers. Clarida received his BS from the University of Illinois with Bronze Tablet Honors in 1979 and his MA and PhD from Harvard University in 1983.

JOHN H. COCHRANE is a senior fellow at the Hoover Institution. He is also a research associate of the National Bureau of Economic Research and an adjunct scholar of the Cato Institute. Before joining Hoover, Cochrane was a professor of finance at the University of Chicago's Booth School of Business and, earlier, in its Economics Department. Cochrane earned a bachelor's degree in physics at MIT and his PhD in economics at the University of California at Berkeley. He was a junior staff economist on the Council of Economic Advisers (1982–83). Cochrane's recent publications include the book *Asset Pricing* and articles on dynamics in stock and bond markets, the volatility of exchange rates, the term structure of interest rates, the returns to venture capital, liquidity premiums in stock prices, the relation between stock prices and business cycles, and option pricing when investors can't perfectly hedge. His monetary economics publications include articles on the relationship between deficits and inflation, the effects of monetary policy, and the fiscal theory of the price level. He has also written articles on macroeconomics, health insurance, time-series econometrics, financial regulation, and other topics and was a coauthor of *The Squam Lake Report.* Cochrane frequently contributes editorial opinion essays to the *Wall Street Journal.* He also maintains the *Grumpy Economist* blog.

CHRISTOPHER CROWE is an economist at Capula Investment Management, a London-based hedge fund, where he covers global economics, primarily G10 plus China. He was the UK economist at Barclays for two years; before that he worked at the International Monetary Fund for five years. He has a PhD and MSc from the London School of Economics and a BA from Cambridge University. He was also an Overseas Development Institute (ODI) fellow, working for three years at the Caribbean Development Bank in Barbados. His work in the fields of monetary economics and finance has been published in a number of academic journals, including the *Journal of Monetary Economics, the Journal of Money, Credit and Banking,* and the *Journal of Economic Perspectives.*

ALESSANDRO DOVIS is Assistant Professor of Economics at Penn State University. He studied economics as an undergraduate at the University of Torino and earned a PhD from the University of Minnesota. He was a visiting scholar at the International Economics Section of Princeton University during 2013–2014. His research interests are in macroeconomics and international economics. A common theme of his research is the analysis of how lack of commitment and enforcement frictions shape outcomes in dynamic economies and the implications that the existence of these frictions have for policy. Currently, he is working on sovereign default, the interaction between trade reform and credit market conditions, and on how credibility affects the gains for a country to join a monetary union.

SEBASTIAN EDWARDS is the Henry Ford II Professor of International Economics at the University of California at Los Angeles. From 1993 to 1996, he was chief economist for Latin America at the World Bank. He has published fourteen books and more than two hundred scholarly articles. He is the codirector of the National Bureau of Economic Research's Africa Project. Professor Edwards has been an adviser to numerous governments, financial institutions, and multinational companies. He is a frequent commentator on economic matters on CNN and other cable outlets; his op-ed pieces have been published in the *Wall Street Journal*, the *Financial Times*, the *Los Angeles Times*, *El País* (Spain), *La Vanguardia* (Spain), *Clarín* (Argentina), *El Mercurio* (Chile), and other newspapers around the world. His latest book is *Toxic Aid: Economic Collapse and Recovery in Tanzania* (Oxford University Press, 2014). Other books include *Left Behind: Latin America and the False Promise of Populism* (University of Chicago Press, 2011) and *Crisis and Reform in Latin America: From Despair to Hope* (Oxford University Press, 1995). Professor Edwards has been president of the Latin American and Caribbean Economic Association and is currently a member of the Scientific Advisory Council of the Kiel Institute of World Economics, Kiel, Germany. He was also a member of California governor Arnold Schwarzenegger's Council of Economic Advisers. In 2013 Professor Edwards was awarded the Carlos Díaz-Alejandro Prize in recognition of his research on the Latin American economies. Professor Edwards was educated at the Universidad Católica de Chile. He received an MA in economics in 1978 and a PhD in economics in 1981, both from the University of Chicago.

CHRISTOPHER ERCEG is currently a senior associate director in the Federal Reserve Board's International Finance Division, where he has worked as an economist since 1993 and has played a major role in developing the board's global macroeconomic models and applying them to policy issues. His research interests include monetary and fiscal policy, open economy macroeconomics, and commodity price behavior. During his career, he has published papers in many leading journals, including the *American Economic Review*, the *Journal of Monetary Economics*, the *Journal of International Economics*, and the *Journal of the European Economic Association*. He served as a senior research fellow in the International Monetary Fund's Research Department in 2012–13 and also as an adjunct professor at Columbia University, Georgetown University, and

Johns Hopkins University. Erceg received his BA from the University of Virginia and his PhD in economics from the University of Chicago.

PIERRE-OLIVIER GOURINCHAS is a research associate in the National Bureau of Economics's International Macroeconomics and Finance Program. He received his PhD in 1996 from MIT and is currently a professor of economics at the University of California at Berkeley, where he heads the Clausen Center for International Business and Policy. He is also editor in chief of the International Monetary Fund's *Economic Review.* In 2007 Gourinchas received the Bernàcer Prize for best European economist under the age of forty working in macroeconomics and finance; in 2008 he received the prize for best French economist under forty. In 2012–13 he served on the French Council of Economic Advisers to the prime minister; since 2014 he has been a member of the French National Economic Commission, an advisory board to the French Treasury. He is a visiting scholar at the San Francisco Federal Reserve Bank and has been a regular visitor at numerous central banks. His main research interests are in international macroeconomics and finance. His recent research focuses on capital flows and global imbalances, the determination of global interest rates and exchange rates, and the international monetary system.

ROBERT S. KAPLAN has served as the thirteenth president and CEO of the Federal Reserve Bank of Dallas since September 8, 2015. He represents the Eleventh Federal Reserve District on the Federal Open Market Committee in the formulation of US monetary policy and oversees the twelve hundred employees of the Dallas Fed. Kaplan was previously the Martin Marshall Professor of Management Practice and a senior associate dean at the Harvard Business School. Before joining Harvard in 2006, Kaplan was vice chairman of the Goldman Sachs Group, with global responsibility for the firm's Investment Banking and Investment Management Divisions. Previously he served as global cohead of the Investment Banking Division. He was also a member of the firm's Management Committee and served as cochairman of the firm's Partnership Committee and chairman of the Goldman Sachs Pine Street Leadership Program.

During his twenty-three-year career at Goldman Sachs, Kaplan served in various other capacities, including head of the Corporate Finance Department, head of Asia-Pacific Investment Banking, and head of the high-yield department in Investment Banking. He became a partner in 1990.

On leaving the firm in 2006 he was given the honorary title of senior director. He serves as cochairman of Project A.L.S. and cochairman of the Draper Richards Kaplan Foundation, a global venture philanthropy firm that invests in developing nonprofit enterprises dedicated to addressing social issues. He is also a board member of Harvard Medical School. Kaplan received a bachelor's degree in business administration from the University of Kansas and a master's degree in business administration from Harvard Business School.

PATRICK J. KEHOE is an international macroeconomist who works on international business cycles, exchange rates, and international monetary policy. He received his PhD from Harvard University in 1986 and has been a chaired professor at the University of Minnesota, the University of Pennsylvania, and Princeton University. Currently, he is associated with the University College London and is a visiting professor of economics at Stanford University. He is a fellow of the Econometric Society and was the senior monetary adviser to the Minneapolis Federal Reserve Bank for more than a decade. He currently serves on several editorial boards and has had more than two dozen articles in the following journals: *Journal of Political Economy,* the *American Economic Review, Econometrica,* and the *Review of Economic Studies.*

DENNIS P. LOCKHART took office March 1, 2007, as the fourteenth president and chief executive officer of the Federal Reserve Bank of Atlanta, where he serves on the Federal Reserve's chief monetary policy body, the Federal Open Market Committee (FOMC). From 2003 to 2007, Lockhart served on the faculty of Georgetown University's Walsh School of Foreign Service, teaching in the master's program. From 2001 to 2003, Lockhart was managing partner at the private equity firm Zephyr Management, L.P., based in New York with activity in Africa and Latin America. Before joining Zephyr, Lockhart worked for thirteen years at Heller Financial, where he served as executive vice president and director of the parent company and as president of Heller International Group. Lockhart held various positions, both domestic and international, with Citicorp/Citibank (now Citigroup) between 1971 and 1988. He earned a bachelor's degree in political science and economics from Stanford University in 1968 and a master's degree in international economics and American foreign policy from the Johns Hopkins University School of Advanced

International Studies in 1971. Lockhart serves as a director of the Metro Atlanta Chamber of Commerce and Commerce Club. He is the former chair of the Midtown Alliance, World Affairs Council of Atlanta, and Carter Center's Board of Councilors. He is a trustee of Agnes Scott College, Atlanta International School, and Georgia Research Alliance and serves on the advisory board of the Andrew Young School of Policy Studies at Georgia State University.

ALLAN H. MELTZER is the Allan H. Meltzer University Professor of Political Economy at the Tepper School of Business at Carnegie Mellon University, a distinguished visiting scholar at the Hoover Institution at Stanford University, and past president of the Mont Pelerin Society. His teaching and research interests include the history of US monetary policy, size of government, macroeconomics, and the relation of money to inflation and unemployment in open and closed economies. Professor Meltzer has served as a consultant on economic policy for the US Congress, US Treasury, the Federal Reserve, the World Bank, and the US and foreign governments and was chair of the International Financial Institution Advisory Commission. He was founder and chairman of the Shadow Open Market Committee from 1973 to 2000 and honorary adviser to the Bank of Japan for seventeen years. He is the author of many books and papers in the field of economics.

LEE E. OHANIAN is a professor of economics and director of the Ettinger Family Program in Macroeconomic Research at the University of California at Los Angeles, where he has taught since 1999, and a senior fellow at the Hoover Institution. He is also associate director of the Center for the Advanced Study in Economic Efficiency at Arizona State University. He is an adviser to the Federal Reserve Bank of Minneapolis and has previously advised other Federal Reserve banks, foreign central banks, and the National Science Foundation. His research, which focuses on economic crises, has been published widely in a number of peer-reviewed journals. He previously served on the faculties of the universities of Minnesota and Pennsylvania and has been a visiting professor at the Stockholm School of Economics, Arizona State University, and the University of Southern California. He is codirector of the research initiative Macroeconomics across Time and Space at the National Bureau of Economic Research. He received a BA in economics from the University of California at Santa Barbara and an MA and a PhD in economics from the University of Rochester.

DAVID H. PAPELL is the Joel W. Sailors Endowed Professor and chair of the Department of Economics at the University of Houston, where he has taught since 1984. His fields of expertise are macroeconomics, international economics, and applied time-series econometrics. He previously taught at the University of Florida and has held visiting positions at the University of Pennsylvania, the University of Virginia, and the International Monetary Fund. He received a BA from the University of Pennsylvania and a PhD from Columbia University. He has published more than fifty articles in refereed journals and served as an associate editor for the *Journal of International Economics*, the *Journal of Money, Credit and Banking*, and *Empirical Economics*.

CATHERINE SCHENK, FRHS, is Professor of International Economic History at the University of Glasgow. She earned her PhD at the London School of Economics and has held academic posts at Royal Holloway, University of London, and Victoria University of Wellington and visiting positions at the International Monetary Fund and the Hong Kong Monetary Authority as well as the University of Hong Kong. An associate fellow in the international economics department at Chatham House in London, she focuses on international monetary and financial relations after 1945 with a particular emphasis on East Asia and the United Kingdom. She is the author of several books, including *International Economic Relations since 1945* (2011) and *The Decline of Sterling: Managing the Retreat of an International Currency* (2010), and coeditor of *The Oxford Handbook of Banking and Financial History* (2016). Her current research interests include the development of international banking from the 1960s to the 1990s.

GEORGE P. SHULTZ is the Thomas W. and Susan B. Ford Distinguished Fellow at the Hoover Institution. Among many other senior government and private-sector roles, he served as secretary of the Department of Labor in 1969 and 1970, director of the Office of Management and Budget from 1970 to 1972, and secretary of the Treasury from 1972 to 1974. He was sworn in on July 16, 1982, as the sixtieth US secretary of the Department of State and served until January 20, 1989. In January 1989, he was awarded the Medal of Freedom, the nation's highest civilian honor. Shultz rejoined Stanford University in 1989 as the Jack Steele Parker Professor of International Economics at the Graduate School of Business and as a distinguished fellow at the Hoover Institution. Shultz is the chair of the Precourt Institute Energy Advisory Council at Stanford, chair of the MIT Energy Initiative External Advisory Board, and chair of the Hoover Institution's Shultz-Stephenson Task Force on Energy Policy. He is a distinguished fellow of the American Economic Association.

JOHN B. TAYLOR is the Mary and Robert Raymond Professor of Economics at Stanford University, the George P. Shultz Senior Fellow in Economics at Stanford's Hoover Institution, and the director of Stanford's Introductory Economics Center. He served as senior economist on the president's Council of Economic Advisers and as a member of the council. From 2001 to 2005, he served as undersecretary of the Treasury for international affairs. Taylor was awarded the universitywide Hoagland Prize and the Rhodes Prize for excellence in undergraduate teaching and the Stanford Economics Department's Distinguished Faculty Teaching Award. He received the 2016 Adam Smith Award from the Association of Private Enterprise Education, the Truman Medal for Economic Policy for extraordinary contribution to the formation and conduct of economic policy, the Bradley Prize for his economic research and policy achievements, the Adam Smith Award from the National Association for Business Economics, the Alexander Hamilton Award and the Treasury Distinguished Service Award for his policy contributions at the US Treasury, and the Medal of the Republic of Uruguay for his work in resolving the 2002 financial crisis. Taylor received a BA in economics summa cum laude from Princeton University and a PhD in economics from Stanford. He won the 2012 Hayek Prize for his book *First Principles: Five Keys to Restoring America's Prosperity*.

HARALD UHLIG has been a professor in the Department of Economics of the University of Chicago since 2007 and was chairman of the department from 2009 to 2012. Previously he held positions at Princeton University, Tilburg University, and the Humboldt Universität Berlin. He served as coeditor of *Econometrica* from 2006 to 2010 and has been the lead editor of the *Journal of Political Economy* since the summer of 2013. He is a consultant to the Bundesbank and the Federal Reserve Bank of

Chicago. He chaired the Center for Economics Policy Research's Business Cycle Dating Committee from 2005 to 2012. He is a fellow of the Economic Society, a recipient of the Gossen Preis of the Verein für Socialpolitik, and a member of the Center for Economics Policy Research and the National Bureau for Economic Research. Uhlig is a specialist in applied quantitative macroeconomics and applied quantitative methods in economics. His research interests include macroeconomics, business cycles, financial markets, economic policy, and Bayesian time-series analysis. He is particularly interested in studying the interrelation of macroeconomics and financial markets and the role of monetary and fiscal policy.

JOHN C. WILLIAMS took office as president and chief executive officer of the Federal Reserve Bank of San Francisco on March 1, 2011. In this role, he serves on the Federal Open Market Committee, bringing the Twelfth District's perspective to monetary policy discussions in Washington. Williams was previously the executive vice president and director of research for the San Francisco bank, which he joined in 2002. He began his career in 1994 as an economist at the Board of Governors of the Federal Reserve System, following the completion of his PhD in economics at Stanford University. Before that, he earned a Master's of Science from the London School of Economics, and an AB from the University of California at Berkeley. Williams's research focuses on topics including monetary policy under uncertainty; innovation; and business cycles. He has published numerous articles in leading research journals and recently served as the managing editor of the *International Journal of Central Banking*. He also served as associate editor of the *American Economic Review*. Additionally, he was senior economist at the White House Council of Economic Advisers and a lecturer at Stanford University's Graduate School of Business.

About the Hoover Institution's Working Group on Economic Policy

The Working Group on Economic Policy brings together experts on economic and financial policy at the Hoover Institution to study key developments in the US and global economies, examine their interactions, and develop specific policy proposals.

For twenty-five years starting in the early 1980s, the US economy experienced an unprecedented economic boom. Economic expansions were stronger and longer than in the past. Recessions were shorter, shallower, and less frequent. GDP doubled and household net worth increased by 250 percent in real terms. Forty-seven million jobs were created.

This quarter-century boom strengthened as its length increased. Productivity growth surged by one full percentage point per year in the United States, creating an additional $9 trillion of goods and services that would never have existed. And the long boom went global with emerging market countries from Asia to Latin America to Africa experiencing the enormous improvements in both economic growth and economic stability.

Economic policies that place greater reliance on the principles of free markets, price stability, and flexibility have been the key to these successes. Recently, however, several powerful new economic forces have begun to change the economic landscape, and these principles are being challenged with far reaching implications for US economic policy, both domestic and international. A financial crisis flared up in 2007 and turned into a severe panic in 2008 leading to the Great Recession. How we interpret and react to these forces—and in particular whether proven policy principles prevail going forward—will determine whether strong economic growth and stability returns and again continues to spread and improve more people's lives or whether the economy stalls and stagnates.

Our Working Group organizes seminars and conferences, prepares policy papers and other publications, and serves as a resource for policymakers and interested members of the public.

Working Group on Economic Policy—Associated Publications

Many of the writings associated with this working group will be published by the Hoover Institution Press or other publishers. Materials published to date, or in production, are listed below. Books that are part of the Working Group on Economic Policy's Resolution Project are marked with an asterisk.

Rules for International Monetary Stability: Past, Present, and Future
Edited by Michael D. Bordo and John B. Taylor

Central Bank Governance and Oversight Reform
Edited by John H. Cochrane and John B. Taylor

Inequality and Economic Policy: Essays in Honor of Gary Becker
Edited by Tom Church, Chris Miller, and John B. Taylor

*Making Failure Feasible: How Bankruptcy Reform Can End "Too Big to Fail"**
Edited by Kenneth E. Scott, Thomas H. Jackson, and John B. Taylor

Across the Great Divide: New Perspectives on the Financial Crisis
Edited by Martin Neil Baily and John B. Taylor

*Bankruptcy Not Bailout: A Special Chapter 14**
Edited by Kenneth E. Scott and John B. Taylor

Government Policies and the Delayed Economic Recovery
Edited by Lee E. Ohanian, John B. Taylor, and Ian J. Wright

Why Capitalism?
Allan H. Meltzer

First Principles: Five Keys to Restoring America's Prosperity
John B. Taylor

*Ending Government Bailouts as We Know Them**
Edited by Kenneth E. Scott, George P. Shultz, and John B. Taylor

*How Big Banks Fail: And What to Do about It**
Darrell Duffie

The Squam Lake Report: Fixing the Financial System
Darrell Duffie et al.

Getting Off Track: How Government Actions and Interventions Caused, Prolonged, and Worsened the Financial Crisis
John B. Taylor

The Road Ahead for the Fed
Edited by John B. Taylor and John D. Ciorciari

Putting Our House in Order: A Guide to Social Security and Health Care Reform
George P. Shultz and John B. Shoven

Index